The Deep Truth

By Johann Rannu

"You cannot expect this book to be the magic pill. Nobody is going to read this book, put it down with a smile on their face and go bang models the very same day, it's just not going to happen. However, it's probably the fastest way to move in that direction. One just has to ask himself, whether he'd like to be there some day or never."

This book will tackle matters such as:

How to read this book?

"Reading a book is much like having a conversation with the author. The only difference is only that instead of you blabbering in-between you'll be observing everything he or she has to say."

Before we start, I'd like you to know that I'm not telling you how to live your life. That's none of my business nor is it anybody else's business. That's your business. Anything that you decide to engage in life, is completely fine as long as you have something to engage in. For those of you who would like to engage in and master the world of dating and picking up women, this book is entirely made for you to explore.

The key point to realize is that nothing in this book is going to help you much, if you're not willing to invest some time in this craft. Sure, you can learn a lot of theory on how to pick up women, how be extremely attractive and how to be an efficient person in general, but in terms of actually changing your life this book will do very little without you putting the energy in. This is the deal with every single online program, every practical book and so on. Famous and inspirational people say we can do anything in life and that is completely true, but the difference between could and would is so fucking big. Yes, we could do practically anything, but the things we're actually willing to do – those matter. For instance, it's possible for you to sleep with 100 different girls in the next 365 days starting today no matter the skill level you're at at this given point. It's possible for you to be the best pickup artist in the entire world, sleep with 10 000 women in your entire life or choose to embark on even crazier adventures. However, if you're not willing to suffer the pain early, like the pain of finishing a book despite all excuses that run around in your head every single day, then nothing will happen. We have the capacity to be the best, but if you're not willing to learn and take action, then we will die out like the rest, which most of us do before actually leaving this world. Killing a man's dreams is in many ways worse than killing a man himself.

This book is definitely not meant to be offensive nor judgemental towards you. The book is simply describing the situation. If you find this to be unpleasant to read, then realize that the author was in the same boat with you, my friend. Don't take this the wrong way and most of all, since conviction is the enemy of truth. If you do find something offensive to you which most of you will, do your best to stay subjective and try to see the point behind it all. This material exists merely with the goal to serve and teach you to become an absolute master of dating. To make an omelette one is required to break some eggs. In this case, the eggs are our negative paradigms that we've accumulated throughout the years and that are not helpful in the field of dating in any shape or form.

"Ultimately, no matter how hard I try, people will learn at their own pace."

Most of us think it's wise to criticise everything we see and doupt in the authenticity of everything. Sounds like a smart way to see things, however it will do the very same thing I've worked so hard to destroy here. This kind of thinking will set limits to yourself, won't let you enjoy yourself and will create a negative thinking pattern that's a plague to anyone who tries to improve. It's one of those half-truth type concepts. It's in your best interests to let go of your judgemental attitude and take everything in this book for granted. The results will be insane.

There are two ways which you can use to learn from this book. One is thinking logically and really examining the information I share here down to its core. This is a great place mentally to be at and will make you see the real truths behind dating, what really sparks attraction and how to apply it into your own life. However, if you're feeling adventurous and looking for the quick fix to your problems, then another path that you could take is believing everything I talk about in this book without any conviction since it goes against our social normalities and will make you question everything you know about women and dating. This is the closest thing to the magic pill of life.

We are the total sum of our habits. If you fit reading this book into your habits, one day you'll apply this knowledge without even realising.

In order to not make you confused I STRONGLY advise you to take everything you see here to heart without conviction. It's a blind spot that you'll want to have. The world is very subjective and depends on your interpretation. In this case the most effective thing for you to do for your own personal growth in picking up women is to believe every word that exists in this book. It's a lot to ask for and might even sound at times really stupid, but to create a positive change that will shape you into something that's known as the superhuman, this step is an absolute necessity. I've used this method on my clients, I've used it on myself so I know what I'm talking about. A leap of faith that will get you the desired results, if you let it help you. Afterall, if you've studied neurology, you know that everything we see in our daily life is brainwashing us in one way or another, this book is just something that's honest with you and tells you exactly what it is.

Critical thinking is something we all want to have in order to really dig deep and find the truth. It's something I'm all for, but since I have strong faith in my content and do not doupt in the authenticity not even one bit and care about you, the reader and wish the best results possible for you, then I must mention this method of learning. Some say it's blind faith, other says it's stupidity. But me? I say it's brainwash, a healthy brainwash that's designed to tell get you results through telling truth.

This is a practical book. It consists of many simple and adaptable rules that cover all areas of dating from inner battles of a beginner to actually living the life of a player. At first when you read this and have no previous knowledge on game, then they might seem quite stupid and you'll wonder why do we have to play these games with women? Why are we supposed to do these things and can't attract girls with the stuff we've been doing so far. Well, tough shit. Without being aware of these mental fixed women have you're not going to get a healthy relationship or even any for that matter. If you do, then it's for the wrong reasons such as money, high status, freedom to buy anything the woman wants and stuff that like. It's not healthy and will not grant either of you happiness. The sooner you'll learn these principles, the sooner you improve your life's quality. Plain and simple.

All of these concepts that I share in this book are field tested and hold themselves up strongly. It's my principle to not write about anything that I'm not completely sure of.

I really advise you to read all chapters with severe focus, all the truths, tips and shortcuts of seducing women are right here written down for you to experience. The more you absorb, the more time you're going to save learning this on your own. This book has the power to make you into the next success story within just months, if you have the drive to finish it. This book is not designed to be finished in one sitting. Pick it up whenever you feel like it, but know that the full power of what this book has to offer will present itself only once you've finished the entire thing. Whenever you've got questions about women and their behaviour, how to get laid as soon as possible through free and non-degrading ways or have some time to kill, just pick up this book and learn the ways of how to sleep with hundred women in one year or less. Everything is in here.

I'm a pickup artist and here's everything you need to know about the game and how it's played.

You're Responsible

"When you fully understand the reasoning for attraction between men and women, you'll be able to adapt these ways yourself almost instantly."

I believe the biggest problem we have in our world today is not taking responsibility for our own life. We tend to let others control the paths that we are able to choose and even the choices that should be left for us to decide. It's all coming from the state of insecurity and the lack of information, the right knowledge, the right education in our modern society. A big majority of us will blame everyone and everything before they get to the point of pointing a finger towards themselves. We think others are to be blamed for our current life situation. Our countries, laws, terrorists, bad and dishonest people and most of all, luck. Luck is the most commonly used excuse in the world we live in today. Sure, it does play a small part in it, but much more is about whether we let the right influence create us.

The New Year is not going to save you. 2017 will not be any better than 2040. Your life will be the same unless you decide to take responsibility for your situation. You alone are responsible for your own life and if you're sitting around waiting for something or someone to come and save you, to fix you to even help you, you're simply wasting your time. The sooner you realize that bad things happen to all of us at some point of our lives, but the way we react to them and what our attitude is like will make us or break us, the sooner you are able to enjoy life. Bad shit happens all the time and but as long as you keep blaming outside factors for your misery, you will never find any sort of relief, no improvement, no change and no happiness.

"As soon as you start to blame, even if you're being right, you'll lose control."

It does not matter where you come from. Just take a look around you. Look at all the successful people and what they had to go through to get there. It's not luck, it's not talent, it's only their attitude towards life. They are willing to take responsibility for their own life. No matter what life throws at them, they will focus on what they can do to improve instead of looking other factors outside of themselves to blame. Yes, maybe you are not to blame, but you are the only one who is able to fix it.

I want you to really be aware of this. Whenever you notice yourself blaming something else for your misery no matter who or what it is, stop. Keep doing it untill your paradigm changes and you begin to see world and success in it for what it truly is.

"The idea is not to fix your bad behaviour by putting on a good mask, the idea is to fix the reasoning behind bad behaviour. Learn the difference. You can't fix a problem by hiding it."

The Magic Pill: Part One

Ultimately we're all looking for that magic pill, the quick fix to all our problems. We act like there is this one thing, that one little secret all rich, famous and successful people know and just refuse to share with us. Many of you even bought this book with the hope of finding one of these pills in here, like I'm able to give you that one secret, that one small step that will transform all your dreams into reality and ends the miserable life you've been living for so long.

I'm not able to give you that magic pill. In fact, no one is. That magic pill does not exist. What does exist is a mindset that helps us get through tough times. Our brain can adapt to literally anything. It's the natural way, this is the only explanation of how we're able to form opinions, learn new languages extremely fast if put into the right environment, become better by practising more and anything else like this. Our brain is like a sponge, it will suck in everything that we expose ourselves to. We can't really circle out the right information from wrong since our conscious believes whatever is in the majority. There is only one thing we can fully control.

The information we expose ourselves to.

If you come from a family where your parents have not really done much with their lives and are constantly criticising the way of things and giving to their "why" a negative answer, then most likely you'll also grow up much like them hence their influence on you. If all your friends are unambitious, then you'll most likely also be unambitious. We all influence each other in one way or another, even if two people are really different, they'll still have an influence on each other and after spending tons of time together, their personality, their belief systems and principles will meet in the middle.

The best way to change your life is to be aware of this principle of we become what we think about, what we read and who we hang around with. Since we can't effectively choose the things we belive in without having some influence whether it's negative or positive change us in one way or another, there is just one way left that fully works.

We are able to choose our environment, the people we hang around with and the media we watch and read.

This is all you need to fully understand. By doing so you'll discover something magical. Many of us say it's easy and we all know this, but do we really? If we did, every single one of us would feel happy all the time! If you think you know this and still feel sad, then guess what – you don't. You might know it, but you do not understand it.

The sooner you adapt the mindset of your life being in your own hands and the information you expose yourself to will be the fuel for the actions you take. Being rich, famous and overall successful in any endeavour is the matter of what information you choose to consume. We become what we think about, therefore ideas are like fuel for our actions. It's up to us to make sure we're getting the best fuel that favours the life of our dreams. Changing the fuel will change your mind, which in turn will change your life.

How does one do this?

By exposing himself to the right information.

This book will teach you the ways how you can start enjoying hard work, and also use this trait in the smartest way humanly possible. Soon enough, you'll be able to enjoy every single moment in your life, know where you're going in life, have the sex life beyond your dreams and be the kind of guy who everybody wants to be, but only a few actually are.

Autopilot

We as humans have the ability to carry out thousands of complex activities every single day from making a cup of coffee to driving mechanically complex machines such as cars. We do all of this without even paying much attention to them, we're on an autopilot. We don't have to rethink every small step over and over again since most of what we do is already automatic. Our speech, eye movement, walking, running, writing, reading and much more.

As a child you learned how to open doors. If you didn't then you'd spend some time every time you approach a door on thinking about how to open a door. If this behaviour was not learned in an early age, you would have to learn it right now and soon enough add this behavioural into your autopilot pile of stuff you're constantly doing every day, but not thinking about.

This is exactly how you should approach this book. I offer you ideas, behavioural ques to which women respond well. I teach you to become the guy who is excellent with social interactions, who is able to find a new partner in just a matter of days not even talking about making new friends, but most importantly – how to become the man in your prime.

Every single idea that you adopt from this book will be carved into your mind and which will stay there just like the example with opening a door. If you keep hitting the iron, in other words keeping at it, reading the material that's presented to you in here, you'll be building your skillset, becoming better day by day and soon enough get the results you desire. All these things I teach you in this book will soon enough be a part of your autopilot section. When you don't even have to think about game, the moment you BECOME the game, you've deeply mastered this topic. This is what we're striving for here.

Some of the linguistics that I use regularly in this book...

- Pulling - getting a girl to come home and have sex with you

- Logistics - The details of a situation, be it transportation, timing of events, how many friends need to get home, how close does she live to the the place met, does she have a boyfriend and is he home etc.

- Neg/negging - A light insult wrapped in the package of a complement

- Set – any person or a group that you approach with the intention of having sex with one of the members

- PUA – Pickup artist

Make an effort and keep these in mind as you move on, and come back to this page when something seems unclear.

My Two Cents

"Pickup artist subconsciously acts as a liberator, a mental healer who will show girls a glimpse of what life of being free and living for yourself really looks like. A great pickup artist is designed to inspire."

First of all – Game & Pickup & Seduction & Dating – For the most part they all represent the same thing. Call it whatever you like, but the meaning will not differ. I will be using all of them with the same meaning throughout this book.

Also, I tend to refer to all women as girls, there is no underage shit going on here. Just to avoid any confusion.

Anyway, let's jump right in…

A lot of people consider or game in general to be something players do to sleep with as many women possible just because they like sex or they want to have revenge on some girl who dumped them or didn't go on a date with them in the past. The terms "game" and "pick-up" are tremendously underestimated. Altho this is usually the main reason guys get into this, to pay back their ex by becoming the man she could never have anymore, to fix their social issues and become desirable, having a sex addiction and other many negative roots , it's not however why most of them stay to this path. There are two sides of this of course just as in Star Wars movies, the dark side and the light side, but only the ones who are doing it out of love have the capability to really benefit from it and change their lives in a positive way.

Game changes people. It changes our values and makes us see the world for what it truly is. It makes them realize their life's calling and gives them the life they've always wanted to have. And I'm not just talking about getting lots of sex with different girls or being labled as a player and „the cool guy" in their social circle. Game makes people find the road to happiness and create the strongest version of themselves both mentally and physically without any unnatural substances what so ever. From my point of view, it's more effictive than any drug, food, drink or any other consumable object in the world.

Have some faith in the process and you'll be there sooner than you think.

Being really amazing with the way of handling women, being able to get laid and be the kind of guy who women naturally want to be around comes down to a principle. It's like with becoming rich, experts say if a certain individual is not able to become rich in today's time, then he or she would not be rich also during a different time. If you're not able to become fit while being just a bit overweight, then you will not be any more inclined to becoming fit if instead are totally obese. The law of being excellent with women is very much the same. No matter if you're extremely fit, rich or just famous for something, it does not mean you're also good with girls and dating. Women might give you a try rather than some other dude who's nothing compared to your achievements, but you in no shape or form will be good with girls from the standpoint of your external values. Being good with girls is about having a certain personality, a certain type of mindset and this is what I'm going to focus on.

After sleeping with hundred women I discovered that it's not even a big deal, since the number itself did not do anything in terms of getting me on the right track. I was a young kid who was chasing his dream of becoming successful through sleeping with lots and lots of different women. I did not become successful because of achieving my goal of reaching the count of a hundred. It did not increase my value as a man. I owe all my success to the ideas and truths that I discovered during the time of sleeping with one hundred women, the paradigm shifts that happened in my head and discovering the new way of seeing this world, adopting a more positive, happy and a successful outlook. By doing so I demolished my ego and built a strong web of understanding, knowledge and started to enjoy every single moment in my life. This is what made me into a high value man and not the amount of women that I slept with. Ultimately picking up women is all nothing more but a mere journey of self-discovery. Fixing your life is done from inside, not from outside. Certain external actions are required, but they are not the cure, they're just a tool of achieving your dreams, just as pickup is.

I was a young kid, desperate to find a girl who would like me back. Instead, I stumbled upon thousands of women who were into me. This is not an accident. This is nothing more but a mere manifestation of being able to take action and shut down the negative fearsome voices in the brain that are always screaming to say no.

The purpose of this book is to motivate you to be an awesome person and always spread positivity to those around you. Funny enough, that's how you get laid. It's also how you become a better person in every aspect of your life, not just with women.

If you were to die right now, what would your last words be? "I was a really good boy and I cleaned my room every day for an hour every single day?" Or is it going to be: "I pursued my purpose." Up to you.

Society vs Pickup

"The very same moment when we lose everything, we become free to do anything."

From the moment we born, we begin to earn lables and are criticised by literally everyone we meet, whether it's good or bad, it's still judgemental. The opinion of judgemental people don't matter, because they don't matter. Judgemental people are of a lower moral authority than those who don't judge. We, people who don't judge, have the responsibility to crush and destroy those judgemental bullies and we do that with an overwhelming positivity and our extreme open mindedness.

Social normalities try to put us in a box. That box is a prison that is being created in our mind and is said to be there to protect us, to be useful, to contribute to the society in a way they decide for us and other bullshit such as this. What pickup does, is it destroys the blocks we've been building inside ourselves since the very moment we enter this world. The things that hold us back, by doing pickup, will be gone relatively quickly, we begin to see the world from a whole different perspective, we understand the dynamics of all social interactions and we begin to see the intention that are usually distracted by sentences. In other words, we learn to read between the lines and see the true meaning of every communication.

The society has labeled "pick-up artists" and the idea of sleeping with many different women as something sinister. Hide your wives, hide your kids, the dark wizard is coming! Do you see where this idea is coming from? Put yourself into the person's mind who's saying it. Where is it coming from? I-N-S-E-C-U-R-I-T-Y.

People who badmouth pickup, are deep down actually afraid of it because they don't understand the whole concept. We are so afraid of breaking out of social norms and belive something that's not so "out there" that they would rather badmouth and fight against instead of trying to understand the roots. If you're one of those people, then of course you should be scared of it, since all you see is some badass looking pickup guy rolling in wearing some ridiculous outfit and taking away your beloved wives. Simply put – people who demonize pickup are blind in

21

terms of how our world works because of their own arrogance and laziness. In this case, blindness can be translated into being uneducated on life and just plain stupidity. After realizing how important pickup can really be for my business growth, mental disorder fixes, getting in shape and much more, I've made it my mission to show everybody what I've experienced and how anybody can do the same. It would be a shame to waste this wonderful oppurtunity to become something unbelievably awesome.

Any person that's truly confident in himself and not with that fake confidence that's easy to break by putting him in a tough situation, has no problem with pick-up artists or any other type of people such as races, genders, levels of education... . A person of this type is one of the happiest and also one of the most attractive people on our planet. Some of the traits these people have:

They don't judge, therefore people feel relaxed with them. They do not have insecurities, so they are valuable for us to be around for their and for our own growth. And most of all – they're confident in themselves for the very same reason – they understand how the law of attraction works.

Do you see the connection here? By educating your social side by going out, talking to the opposite sex, figuring out what their sticking points are and what triggers attraction in them you'll have a high possibility of stumbling onto a gold mine. By doing this you have the potential to unlock in my mind the most powerful tool you could ever posess – the universal truth of what attraction really is. Once you have a clear sense of understanding attraction and how our minds really work, both men and women, you can do literally anything let alone get many hot women to sleep with you. This stuff is just a bonus. You will know how the world works and what it takes to achieve any level you desire.

But why would our society make us believe such lies about the dating industry? No society or country wants you to be that smart, because we don't need everyone to be like Steve Jobs and Gandhi in the world. The biggest proportion of our population is working on 9 to 5 jobs and live for the weekends and holidays. If there were a shift in media and everyone would start telling the truth, then what would happen in a society that's been built on lies over thousands of years? More people would start to realize what life is really about and get smarter every single day. In the end there would not be enough labour force to keep the industries and companies on float. Mediocre people are in high demand, because they work on jobs that a smart person would never even dream of doing.

Here's my question for you:

Why would You settle for a low, normal, just okay, mediocre life? Last time I checked all life ends with death, this is the only version that has been proven. All these theories about reincarnation and life after death sound good of course, but we cannot just take it for granted without any proof. I don't think it even matters what will happen after our death. Much more important is what is happening while we're alive! This is the only thing we can take for granted. Our time on earth matters and should not be wasted doing something we don't like. Even though our world is unbalanced, could be organized much better and most of us are not able to follow our dreams, it's not really our problem right now. The real problem is we're unwilling to step out of the rat race and become the heroes of our own story. If you're set out to change the world, start with yourself.

This is why learning the ways of seduction are so life changing. It shows us what's truly possible in life and that the limits are far beyond than where we expect them to be. The game teaches us to live a fulfilling life by having positive effect on LOTS of people and becoming the best version of ourselves in the process. Pickup teaches us to be free and do whatever we need to do and how to have fun while doing it. Oh and did I already mention mastering social interactions? This just keeps getting better and better.

Funny enough, to illustrate my point even more, the things a guy who learns game in a healthy wants to do are always about self-development such as taking care of his health, making more money, having a positive impact on the world by teaching other's that need some guidance. Simply put – getting laid will make you into everything you could ever wish for. It all starts with the desire to attract women and moves on to something that makes most of us legendary and some of us even remembered in history. The mastery of self-discovery…meaning that we finally understand what the right road is and starting to walk on it. Not the end result, it's all about the process. Pickup industry might just be the very best place for you to invest yourself in.

Is this life for me?

"In five years you'd wish you had started today."

Some guys have it naturally and some just don't. Some guys are good naturals, some are average and some are bad. Some are not socially awkward, but don't know how to have sex with different girls almost every single day and some are socially completely terrible in every single interaction including with their dearest friends and family. Some guys are just talented in a specific field and some are not.

It does not really matter in which category you belong to. Even for the talented natural guy he still has tricks and tips to learn on this, nobody, no matter how good he is, is ever going to know everything about game. There is room for improvement no matter who you are.

But is it really worthwhile to go out and practise expressing yourself with women and to practise sticking up conversations with women?

Many guys are afraid to approach women they don't know. Fear of rejection amongst many other things is to be blamed here. Game will destroy your little bullshit stories that you make up for you „being cool for all your life and not needing any practise" type of shit. Let's use Bob for an example.

Bob sees a woman he likes right off the bat. She looks so good that Bob can't resist to fantasise about their life together and what would happen if they were to get married let along many other sexual thoughts. There is an obstacle though. Bob does not know the woman nor the woman him. In order to meet her Bob needs to go up to her and talk or the woman might dissapear forever and he will never see her again. It feels like taking a risk. A big risk. Bob's mind is filled with insecure thoughts. Maybe the girl does not like me back? What if she laughts at me? What if I look weird in the eyes of society? Maybe she has a boyfriend? Maybe the boyfriend is spying on her and will kick my ass right after I go talk to her? In the end, it's all a generalisation of failing thanks to your ego that ultimately tries to protect us from harm. The thing about ego is that it cannot tell the difference between real threat and fiction.

There are two things most of the guys in the world think they excel at – winning a fight and getting the girl they crave for. When the time comes to actually prove it, they get frightened and bail out. The thoughts of failure come to the surface? And even if they fail prove the authenticity of their ego's theory that they are able to excel in these two things, it feels like they have been lying to themselves for so long. The next step is failing into a depressive state because they are realising that they are not that cool, badass and successful guy that they had in mind. This is why approaching a stranger always seems like a big risk since it plays with your reality exposing your true colours.

Let's take a look at what would happen if Bob did not approach that women on the street. The woman would dissapear and he would probably never see her again. Seems like the risk is gone, right. Is it really? If Bob does not have the courage to approach, then what is he risking? Staying lonely for the rest of his life. Not progressing as a person. Slowly dieing inside. Not taking action leads to not building willpower and strengthening your weak character that has been developed through many other failures to take action not just in pickup, but with all areas of life.

It really comes down to just willpower and how bad do you want it. If you want it bad enough you'll find a way, if not, you'll find an excuse.

You're always going to have fear in life, if you did not know already, then sorry to break this to you, but this shit won't go away. Never. No matter if it's talking to a girl, guy, getting a promotion, public speaking, whatever it might be – you will always have fear. We are able to expand our comfort zone by doing many fearful things and by doing these the fear will slowly fade away over time. It's not called destroying a fear, it's just expanding your comfort zone. Even if you're completely fine approaching any woman in the world, do all kind of weird activities on crowded streets and are willing to have people laugh at you, there will always be something that is scary to you. Fear will never go away, but it can be drastically diminished.

"Start with small and simple things."

Courage does not come from not having fear. Courage comes from acting despite fear and destroying it though action. No matter what you do, you're always taking a risk. In Bob's case, it's either becoming a stronger man through fear and rejection, but having a great reward in the end OR staying the same, not improving and living a small and pointless life that you don't even enjoy. You might enjoy part of it such as eating pizza, watching mindless entertainment movies and such, but that's about it. There is no fulfillment, no victory and no purpose. It's coping, not thriving.

Now put yourself into Bob's situation. What would you do? Which risk would you take? Both roads are painful. Both inclue tears, sweat and and most of all - fear. One of them will give you instant small satisfaction, like eating chocolate or not approaching and feeling good for a moment but knowing deep down inside that you failed to act. If Bob does approach and takes the so called high road, he will get a different reward that comes in two parts. The first part is instant satisfaction just like in the first situation. You will be rewarded right away, whether it be feeling like a badass for acting despite fear. The second part is growing as a person and feeling like on the top of the world every single moment for the rest of your life!

So as you see, both situations can reward you, but only one of those rewards will last a lifetime while the other one barely even exists. It might be a bit more difficult and will require willpower to take the high road, but in the end, nobody has ever wrote a book about how thankful and happy they are for not improving their life and being mediocre. So here you go. We get what we deserve.

Pickup is definitely not the only way how you can improve your life, but it's defenitely a great way to start your „recovery" from the social conditioning that we have been taught to follow and which has suppressed us for so long. It does not matter what you believe and know or what your background is. Paradigms in our brain are formed by the environment we are surrounded by and we are able to shape them by increasing self-awareness and choosing which type of influence we want to influence us. It's like brainwash, but the one of your choosing for your own benefit. After all, that's what learning really is all about.

Do I know whether it's the right path for you exactly to take?

There is no way for me to be completely sure of it, since life is very random and has the trait of playing tricks in most unusual times. The best way to describe life is to picture a guy pushing you down the stairs, watching you fall down, then starting to laugh it off while sincerely calling it a joke and sending you an elevator to climb back to the previous floor and even one higher, if you let him. Do I know the real answer behind this question?

I don't. Regardless, my philosophy is that in life I go where I feel like going. At the moment it's writing my ass of to produce value for guys in who's situation I used to be at. Will it be the same next year? Or the year after that? In 10 years? Who the fuck knows. Franky, I've stopped caring about it, the real answer of whatever you'd like to call it. I do what I feel like is right for me to do at the given period. I believe this is what we all should, and can do.

This is life.

It's random, it's tedious, it's fun, it's electrifying, it's boring, funny, difficult, painful, easy... The idea of life, living, is everything, the greatest thing we are able to ever own. Enjoy the struggle, embrace the chaos of unknowingness, of being inadequate and strive to be better, yet at the same time do not make it into something you're not happy with.

Myths of Attraction

"Anything that's not actionable right now is irrelevant when doing the approach."

When you see a cool guy at the club, he might pull girls against himself from left and right. You'll immediately start rationalizing like he is a cool guy and I'm not. He can do such acts and I can't. He is cool and I'm not. Most guys would quit right here. The successful ones, those people who are determined to find out what's wrong with them and look for solutions instead of coping with their pain, however start taking this concept apart piece by piece. Why is that guy considered to be cool? Why am I not cool? It's his paradigm of thinking that determines success in any field.

In pickup, regular dating and men-women relations in general, there are couple of things that you need to realize that are not true and exist purely to give an explaination to the guys who don't understand the ways of seduction. A lot of people have influenced your life and the way you see man to woman communication, especially your parents, friends and movies. What are some of these paradigms that come to your mind?

Women like guys who look good meaning fitness plays a big part.

Women go for the guy who's rich, meaning money plays a big part.

Men need to buy flowers, gifts, pay for dinners.

Being really good at your job will trigger attraction.

Abdominal muscles must be in check.

These are just some of the things we've been led to believe. Some of these even reach out and scratch the surface of truth, but are still half-truths at best. In reality, having these traits, acting this way and thinking it will trigger attraction is completely wrong. Knowing everything about the French revolution, being really great at accounting, having lots of money in your hands, looking like a male model or Brad Pitt, being really muscular, showering the girl with flowers and gifts – these are absolutely not necessary at all. In some cases and at certain times they do help and some of them are even good traits to put your focus on, but as far as dating goes they do not play that big of a role.

Dating is NOT based on logic. It's based on emotions. Being too logical will kill the attraction by reinforcing to overpower emotions which we've been working so hard on to bring out in her. If there is no emotion, then there will be no sex.

The comments I typically see on some pickup videos on YouTube:

"Two fit good looking rich guys sharing tips on how to get a girlfriend...nice."

Men are logical thinkers meaning we need a reason why the girl likes us, we need action-result type of knowledge because that's just how their brain works. This makes it so easy for us to keep thinking that buying gifts will make her happy, being in a great shape will make her happy, being rich will make her fall for me. It's really easy to believe that. This is however not true and the product of lacking information on this subject. The real truth is that women will fall for you, if you fall for yourself, figuratively. Here's what I mean by this:

Women like a guy who's living an interesting life, who is okay with expressing his own kind of humor and does not look for approval from others (looking for approval from others will show that you're not the most high value guy in the room). Looking strong and fit will make you feel good about yourself and so the girl will like you for your self-confidence, not for your body. **These godlike traits like being rich and famous and fit are for you and for you only, the girl will like the person you are because of them.** Don't get me wrong, women do like a guy who looks good, but that's never the deciding factor. There have been many surveys on this where an interviewer hits the streets and asks around from women about their ex boyfriends and their desired types. The results are always the same – women date guys of all shapes, all sizes, with all kinds of financial records, with cars or no cars, stutterers and radio speakers. Women date guys of any type, because the type does not matter. The only trait that matters as far as dating goes is your personality, the way you carry yourself, the way you treat others and her and how you live your life whether it's in fear or in satisfaction. Dating experts have noticed that women think they have a type of which they like, but in reality they don't. Women do not know what they like or want because they are unable to explain it. One being unable to explain something means not being able to fully understand it. Once again, this is caused by the lack of knowledge on this subject and the fact that this area of life has been kept hidden under the table due to schools not teaching this, academics, entrepreneurs being busy with their own lives creating value, making money, focusing on completely other areas of life. People think they have dating all figured out which is merely because of ego and we just don't care to look any deeper on this. Humans mind is a funny thing, the majority does not dare to examine it since most of our lives are built on avoiding our insecurities. Learning pickup and all dating in general will make you exposed to your own weaknesses and shows you the fastest way on how to improve on those very same traits that you've been avoiding so hard to develop.

Being rich, looking totally ripped like a Greek god – since I do teach how to be attractive without these traits, it does not mean you should not have those or not work towards them. We should want to have those things for you, to live a better life, but as far as dating goes, they do not matter at all. In music videos, especially in rap videos they have those sports cars and are „making it rain" and provoking us with the so-called high life. In reality a guy with no hair, no job, without even a HOME can get a model looking chick and not just one, but as many as his soul desires. That's not even rocket science. It's not about learning certain mechanic behaviours. You don't need to remember endless rules on how to act in every single situation. It's a simple shift in your mind. Pickup does not teach you to become James Bond or Casanova, it teaches you to become the best version of you. You will be your own brand and the opposite sex will love you for it.

Alcohol

Another big misconception is that if you go for the drunk girls every night, then getting laid is the easiest thing ever. I can tell you from my professional experience that this idea is certainly not true. Alcohol does give you beer goggles, but not in the same way as you might think. Alcohol makes us free of social pressure and fears. The more we drink, the more of this effect we start to experience. Alcohol does not make men more attractive to women, it just makes women more receptive to cool guys and eliminates the bitch face, if you get my meaning. No beverage of alcohol is able to make an unattractive man into a pickup artist, all it does is make it much easier to get to sex and skip a lot of bullshit in-between, both for girls and guys. So if a guy comes up to me and says it's easy to sleep with hundred different women in a year, I'll know exactly where the guy is at in his path. The man who relies on drunk girls to increase his batting average, will never reach the mark of hundred because it's more to it than that, but also less than you might think.

For those of you who are really keen on the topic of alcohol, there's more on this in an upcoming chapter.

It's really easy to learn if the right action is being taken

"Only one who does not question is safe from making a mistake."
– Albert Einstein

One day after a long night out, after sacrificing a good portion of my sleep in order to have wild sex with a random one night stand that I picked up at the bar not more than just several hours ago, I was left with a sinking feeling, right after the girl leaving my place for good. It was almost noon, I had skipped breakfast, as you do in these occasions, laying there staring at the whiteness of my plain and utterly normal sealing. But, as it was a sealing for me, someone else used it as a floor to walk on. The woman who was living on the top of my apartment, relatively young and quite hot if you ask me, took the liberty of wearing high heels, for what it seemed to me, just as a joke to piss off neighbours that were living downstairs. Pissing off me. Yes, I heard it. I heard the action that was taking place upstairs, woman walking back and forth, enjoying her little show that was just for me to hear, supposedly. I was in a great mood thanks to my extracurricular activities that took place just a few hours ago. My self-esteem was quite high, needless to even say. I took the liberty of getting my ass to her door while having just one intention in mind. Feeling the sense of accomplishment through sexual activity with a new potential dame. So I knocked on her door. When she saw me, someone she did not expect to see at all, she was tremendously surprised, asking me what I'm doing there. Me, being calm and everything, looking at her with the sense of tranquillity, asking if she has a reason why to wear high heels in her own apartment and was waking me up part of her plan. She started to laugh, thanks to my skilfully witty and relatable way of saying these things. You see, I did not express frustration or anger or any kind of displeasement. I was merely trying to be funny. She asked if she had broken any laws, to which I replied: "Yes, you made me hard." After a few more sentences back and forth with the interaction tonality of man to woman conversation, she invited me in and we had sex. As you see, sometimes all it takes is a little bit of luck, a sense of entitlement, and major balls. Skill is overrated, confidence and willingness to fail however are perhaps the best character traits any aspiring success story needs.

"You don't need much skill to get laid, you just need balls. Skill is accumulated through taking action and increases your chances."

I'll take a wild assumption and say you're not very good at seduction, hence why you bought this book. Or maybe you're an expert and are just interested in what I have to say about all of this. Might be true, might be false, but the for the sake of making a point let's say you are a beginner in this. As a beginner, your openings and approaches in general are really uncalibrated, feel forced and also a bit insecure, if not very, depending on your level. If you're naturally good with women and have a social personality, then it won't be as bad as for someone who hasn't had a solid interaction in three years. Either way, it's not optimal. Let's say your approaches are terrible. Now, if you continued to approach day after day, night after night, hitting the iron untill all energy has been depleted and you can't wait to just go home, if you're tremendously dedicated and don't give up no matter what, even knowing that your approach is going to fail, but not giving up and still approaching no matter what - do you think your skill level, when it comes to dating, is going to stay the same? The chances of it happening are literally extremely slim to none in the case of a guy who has adopted the ways of self-improvement and follows them like a religion.

Our brains have a mechanism that helps us to be adaptable to any situation life may throw at us. Meaning if you don't know how to swim and you get thrown into water, your mind will start finding ways to keep you on float, and surprisingly enough you'll stay on the surface longer than you'd expect from someone with no experience in hard contact with water at all. We don't just sink like an iron bar, which cannot swim either. We can stay on the surface for at least ten times longer than a lifeless object. If we were to give up, we'd be nothing more than a rock or a tree branch. We would not deserve the title of being a human. There is a great force hidden within us, which can only be revealed by life threatening occurences. Forcing yourself to approach a woman and take the first action-based step towards self-improvement, in this particular case our brains act as if our life was on the line. This is what makes pickup such as great tool to use to turn a man into an absolute beast, someone who's a wolf amongst sheep, who gets what he wants out of life and who is an inspiration to every single living soul on this planet.

My openings used to suck a lot. I did not dare to look the girl in the eyes. I did not know how to control my body language in the manner of not looking socially awkward and overly weird. I wasn't comfortable around any female, therefore giving off a negative and unpleasing vibe. I tried to be fun, but it always felt forced and overall fake, so nobody really wanted to spend any time with me. Although I did not understand that I sucked at all. I felt so freaking alive doing the approaches because it felt like the most productive thing to do in my life. It was like I was stepping up as a man and creating something beautiful for the world to see. I literally felt like I was godlike, in the movie. But did those women see it? Maybe. It's said that whatever you feel, the girl feels. Since I felt so awesome, I was uncalibrated and still a bit insecure having nothing to say most of the time. Now I can see that the girl actually liked me because I felt so positive, but I did not have the experience and the knowledge in general to back my actions up. Either way, I kept approaching every single day. I believe I hit at least 40 new encounters every night in a bar plus not even counting my daygame approaches. Do you think a guy with my attitude would stay the same after living like this for a year? No fucking way. My brain adapted to the situation, I learned to calibrate myself and became more confident because I had all these experiences of talking to women and it just began to feel normal doing it. I felt better in a bar than I did in my own home. These higher level of states are so powerful that once they have been experienced, they are never forgotten, and therefore, are sought ever after.

The point?

No matter how hard you suck, no matter where you are in terms of learning seduction, if you keep going out and putting yourself in these situations through approaching, then you will become better! There is no way around it. It's simply how we're built. We're built to evolve and learn new stuff relatively quickly when in tough situations. It's the will to survive that taps into us and begins to work its magic in the world of seduction.

All we can ever do in life is choose our environment and choose the people and influences we let in our life, including television, books and most importantly – out attitude. If we create an environment for ourselves that is positive and informative, our brain will pick up everything we need to know on its own. We don't need to do any hard studying nor remembering rules or any other principle. We just need to expose ourselves to the information, because the information will stick to us no matter what. Our actions are in our control, everything else comes naturally.

In pickup when we're learning, then what we can control is putting ourselves in the situation and say hi. You don't need to have anything else in your mind ready to be said other than a simple "hi". Everything will be taken care of itself when we're just exposed to the thing we're so desperately trying to learn. Same with books, same with making money, same with literally everything. You want to learn game? Read books about it, go out and approach, put yourself in the life of a pickup artist. You don't need to be a pickup artist right away, you just need to act like one and the knowledge will stick no matter what if you keep yourself in this kind of life. Trust me on this.

Pushing yourself to go out and approach is the only thing that matters, everything else will come naturally if this first step is being done over and over again.

I've found that the easiest way to know whether you should be learning game, approaching a girl, going for the kiss, taking a girl to dance with you, buy gifts and pretty much everything else that you can think of are decisions that come with resistance. Meaning you will not be able to make these kind of decisions quickly unless you've practiced and are completely comfortable doing them. Every time you're on your way to do something that's outside of your comfort zone, you'll be feeling resistance and run into a debate. With who? Yourself!

It's funny how we are the only problems on our road to success. The problem is never anything external, it's never about the situation, every single debate we have over anything is always internal. Mental debates are frustrating, they are always in high demand of energy and will make you less productive in any endeavour. Thankfully I've been using a method for years now that's designed to specifically make you spend little to no energy on shit like this.

What's the method?

It's really simple. You've heard it before, but only a small percentage of us has actually implemented this in their lives. It's literally life changing.

Every time you're not sure of whether you should do the deed, pick up that hobby, ask out that girl, make that business deal – every single time just ask yourself one simple little question.

In five years, would I regret my decision or would I be happy to have that experience?

It sounds so damn simple, in reality it's something a highly functional human being will be able to do daily.

Should you learn pickup?

Should you go out tonight?

Should you ask out that girl you like?

Should you try to be more than friends, but risk losing her in the process?

The answer is really simple. Would you rather live a cool life and risk a little or play it safe and settle with mediocrity. Don't get me wrong, mediocrity has some cool benefits such as comfort foods, trash TV, computer games, which come with the price of not learning to be charismatic, not exposing the limits of life as a successful human being is supposed to do, and most importantly – having grand regrets later in life about not being courageous enough and not having no chance to live the life you've always dreamt of, and which now you can't. Not anymore.

What Women Like

"The Woman sees the Man only as he sees himself, doesn't question and nourishes only what he produces and expresses what he impresses."

When I first got into pickup, my first goal was to get a girlfriend, someone who's loyal, nice and devoted only to me. My experiences with girls at that time during my early 20s was extremely limited, while other hot girls of my age already had several experiences dating other guys. The most attractive girls had usually dated the cool guys in high school and other guys who were considered to be high value from teenager's standpoint. I was competing with those type of guys, at least in my mind, and it felt like I just don't have the goods.

When I got to the point of actually getting laid, dating these really attractive women who have been with many desirable guys, and I found that out, I was a bit annoyed that they have had a cool sex life, have no problems with finding a partner that's actually considered to be high value of some sort and just gave herself away which seemed to be with such ease. Needless to say, many negative assumptions and comments started to take over me. Why would they do such deeds? Why would they hook up with some guy in a car? Why would they give themselves up for some douchebag in school? Why don't they have any self-respect? This sort of thinking led me into breaking up with every single girl who I treated this way. It was not because they felt guilty, I don't even think they have any regrets about their past at all, it was just because I'd be nagging on them, trying to slut shame and being an overall mood killer. So when my girls would go to the club with me, meet a cool guy who did not care about what they've done in the past, did not judge and put himself out there with the intention of sleeping with my girls, they'd most likely accept that offer and just let the guy run all over me. The girls were looking at me like the little sour guy who's not happy with his girlfriend having fun and enjoying herself, and then she's having fun with those other dudes who are much cooler and popular than me. The choise always came in favour of the other guys who had the sense of being able to not care and focusing purely on having fun with the girl. As a result of this I lost some of the best girlfriend I ever had and wound up hooking up with the ones for who I was their first or who were denying their past since they had a sense of seeing through me into the sour sorry little soul. Those girls are usually less attractive, less good in bed and overall isn't high quality.

There are only 2 types of people who would shame girls for acting as a slut:
1)   Girls who WISH they could be having fun, letting loose, and being sexually open, but are jealous and can't due to their own mental blockages.
2)   Guys who WISH they were getting the girl, but are jealous because some another dude, who is happy about life and who devotes time on learning the ways of seduction, is having the fun.

There is no such thing as a slut. People like to fuck. Get over it.

On a personal level, it used to bother me seeing guys date best quality of girls they can, beautiful, fun, popular, and get intimidated that the girl had more sexual experience. On the level of game, girls can detect what you want them to do. The girl will fit whatever mould you'd like her to fit. If you want her to be a total sex maniac, she'll be a total sex maniac. If you want the girl to be shy and polite, she'll be shy and polite.

When you're talking to a girl at a bar while you're fun and every part of you does not judge her in any way at all for what she's done in the past, she'll probably come home with you and have fun with you, if this is what you want. If you judge her, she'll sense it and hit you with a giant web of lies. Women will absolutely and without any kind of shame, lie to you as much as it takes with anything you want to hear, and the crazy thing is she'll probably even start believing it herself. Women are socially adaptable. They find out what the society expects of them, and they'll live up to that role.

From a girl's perspective, she has a conservative and an adventurous side of her personality. Depending on which side you'll ask, which depends on your intention behind the question, she'll answer with whatever's suitable for you to hear. If she gets the sense of you not liking sluts and that you prefer a girl who's loyal and nice, she'll lie about her partners. However, if the cards are played opposite, she'll tell you everything you want to know and also truthfully.

Which side of her should you listen to? Adventurous side for sure. For a guy who is not able to handle the truth, you might want this as your blind spot to go on with your life as it stands right now, but if you're looking to have crazy hot sex with her, explore the limits and maybe even hook up with her friends on her own will, you'll need to focus on her adventurous side and be okay with her bringing it to the surface. When you stop worrying about how many guys she's been and start focusing on your experience and having an amazing time, that's when your life starts to improve.

When you're failing with women, have no skills to get a solid relationship or even a one night stand for that being, the slut shaming card is the easiest to pick up and blame your dysfunctionality on. It's really hard to snap out of that place since if you let go of the lies you've created in order to feel better about yourself, for an example if you don't get laid, then you have to take the responsability for it. By letting go of the story you've created as an excuse, you'll start getting laid, but the fear of the unknown can beat you down nonetheless and keep you from ever stepping out of the false world. Blaming yourself is incredibly painful ad that's why excuses feel so good. It's the road of less pain, but also rewards you much less, whether we're talking about getting laid, earning money or even as simple as just getting in shape.

What do women really look for in a man? The way how a man carries himself. How he treats other people. Is the man secure of himself, is he confident?

There is no point in going around and asking women what they like in a man because a woman cannot explain that. It something she does not even understand. They feel attraction and justify it with the guy being rich, confident, caring, sincere, good looking and much more since they do not know how to explain it themselves. They do not even know why they feel such attraction towards some men.

Here is the best definition I've been able to find. Women are mostly attracted to a man of <u>masculine characteristic</u>. A man of this caliber would be confident in his own abilities, be okay with expressing his own personality without changing his core ways to be accepted, finds or creates his own social circle that's suitable for his character, and is overall a man of purpose since when you have a strong sense of purpose, then it takes care of your insecurities and confidence and everything else by itself. Whatever you choose your purpose to be does not matter at all, what matters is actually having something to work towards.

Steps to Masculinity:

1.) Be very purposeful

2.) Control - be grounded in who you are/depth

3.) Flowing; be relaxed and at ease - Free & Entitled

4.) Self-Amusement; enjoy your own behaviors (internal) over her reactions (external)

I could write so god-damn many chapters on being the man of purpose through self-discovery and becoming someone of really high caliber, but I've already done it once and besides, that's not what this book is about. This book is about developing the skills and the mindset of picking up women. There are many different ways on how to skip many steps in becoming a man of purpose and get women in your current life- and mind situation without so-to-say "handling your shit". This is what I'm here to teach you.

Remember when I mentioned the guy who knows everything about the French revolution in the last chapter? If a girl likes the guy who keeps talking to her about this subject, then it's not because of the words the guy is saying. Girl likes that guy because he seems passionate about the subject and that makes him looks like a man of purpose, someone who knows what he is and where he's going. It's not in the words. It's in the subliminal messages. You have to learn how to read between the lines.

Next example is the guy who is extremely muscular and looking like a fitness model. Girls do like guys who have a nice body, but that's definitely not a deal breaker if the guy does not have this trait. The main reason why girls are attracted to a guy of this caliber is mainly because they look confident and overall satisfied with themselves. Do you see the difference? That nice body is there only so that the guy can feel good about himself, not for the girl. Girl is attracted to the mind that the guy will develop through having that nice body, that confidence, that leadership like attitude, the masculine vibe coming from that guy. So if I were to teach you the ways how you can feel just like that shredded ripped totally awesome looking guy without going through the same path, then you'd be a chick magnet without having that nice body to blame your success on. And guess what? Teaching this mindset is exactly what I'm here to do amongst many other things. You are able to get sex every single night without having a purpose nor even the mindset. Being a man of purpose will be the ultimate thing to attract high value girls to be with you for a long time, but to have simple sex with the girls of same caliber is actually much easier. In conclusion, getting in a relationship is a lot harder than having casual sex regularly.

Women appreciate who you actually are, not who you imagine you are. At the same time if you're weak on the inside, then they will not find you attractive. Being nice or being an asshole won't get you laid. The only behavior that will get you results are your masculine manners. Having a purpose is one of the most masculine traits, if not the most important one, but can be overlooked easily if everything else that is the result of you having purpose without actually having it is in check.

How can I do this with my life? How can I have a purpose? Or even more important - how can I not have a purpose and still have a shit loads of sex with different girls?

Everything is cultivated over time. This goes for the pickup skills as long with everything else. For every work you put in, there is a reward. The reward for learning pickup is a universal skillset that will help you to reach any amounts of success in anything you decide to throw yourself in, taking care of your sex life is just a nice bonus.

By learning pickup it's also very possible that you'll find your purpose or even create one. Even though the journey starts by faking most of these traits, if done enough, they soon become a part of you meaning you will transform into something you're not. For that you need to be able to change your belief system, to adapt some behavioural ques into your day to day life and be open minded since the stuff I talk about here will step on more than a few toes. This is the material that by understanding and cultivating will be phenomenal and will bring you the results you so desperately crave for.

Having a purpose is something that makes the woman stay after spending some time (few dates) together, but the things that attract her are mainly confidence in himself, not being afraid of expressing who he is and fun that he provides also known as stimulating the girl with positive emotions.

Income and power are related to attractiveness. This is because of many reason, not necessarily people being gold-diggers. It is called costly signalling, that's the evolutionary, the biological term. When you have the ability to do something that's hard like becoming rich, being funnier than other guys around you, looking better than most people on this planet, then you will signal that you have other traits too, therefore you're valuable. You don't need another human to be funny, there is so much entertainment out there.

The real reason girls said they life humorous guys is not because women actually like jokes, since they could just watch a comedy show on YouTube at any time they like. Women like funny guys because it's a costly signal meaning people have to use glucose in their brain to exhibit IQ and wit and all that stuff. All humor ever does, is showing the girl that the guy is witty, smart and worthy to keep around. It's the same with power, money, fitness and all those high class traits. As much of a cliché as it is, for a woman, it's the inside that counts, always has been and always does, and that's the ultimate truth.

Costly Signalling

"Sexual experiences happen to you on a regular basis if you continue to put yourself out there, continue to say yes to the experiences that lay outside of your comfort zone. It's never about the right decisions, it's about how well are you sticking to your decisions."

Every single person has been exposed to the fact that rockstars and famous individuals overall have a big swarm of women who endlessly circle around them and are totally ready and open for a sexual intercourse with them at any given moment. It's like they have this aura around them that just attracts the opposite sex and does it with a major success. Or maybe those guys are just rich and all the women that wish desperately to get their attention, are all gold-diggers? Let me explain you a woman's subliminal thought process behind all this by using the example of rock stars, since most of them are overly known to have slept with thousands of women. This is an important piece of the puzzle of game and an idea that will give you a better glimpse of a natural guy, who is able to attract many women.

A rock star has many quality traits that make him EXTREMELY attractive to pretty much all women. Many of them don't even dare to admit this, but the more likely the chances of her to sleep with a rock star are, they'll most likely take it. Rockstars posess more than just one trait that makes them attractive and puts them in the top list of guys out there. Let's take a look at what they are.

A famous singer/rock star/musician…

Is expressing his true self through the music he creates. He is putting his personality out there and risks everything. If it's not fake and also something that he is outside of the stage life, then it's attractive as hell. Major confidence, not giving a fuck attitude and doing something that he loves for a living. An authentic self. All quality traits of a successful and smart alpha male who knows what he wants and how to get it.

Is rich. Money is not the deciding factor here because he is able to provide, it's more of a signal, an indicator that the guy has mastered something in his life, and therefore most likely has other valuable traits to offer. It's called costly signalling. When you have the ability to do something that's considered hard, you signal that you also have other successful traits. The real reason girls said they life humorous guys is not because women actually like jokes, since they could just watch a comedy show on YouTube at any time they like. Women like funny guys because it's a costly signal meaning people have to use glucose in their brain to exhibit IQ and wit and all that stuff. All humor ever does, is showing the girl that the guy is witty, smart and worthy to keep around. It's the same with power, money, fitness and all that kind of high class stuff.

Is overall chill and confident since he is respected, most likely financially rich and sexually experienced. The have their shit together in terms of creating attraction in women. Girls are designed to follow guys meaning they're attractive to this function, this leadership like personality. They care a lot more about man's ability to lead and be cool, looks and money and fame will always be secondary and viewed as a bonus, not the actual reason why to sleep with you. If you have the first level of attractiveness cleared up in your own head and you fall into the category of having your shit together, then these secondary traits will not be necessary at all. Once again, this is a costly signal of a high value guy.

Is loved by tons of other people. This is social proof that the guy really is something special. If so many others like and even love him that much, if so many other women want to be with him also, then he must have something to offer, something of high value. Social proof also eliminates the factor of fear, meaning the guy is probably not a killer or a rapist, so the girl will feel much more safer without the star actually needing to prove it.

We can't deny the fact that there are also many gold diggers that really go for the money, but at the end of the day, they have feelings and emotions as well as the rest of us. They're also human. So even if they're going after financial values, they cannot help to notice other traits that were just described and that the stars usually have, or at least signal to have.

Pickup – The Beginning

"Behind every successful person, there are many unsuccessful years."

A lot of people tell me I am talented. I'm not talented. I just failed many times while working every day including birthdays, weekends, sick days, holidays, and got better at the stuff that I was not good at.

"As your knowledge goes up, your anxiety goes down."

I had been terrible with women and all social interactions in general untill I turned 19. I did not know how to get a girlfriend, let alone how to even talk to one. I had no idea what attracts woman and I did not know that pickup artists nor this sort of craft even exists. For few years after I turned 17 my view on the dating world was that I need to have a good fit shredded body in order to get a girlfriend or any kind of attention at all. And it worked, but only for the attention part. None of the girls who saw me daily would like me any more than before. Maybe some did, but they sure as hell did not show it in any way what so ever. My interactions with friends were also bad, because I did not come from the frame of offering value back. I was trying to leech off them and get their approval by making jokes about stuff that I did not even find funny. If they response was positive, I would feel better. Not good, just a bit better. It's like I eliminated a little bit of pain with every good response that I got. This type of behaviour did not allow me to share my true personality. In fact, I did not even know what my true personality really was. I had never been completely real with anyone. My goal had been to just fit in and avoid the negative attention or even any attention for the most part. I belive this is a problem most of the people on our planet experience every single freaking day. They might not see it as a problem though and more of as a tool to survive and not cause any trouble, because they simply don't think on a higher level. Most of us just see it as a tool to exist in this world and not piss anyone off. It's our brain guiding us to survive, but without seeing the full picture. It's like running away from a tiger when there is a friend with his car driving right next to you and waving you to get, but you simply just don't care to look in his direction, completely miss out on the oppurtunity while eventually getting eaten and before that living a shitty life in fear and inability to think because of the stress thanks to this tiger. But once one realizes that this tiger does not need to be feared, but to be played with, and that the friend is merely there to show you where you went wrong and has a solution, everything becomes clearer.

What we've failed to understand is the difference between true threat and the one that our mind makes up just to avoid painful growth. Since growth can only come from pain, listening to our emotions can be deadly to our career, to our dreams and to our overall happiness. Part of our system, our brain mechanism is flawed, outdated and the sooner we realize this, the better. Luckily we have been given the tools to fix it – prefrontal cortex, the ability to choose. The tiger is a real threat, looking around for your friend and taking some time off from escaping from the tiger however is not and is a valuable leap of faith, it's exactly the opposite of threat, it's the cure. We often tend to ignore help because we do not believe enough in it. Lack of information and faith, not in god, but in the process. In reality the tiger represents your own deepest fears and friend with the car the helpful information and the new path that will help you to escape from the tiger. We are unable to see this because of our ego and our preconceptions getting in the way. We are too caught up in stress, work, familty, money and other insecurities that take our mental energy from being used for something that would actually help us instead of delaying the inevitable. The act of running away from misery and disaster actually is disaster and misery itself since living in constant fear and anxiety - it's in no way good or healthy life.

This was the concept I realized once I took up learning game. Through countless hours of trial and error and with the help of books and educational videos, I had the privilege to finally realize what really creates attraction in a woman and how a guy like me can achieve that level of being desired. What did I do? I sucked up all the information and experiences I could fit into the 18 hours of being awake, watching videos, reading about the laws of seduction and most importantly – I took the leap of faith. I stepped out of the house with a single goal in mind – finding a girlfriend. Little did I know the principles behind it are universal and apply to any other area of life.

At first it did not go as well as I thought, but then again, nothing ever does. I had no courage at all, so I just strolled around the city at nighttime picturing all kinds of social interactions and were working on a game plan in case I interact with someone. The damnedest thing was that I could not even ask for the time nor directions on the street from a woman I was not attracted to. Every kind of social interaction, any kind of attention what-so-ever was really fucking scary to me. It literally felt like approaching someone, anyone in fact would put my life in danger. In a way having to approach someone was my tiger that I was running from.

Another reason why I failed to have a great social upbringing was due to having a severe stutter that I had developed at the age of 9, which made it even more difficult to put myself into social interactions. The knowing of I'm going to fail regardless of my effort is one of the most devastating feelings one could ever experience. Yet, there was no other choise. It was either living in fear for the rest of my life or to take action and go for more than I already had.

Everything I had experienced and felt so far was just pure pain, which I thought to be life. I saw life as hell that needs to be gone through. Looking back now I realize it was no life, it was living in hell. Later on I came to a realisation that life is always neutral and we are the ones labeling it to be either hard, easy, fair on unfair, good or bad. When it comes to lables, I had made my choise long time ago. Taking action and escaping my own hell by approaching a random girl on the street felt like committing suicide. Finally, after days of walking around, seeing people all around me from which some even did even smile at me, something in my mind clicked and I approached the first woman in my entire life. An act of impulse. Taking that step…I was literally ready to die. This is how tough this situation in my head really appeared to be, when in reality it was a mere act of saying hello to a stranger. Not that tremendously exciting for the most of you, I'm sure. To me, however, it was ignoring my survival instincts and go for the leap regardless. It was death. Now, it's my belief that we need to die in order to be reborn as something grand. To become something we're not it's essential to kill the thing we used to be. Then kill that thing and transform into some other thing, and then kill than thing to transform into some other thing. That's how progress is made by jumping from one level to the next. In my case, the next level was to kill this fat, mentally slow, insecure guy full of sadness and fear. One of my most praised mentors always insists on enjoying the process no matter what it might be. Progress is meant to be positive regardless of the deed that needs to be done in order to embark on that journey. In my case, the process was about letting go of everything I had believed before, let go of my ideas, principles and rules, and do the thing I felt the toughest resistance towards.

Here's a super short exercise. Take a serious look on your life right now. If you're not exactly where you want to be, then your belief system whether it's right or wrong is simply the only thing in the way of your goal. The only thing we really have to fight in life is with our own belief system. If you're not getting the results you'd like, then it will keep happening untill something in your brain/personality/mental religion is changed.

What do you need to change exactly? Your paradigm. The pattern which we all use to influence our thoughts. That new paradigm does not need to be truthful, it just needs to be helpful in the right direction. I'll explain this a bit later. For right now the only thing you need to reach the conclusion of is whether you're satisfied with your life in this very moment or could you use more.

Anyway…

My first approach took place in a gym, lobby to be exact. I don't know where I found the courage to approach her, it was something that came from deep within, a drive that made my body go in the right direction while my mind was telling me not to do it. It is my understanding that you can't always fix the problem with your mind, if your mind is the problem. For the most part you just have to tell your mind to shut the fuck up and move your body in the right direction. The mind will catch up.

The woman was a receptionist and she was working there, this is probably the reason why she was so nice to me. We talked, she seemed happy, I seemed happy, everyone around us were happy. Yet, when I asked for her to go out with me, she refused and used the boyfriend excuse. Either way, at the time it did not matter to me at all, I was just patting myself on the back and thinking it's not even as hard as I expected it to be. Once you've been thrown into the pool, you'll find in yourself an element of chillness, of being at ease with the situation. The worst moment is the last moment before taking action, everything else from there will appear alright, even relaxed.

After the approach I felt better, yet not amazing. I knew I had not given my all to the cause since I left too soon due to feeling uncomfortable. I can imagine most guys in my situation after such deed would be close to dieing from excess happiness, but not this perfectionistic guy right here that's writing about his first real interaction with a woman in his entire life. Most guys who have had no courage to talk to a girl for 19 years and then finally burst out the bubble, would feel really fucking fantastic, but not me. I was just alright. I knew I had to try again, and this time do it better.

On my journey, or as Elliot Hulse likes to call it a hero's journey, I got to know many pickup artists, who all said that their first approach was game changing and made a huge impact on their mental state. With me however it was not like this at all. I still felt like a chode, a disastrous degenerate. Don't get me wrong since I definitely felt better than before the approach, but it was definitely not the breaking point. Now, when I think back, I'm deeply glad for taking that leap of faith. It was the start of something magical, of something truly amazing. Without that one approach at the gym that only lasted for about 15 seconds and went nowhere, I would not be here today, at least not in this shape or form and nowhere close to the mindset that I'm rocking right now. Without this experience I would not feel as alive as I do nowadays. I would not feel hope, I would not have these amazing experiences with women that I do now and I certainly would not be happy. Lesson – do the thing you're afraid to do. It will embark you on a journey of something that's more than just getting women. It's the most amazing thing I've experienced in my entire life.

I did not approach anyone else that day.

My first interaction that happend in a gym with the receptionist took me three days to create. Before this I was walking around on the streets every single day for countless hours just thinking about how to lose this fear I have. At one point in my journey I realized something that laid the foundation of who I am today. I learned the definition of fear. Fear will always be there. It's all about your choise of whether you're going to act despite fear or not. This idea made me approach like mad while having a tremendous amount of fear still inside me. It was like going for suicide every single time at 8 pm and being reborn fresh and a lot stronger in the next morning. I approached at least 50 different women every single day. I got so many reference experience in my first month after the first incident at the gym, spending all my time on learning the ways of a pickup artist for the entire day, every single day through video programs, books and most importantly – taking action myself. This is how my fundamentals of game were created, on which I started to build on to create my own style, my own brand. Loads of self-discovery, tons of fearful moments, throwing myself in cold water without having the ability to swim, a good portion of my anxiety being destroyed every day while finding new fears and then destroying them also, over and over again. I found an extreme amount of courage in myself through silencing my mind through force and using my body to put me into the situation before my ego had a chance to even talk back. Taking action despite feeling like fear killed me over and over again, then created a new and strong Me, which was destroyed once again to create an even better Me. This process just kept on going. I started to realize who I am, what my personality is like and how to build my life around it, focusing on my strenghts and minimalizing the amount of weaknesses. I discovered myself.

"In order to be loved by some people, you have to risk being hated by many."

And on it went...

I had loads of fun every single day. Having fun did not come because of having routines to follow each day such as memorizing jokes so I would have something funny to say, or because of the women I slept with. Fun came from living the life I loved, a life that's not controlled by fears and run by courage and knowledge. A life run by love for living.

Living is really fucking fun! I learned to express my personality, learn about my true character and see the world for what it truly is. When someone did not like me for who I was, it was not a big deal. Some people will like you, some will love you and some will plain out hate you. What's the big deal? Accept everybody for what they are. Not being able to tolerate someone is not due to that guy or girl, it's because of you and your inability to enjoy life for what it is.

Women I approached began to see that ultimately I do not need the approval from them and I can create the fun on my own, since I enjoyed life. I did not need alcohol to have fun, all it took was loving life. When one loves life, he becomes unjudgemental and does not critisise. A guy like that is a high value guy, he is having fun on his own and if the girl happens to be into him, he will take her along as a bonus that he could easily live without. Plus, while seducing women in one corner, I had another groups of women backing me up by screaming my name and inviting me back to their table, therefore giving me social proof that I have friends, I'm liked by others and that I'm not there to leech the fun, but I'm the one that's creating the fun. A guy like this is in high demand.

Having value is attractive. Not just for women, but for all people.

How to have true value? One way is to be rich, good looking, funny etc. I call these having plain value. True value however is something different. The key word here is improvement. Make every year better than the one before. The concept of true and irresistible value will be explained in depth in the upcoming chapters.

After few months of going out and playing a pimp, I became the soul of any club. The ability to outgame other guys came almost naturally, including real boyfriends, male friends, strangers who also practiced pickup, or those who are simply companions waiting for their moment and take their girl just like that by just applying simple tactics that anyone can easily learn.

I felt like there is no opponent for me. So I took a break from night game (clubs, bars). I started to go out more in daytime, because I heard that's harder. A new challenge, which I had been looking for with both eyes open. And it was, well, at start. The truth is daygame and nightgame are both the same. The methods of approaching and the energy needs to be adjusted to the girl's energy, which is usually a lot lower in daytime, but the overall vibe was the same. I got phone numbers, went on dates, had one "day" stands with random girls who I wonderfully respect for being open. Daygame and nightgame are the same with a small exception – be aware of your surroundings and their energy. Does a football star care if he plays in the left part of the field for a change? No, game will still be the same, he just has to approach the matter from a different angle. After few more months, the results were the practically same as in nightgame. Able to get laid every day with women of quality, if I put in the right amount of effort. The last playing field that I got into was online game, especially Tinder. Tinder game is simply just the ability to combine texting skills and common sense. One needs a bit of both to succeed in there. I'll be explaining all of these topics very closely in the upcoming paragraphs.

So where am I now in terms of game? I'm having regular sex with different women, from which some are older than me, some younger than me, with some I can connect perfectly and with those with who I can't I just use for the reference experience and offering a good time for both of us. Have I completely mastered this topic? Most likely not. Am I getting amazing results and do my methods work? Absolutely. But am I qualified to be teaching this to you?

Let's look at it like this: What I'm sure of is that I've seen lots of different men from different backgrounds getting amazing results thanks to my teachings and being deeply thankful for my time. Can't say if I'm qualified since it's extremely subjective, but if you're looking to get results and not waste your time on programs and books that just spin around the bush, then reading this book is most definitely the right move. I'm probably not the master of pickup, even though I've put in way more hours than the experts say it takes to be one, which is 10 000 for those of you that are interested, but I'm a lot closer than a grand majority of people claiming to be pickup artists. For sure there are people better than me. Loads of people. But our differences are not that big. There is no "best pickup artist". There are only people who dared to take this road in order to become a stronger man. We are all winners here. There is even no need to find out who's the best. The better you get, the more you realize how stupid these "pickup beauty pageants" really are.

The following paragraphs are small guides and ideas that game is made of. I've worked my hardest to keep it as compact and to the point as possible. I do not talk about every little detail and it's not a complite step by step guide. These ideas are meant to help you with your dating life no matter what your goal is. It contains extremely valuable ideas thay are massively useful whether you are or want to be a master of pickup, looking for a healthy relationship, trying to understand women or just wanting to better yourself without having any goal in mind. Once you understand them all, you'll see dating from a whole new perspective. And this time you'll get the real and relevant information, which will hold the test of time.

This can work for anyone!

Waiting For The Perfect Girl

"Women are naturally social chameleons. They need to be liked."

Many guys are stuck in parallel thinking. In this case, what I mean by that is living your life without taking any action in terms of dating and such and waiting for the „perfect" girl to step into their life just like in a romantic comedy movie with Hugh Grant. I'm not here to diss those kinds of movies. They are fun to watch and give hope for many of us. Although, this kind of thinking is not healthy and sure as hell won't help you to achieve your goals. If you are such a softy with your dating life hoping that everything will work out eventually, then it's more common that this type of bahaviour translates into other areas of your life. Let's say you're not working as hard as you could in the gym. You feel a little bit of tired and you quit. If that's the case, then it's highly likely that you will act such way also with your job -not going to the limit and settling for mediocrity.

The more relevant problem for this topic with this type of behaviour is that even when that girl shows herself, then you would not know how to act the way she finds attractive, since you've been waiting for her for your entire life and haven't talked much to the other girls, because in your mind you were not so interested in them and not „right" for you.

Pretty much all my friends have this problem. They rationalise not talking to the opposite sex with sayings such as girl that just walked past them not being as cute as he'd like her to be, as beautiful or nice as their taste desires. In result of that they do not get the reference experience of talking to girls or just have very little. So in their mind when the right girl comes, they can just chat her up and get her to like them. In reality this is definetaly not the case. Besides, judging a person by her looks and being so superficial won't do well for your mental health and sure as hell won't get you good results in the dating field.

If you have not done pickup at any point of your life and been successful at it, then the chances are the girl is not going to like you because you just don't know how to attract a woman. At least not a high quality woman who is suitable and accustomed to fit your desires. We tend to settle for less instead of going for something that we really like and then

54

later on in the future rationalising and bringing up excuses blaming everybody else exept for ourselves.

Women can see what type of man you are by just listening to you and looking at your body language. Even if you had the courage to go and talk to the so called girl of your dreams, why would she pick you? Without knowing game you'll have little to no experience, you probably don't know how to trigger attraction and the only thing you can do somewhat right is to ask her out for a drink, because you read somewhere or saw in a movie that guys always buy girls drinks. Now that is just ignorance and screams of you being inexperienced. Why would a woman like that choose a man like you? Mostly they do it only for the „provider" role which I explain in another chapter. That's if you're lucky...somewhat, because you attracted her for the wrong reasons such as "free money" and there can never be real love since your man status in the eyes of this women has been taken from you. It's more likely that she does not want to have that kind of relations with you at all.

So what would be the ideal situation? Talking to every woman you see in terms of sexual encounters? Almost.

The idea is to have an abundance of woman to choose from. This allows you to actually see, what you like and not choose your next girlfriend or a wife to be from the state of scarcity, desperation and frustration. In this scenario you can actually figure out, what type of girl you like most and you can choose the coolest, beautiful and to you most appealing female companion. Most guys choose the woman who they can get. That's desperation and feeling like you have no other option because no one else is going to love you. This is scarcity. It will not bring happiness nor satisfaction, not for you nor the girl since she can sense you being unease with the situation.

If you're a beginner, you'll definitely like a majority of the women you talk to. The more you do this, the bigger the chances of meeting a girl who likes you back are. Besides, every single interaction is building your mental skyscraper that I like to call personality. Each approach and interaction will make you better and stronger in every area of your life simply because your confidence, your sense of entitlement and everything else will start to fall into place.

How many girls will like you back out of the ones you approach? You will never know before you try. If you learn game, then one day, when you meet that dream girl of yours, you'll have the reference expreirences, you know what sparks attraction, you know how to not seem weird and creepy, you know what it takes to be a real man, a cool human being who she could like and love. Game is about learning how to meet women and optimize your chances of getting laid, but at the same time it's about making you a better, stronger and more effective person in all of your endeavours. It's self-development and focuses on improving your life upon anything else.

It is possible to truly find someone very special to you without learning pickup, but think of the chances of that happening. Pretty damn low. You can meet a woman alright, but the chances of her being the right one for you – really fucking slim. You will most likely choose the woman you can get, not the one you actually want just as majority of the guys in our world. Maybe she's a bit too chubby and you're much more attracted to hot girls, yet you still marry her. Well, say hello to years of misery and sadness. Also, think of all the experiences that you're going to miss when you don't learn game. You will miss all the epic stories such as dating celebrities and all you will ever talk about is how you won that beerpong contest twenty five years ago. This will not be the case for everyone, but it's the reality for a great majority of us.

In order to have great experiences with all kinds of women without letting fear control you and just being in peace with your own emotions, it's a necessity to not fight against your own soul. Fear is nothing more but a signal that's showing you where you need to improve on and will feed you pain untill you man up and finally do it. We feel fear in different areas of our lives. If you feel fear approaching that cute girl at the coffee shop who you see there every day and the woman who works at the same company as you and even sitting right next to you, then please, with all your heart just listen and most of all, trust me to me on this. Give them a try, see what they are like. Break the barrier and see where this path takes you.

Nothing worth having comes easy and without failing countless times before.

How Do I Start?

"Desire is the starting point of any great achievement."

There is no fundamental key that you should know in order to start other than this one word:

Start

Many of us spend years doing research on this topic without ever going out to try it for themselves and see, if these "laws" can actually stick. Some go out without doing any kind of research and just freestyle it, drinking alcohol, parting like there's no tomorrow and being a part of the high life as we like to call it. A few of them might even know some basic principles of game like have confidence or be funny, but that's about it. Funny enough – the person who has no knowledge on this topic and just goes out, has a much better chance at getting real and solid results than the guy who knows everything about it thanks to years of research and practising the couch sport, but does not have the drive to take action himself and actually live the life he sofar has only read about.

The person who is watching all types of educational pickup videos, reads tons of self-help books on how to get girls, how to make out with them and how to fuck them, has a good chance to be completely scared off. Because let's be honest, even after being done with this book right here it might seem like a lot of hard and painful work needs to be done to achieve the level of mastery in this. This is especially so when you watch some guys showing high class skill that takes many years to develop. Hard work has the characteristic of scaring people away from even trying. Just mentioning it makes so many people have negative assumptions, since work for them is equivalent to torture. All those tedious Monday mornings in the office, all these countless hours spent working for someone you don't like doing the job you hate. All of this combined will make the word "work" a trigger for negative emotions.

Someone who does not care about the knowledge, the techniques, someone who does not want to put in the work and just wants it as soon as possible, will go out relatively quick without paying much attention to tips and teachings that could shorten the learning curve. It's like trying to break through a thick plastic door by headbutting it instead of learning the ways on how locks work. It will work eventually, but it will take time and you have to endure a tremendous amount of pain. If you don't know how attraction really works, have no direction due to lack of knowledge after getting home you will be kicking walls and screaming from the top of your lungs, because the world seems unfair and women look like manipulative demons.

So how do you start? In my experience you gotta find a middle ground with everything you do. You have to balance eating with sport, not just do one thing over the other. You gotta work, but also take time to rest and take perspective on it. Same with pickup. I'd deeply advise you to finish this book, it will provide you with the fundamentals of game while also giving you some really deep insights on advanced parts of the game and on how you can really become a masterful communicator with charisma and massively grow your potential influence. If you feel discouraged, take a break, but come back to this book eventually. This knowledge is well worth it. Also, don't think too much. It's not science, it's art. The art of pickup is loose and has many different ways of approaching it. Principles are the same, but the methods vary just as you can either use a pencil, a paint brush or your hands. They all create art.

To help you even more, I'm going to give you these starting tips so that even without doing any research on your own, you'd still be able to get the maximum out of your every interaction and not waste time on figuring Prepare yourself.

Whatever you are at the moment, whether it's a bit overweight and out of shape, not lucky with the genetic pool and therefore ugly, broke, it is totally enough. Meeting women and having sex with them is not something that's about requierements nor rules, it's a bonus of life for anyone who has the capability to believe this.

Whatever kind of a person you are at this given moment, it's enough to meet girls.

The ship is safe in a harbour, but that's not what ships are for. Same with you. Right now while reading this book you're in a safe environment, feeling relaxed and comfortable. However, in order to do something cool with your life, get the bonuses that movies provoke on us, achieve the life that could be pictured only in dreams and that most of us call unrealistic, use your body and your mind to the fullest by just stepping out of the comfort zone and exposing yourself to new experiences.

As far as techniques go, be sure to start by taking small steps and then eventually move on to bigger ones. For an example if I haven't been social for the past month or so, I'll start out by chatting up some people at the book store, then the next day I'll go out with the intention of socialising at the bar, and then finally on my third day go to the club move on to some real pickup shit, going for make outs, sexual activities and much more. It might take me few days to ease myself into it, but I will get there eventually. Pickup is not an Olympic race, it's more of a marathon with a clear intention of where the finish line is. Take baby steps if you need to, but be sure to make progress and move in the desired direction of where you want to go.

On clothing…

I used to wear the same outfit to any club, bar, venue that I could possibly find. Putting on that good old hoodie of mine was like a wakeup call. Every time I put it on, I knew shit was about to go down. Depending on the classiness level of the venue I spend my time in, everybody else were wearing something that matched the vibe of the place. High end places had guys wearing suits and high quality trade mark clothes. Women had sparky short skirts, lots of makeup and tried to be as noticeable as possible. The entire place was like a beauty show, the most beautiful one got the most attention. At the same time, the low end places had people wearing usual clothes that I like to call the chill flips.

Pickup artists emphasize a lot on the fact that your looks do not matter, which is completely right, but only for those who actually have accumulated at least some level of skill. If you consider yourself to be relatively skill-less and are just starting out, maybe even experience lots of insecurity and anxiety, then clothes are going to play a part in the interaction. If you don't have any personality to admire, they'll compensate your lack of skill with your external values, into which clothes fall in perfectly.

There are a few different styles in pickup that regard clothing of which you can choose from. There is this whole concept of peacocking, which revolves around you being the guy who completely stands out from the crowd by just wearing something that's supposed to shock others who are around, but I wouldn't go that far and simply dress in a way that's the most comfortable to you. The idea is to be okay with yourself, but also dress accordingly to the venue you're about to hit. A high end bar would probably not tolerate slippers and dirty hoodies as much as some low end unconventional beer garden.

An insecure guy wearing a ten thousand dollar suit will still be that very same insecure guy, so the idea is to wear the outfit that you're most comfortable with. Later on in your pickup journey it would be a great idea to expand your comfort zone and wear stuff that's really over the top, not really appealing or just plain stupid. It's about expansion and growth, but for a new guy going out is already growth, therefore in his case the ability to choose the right clothing is not emphasized at all.

Power vs Force

"Use the force, but strive for power."

Let's talk about the state of power and the state of force and how it all correlates into pickup. As you've all experienced, starting to do something that you feel strong resistance against is always extremely difficult. It's important to understand that resistance is always bound to be there no matter what you're trying to accomplish. Resistance comes from your primitive side of the brain which is quite outdated in terms of the world we live in today. This side of the brain is trying to keep you from harm and it's doing it by sending you many blockages to avoid discomfort and pain.

As we all know, pickup can be really damn painful thanks to the fear of rejections and being socially unaccepted amongst many other things. So it is no wonder that we feel resistance when trying to approach a random girl on a street. It's a new situation and new situations always bring growth, which is painful. In order to break through that resistance it has come to my understanding over these years that as we begin to do something, anything for that matter, we need to apply a tremendous amount of willpower also known as force. We need force to break through these barriers that our own mind creates whether it's approaching a girl, going to the gym for the first time or on the day you're dead tired and don't feel like doing much, starting a project to create a new business plan that will take years to develop, whatever it might be – resistance is present with all of these progressive, yet at first seemingly tedious activities and can most easily be broken by using blunt force.

On the other hand once you've cultivated force and have broken through these first barriers, you'll arrive in a state of power. Power is understanding and a way of life meaning you do not need to apply force to get the thing done since you have developed a deep understanding of this part of your life and you've accepted the fact that this is good for you and will be done anyway. Power is the state of being, when in the beginning you struggled to find courage to approach women, then now you've adopted this lifestyle, it's your way of life and you know it's good for you no matter what your primitive side of the brain might tell you. It's the state of which does not require energy just like opening a door, brushing your teeth, washing your hands and so on. It just feels normal for you do that and you don't even have any more debates whether to do the deed or not.

The state of power can also be described as comfort zone. We use force to expand our comfort zone and make the circle of things we feel comfortable doing bigger. In reality the concept of power and force goes much deeper and takes a lot more than just one chapther to explain, but this is the basic idea of it and how it applies to pickup. We must first use force to acquire power. Also, using force should never stop. If we get stuck in our comfort zone no matter how big it might be, we lose our sense of drive and begin to settle. In order to live a fulfilling and happy life, we should never settle and always strive for more. Do one thing that you're afraid of every single day to expand your mind and the zone of which we've all created. Acquire more power through force by approaching that girl you're scared of, going to the gym even though you don't feel like it, taking the responsibility when it's due. In order to get power we must first apply force and keep using it to break through resistance. Force is the tool to get power, and by having it your life will be free.

Power and force go hand in hand, both complementing each other and essential for a fulfilling and happy life.

Cold Approach, Part 1

"Plan for success. With no back-up plans, no ripcords, no fail-safes – or you will fail." - Dan Pena

Cold approach – approaching a random woman who you have never met before with the intention of reaching sex. This is how the main skillset of every single pickup artist is forged. Cold approach is essential and one of the main parts of game. Without this, pickup would not be what it is today.

Every pickup journey starts with learning to do cold approach.

Pickup is in many ways just a game of numbers. The more you approach, the better you'll get and the less afraid you'll be. I'm not familiar with your specific situation, so if you're just starting out, start with small and simple things such as walking up to random people on a street offering them free hugs. In time, scale it up and do something a little bit more difficult like introducing yourself without stuttering. Life is all about progress, what matters is the length of the road we travel and not how high we climb.

The guy who is able to do a so-called cold approach will have more initial attraction than you did meeting through a social circle. Why is that? The fact that you're doing cold approach, which is being seen as something that's a little bit unorthodox, you as a man will demonstrate value right off the bat. It's slightly breaking social normalities of interaction. People don't just expect some random dude to come up and talk to them out of the blue, so when you'll do it, it's instant attraction at least in some way even if you're bad at doing it.

The key in cold approach is to not be attention seeking. It's not about being a clown that's just trying to get some attention nor about begging the girl to date you just because you came up to her. The fact that you approached her just like that will be just demonstrating value. It does not mean the girl is bound to fuck you right there. Think of it as a good start, not something really game-changing. So the basic idea is to first approach a woman while being non-reaction seeking nor begging. It's done to demonstrate value, to put yourself out there and to give the girl a shot to demonstrate her own value so you would pick her. It's not about whether she has value or not, since most of the guys don't care and would sleep with her either way. It's about making the interaction look like you're screening her for a potential partner, to look picky so the girl would feel special for you approaching her, not anyone else.

How can you come off as being a high value guy? First part is already done by approaching. The other side of it is to show her, why you did it and where does it come from – from a begging, insecure state, a reaction-seeking state or from the state of being cool.

How can we be cool?

By just being mentally strong, controlling our frame without letting external influences sway us and not taking your own self, your self being too seriously. As you see I haven't mentioned being great looking nor funny. The woman sees how you look like, what you're wearing and does it suit you, but she is looking for your personality, your value system, your energy and your mentality. That's also a reason why so many women go for the guys that the social media lables as not the beauty queen, it's especially seen amongst famous soccer player's wives. It's not about the looks, it's about who you are. If you're insecure and hoping, begging, asking for a relationship, and with this mindset you practise cold approach, then the girl will sense the neediness, the negativity in terms of your self-esteem and just plain weakness as a man. But if you're cool, know who you are, know what you want, have plenty of options to choose from and come from the state of giving the girl a chance to prove herself in your eyes, having the freedom of outcome since you can just approach anyone else right after the interaction which is also called having abundance, then the girl will subliminally feel this also whether she's actually aware of it or not. There are certain traits in which by having these females will automatically be attracted to you, and most of them not even understanding why it is so. It's these kind of subliminal messages that women will pick it up no matter what since we're conditioned to notice them and women's emotional state towards you will be influenced by these alone. How to convey these traits? By living up to the standard of being a high value Man, which I will fully explain to you in this book, if you have the desire to finish it.

In game, pickup, dating or whatever you like to call it, it's mostly not about what we do, it's about our intentions behind the deed. Pick-up lines, fancy gifts to girls you don't even fully like, tremendously fawn compliments that serve the purpose of being liked by the girl – they do not matter and can easily harm the opinion she has of you. It's all about who we are, and to even take it one step further to give you a glimpse of what you will learn throughout this book – what we truly think we are. The only currency any guy can use to attract women is to have value as a man, not the words you say to her nor the gifts you buy. Women love gifts of course, there is no doupt about that, but it's the place where the gift it's coming from that really matters. Women are extremely reliant on feedback and validation, which these sorts of gifts offer with ease. If the woman receives gifts just for being a woman, as leverage so she would not be inclined to leave you, then it's coming out of neediness and being scared to lose her, which ultimately conveys the idea of nobody else wanting you. The idea of scarcity. But, if the gift coming from the place of she deserves it, then it's simply an act of kindness and love. See the difference here? It's about who you are, which is projected through your intentions, your body language, the way you look at her and many other factors which I'm all here to teach.

Let's move on to the technical part, the foundations of what it looks like from an outsiders perspective, if you will.

Cold approach during <u>daytime</u> works in three layers:

1. Get her attention.

   Be sure she notices you and demand attention if the situation calls for it, it's important that she focuses purely on you and is not on her phone, talking to a girlfriend or anything else like that. Don't even start talking if she is not focused on you, otherwise you will instantly look like a guy who's easy to step over and this is the last thing you'll need.

2. Establish comfort.

   There are two frames which you can choose from. You can either make her feel comfortable around you, emphasize and recognize the weirdness of this situation of you approaching her just like that out of the blue. Since it's something that's a bit outside of social normalities, then also act like it. You understand that this is unorthodox, but she got your attention and since you're the guy who goes for what she wants, you decided to give her an oppurtunity to impress you. Now keep in mind that when the girl is too comfortable with you, then it's a bad sign, meaning she will not be sexually aroused. The right amount of comfort is when she feels like being with you is more of a win than a loss.

The other option is to be completely confident in the frame of yours, believe that this situation is absolutely normal to you and she should feel like this too. The girl will be sucked into your reality, this is how female brain is wired to work and you can go on from there. If you feel like she is not buying it, then your frame is simply not strong enough.

Ultimately you can even mix these two together. There are no firm rules in here as long as you make her feel comfortable in this singular situation.

3. Ask for an instant date/number/Facebook profile.

   Once you've gotten her attention, comfort is built and she has accustomed to you in this brief moment, move on to the third step and do whatever you want with her. If she's busy, arrange a meetup or ask for something that would help you two to stay in contact with eachother, either her phone number or Facebook information. If she does not look very busy and gives you the vibe of not having a certain destination in mind right now, then you can implement a plan to hang out, get a quick cup of coffee, whatever you feel like is suitable for the situation. No matter where your game level is at, you can always come up with something that you feel is best. No certain rules, trust the feeling in your gut. Ultimately it's about testing the limits and building your skillset through interactions yourself since it's practically impossible for the teacher to do all the work for the student. Information won't stick if it's not being practiced.

Another key concept in cold approach is you making it perfectly clear that you got her contact information with the intention of meeting up with her some other time, not just for the sake of saying hello and being done with the interaction as quickly as possible. Make your intention clear. How? Express your interest in meeting up with her by just telling her the very same, make it a man to woman interaction opposed to creepy guy to a hottie or friend to friend. You can play around with it once you start experiencing the momentum of approaching many people and get comfortable in the flow.

Cold approach during night time works also in three layers:

1. Get her attention.

2. Stimulate her, offer fun, dance, talk, be in a non-judgemental state of mood and just have fun with eachother regardless of your personality types, since they will vary a lot. It's not about finding the girl who fits you, it's about feeling the man to woman connection. Evolution has made us be attracted to each other regardless of our personality types and the best place for this to experience is of course the club and bars. Places where logic and reason hold little to no effect are being run purely on emotions and attraction. If you're a guy, she will be attracted to you as long as you offer stimulation.

3. Isolate her by taking her to your place, a hotel, a public bathroom, street corner, her place or just about anywhere, where sex is a possibility. If you feel like the girl will not buy into you in terms of sex right now, if she's the one that has deep moral values and will not go home with anyone by any chance or just has bad logistical situation, then just go for her contacts and meet up with her later on the same night or some other day completely.

When you're done with your night, take 10 minutes, sit down and just think about your actions. Think about what you did extremely well. Think about what could be improved. Maybe you did not kiss the girl´. Maybe you were too much of a dick without any playfulness so it came across too aggressive. Maybe you did not fucking approach at all. Think about your night. Break it down. Pat yourself on the back for improving and giving a try. And tomorrow just fucking repeat.

In your interactions, whether you're right or wrong, you'll have influence. All kind of publicity is, in this case, good publicity.

"Fear deliberates. Once you realize there's no benefit in holding back, every single situation and every person you meet, no matter how seemingly beyond your reach, becomes an oppurtinity to succeed."

In this chapter I laid out the principles of cold approach pickup, which can also be considered to be the guidelines of how, where and by doing what one should start. Although, even if a guy understands these principles and is completely aware of how it works, there is a high chance he will not execute these steps. Many guys are not able to execute these simple guidelines of picking up women. Why?

Every time when I run a boot camp, my training program, which is for guys who are eager to learn under the direct hand of me, I start off by first letting guys do their own game, to use everything they know so far about meeting women through cold approach, and then direct their attention to the factors that could use either improvement or change. I'd ask them if they understood, to which they'd say with an absolute certainty – yes. Then, they would go at it again with the new and correct information I've just taught them according to their level of needs, and despite this they'd still do the same thing as before over and over again. One might ask why? Are they stupid? Why would they not fix the mistakes, even if they were tremendously horrible and devastating for the interaction? Why isn't he able to execute this?

The reason is quite simple. We got emotional blocks that are preventing us from success. So in conclusion, you can have literally the best program out there, the best tactics, the best game plan one could possibly have, but it does not count even for shit, if the guy is not emotionally ready to apply these. For this mere reason I've decided to put most of my focus on teaching inner game and rather becoming the guy who gets laid rather than doing the things the other guy does to get laid. Become the high value man by learning the ways of a high value man. The book that teaches you to overcome your own inner barriers and become the kind of person you've always dreamed of becoming has ten times more value than a book that focused merely on pickup strategy and techniques.

"There's a cute girl sitting all alone at the bar, waiting for a cool guy like you to approach her and have a great time with her. Now why in the hell would you not take that oppurtunity? You're not just rejecting yourself from pleasure, but you're also rejecting her."

Cold Approach, Part 2

"If you know what the outcome will be, then you wouldn't even embark on the journey. Fun lies in uncertainty and gamble."

Cold approach is about offering value, not taking. This is a big key in being successful with cold approach. In fact, this translates into many other areas of pickup as well, since nobody wants to be around the guy who is not offering anything back and just tries to suck the fun out of everyone.

When you've finally had enough of walking around being scared of interactions with random women on a street and decide to do your first approach, it's important to remember that you're not here to get something from her. This is definitely not the mindset you should be having. The mere focus of yours should be to offer yourself to her as a cool, confident character from who she could benefit from in terms of value exchange. You're here to offer her your personality, you're there to have fun with her, to make her feel good, desired and all that. You're not there to beg her for a date, you're not there to manipulate her into sleeping with nor dating you. You're simply there to offer value. It's about giving, not taking. Once we let go of our <u>need</u> to sleep with her, our results will triple. Women are attracted to who you are and if you're someone who's desperate to have sex, then it will scream of not having abundance meaning having no other options. If a girl gets that vibe of nobody else wanting you, then why should she? It's like searching for trash. Only the lowest will go for it. So in order to make her attracted to you, it's a must to let go of that frame of needing the girl. You're simply there to have a good time, yet being goal oriented and not keeping the act of sex in your list of goals. Do everything you can to get sex, but if it does not happen, then do not beat yourself up for it. Move on to the next set and make something happen with the next girl. Have a positive mindset, not attached to the outcome while at the same time being goal oriented. Keep this in mind.

Dealing with rejection

"The biggest mistake I've made in my pickup career is thinking that rejection is a real thing."

A grand majority of guys who have just gotten into pickup or is thinking of doing so will ask questions about the topic of rejections and typical success rates. Some of the regular ones that I get almost daily: "What is your success rate? What is your percentage? How many girls do I have to talk to before I can get a girlfriend? How many times do you get rejected by a girl?"

These questions might seem like they're good and to the point, but in reality they're just letting the other smart individuals and especially the professional pickup gurus know where the questioner in his journey is at. Let's start by defining rejection. Is it when you go say hello to a girl and she turns her back to you? Because you could still tap her on the shoulder and pull the whole situation around. Is rejection talking to a girl and getting a bad reaction? Is rejection asking for a phone number and not getting it? Is calling a girl and her not coming out with you a rejection? Is it not fucking the girl? Because even if you fuck the girl, she might not wanna see you again. Is it not being in a relationship with the girl? Is it not making her fall in love with you? What the fuck is rejection?

Ultimately you will realize that there is no such thing. Rejection does not exist. I could go and talk to a girl who would not pay attention to me, then see her again later that night or even the next night and fuck her. Everything is subjective. Step out of that frame of certainty. Pickup is not science, it is art and art is very subjective. You can't measure it or know the outcome. Once you get good at it, you can predict the reactions and even outcome, but it's never as sure as in let's say math or chemistry and you sure as hell will never get it all down so you would have a bulletproof method that works every time. There is just one rock solid rule you need to know in pickup, and that's going out and talking to girls. This is the only universal method that works every time. You just gotta be willing to put in the effort.

There are so many elements of randomness in an interaction. You could roll up with the best pick up line and be the most awesome guy in the bar in terms of being purposeful, controlled, confident, and the girl wouldn't talk to you because she just had a terrible day like getting fired or someone in her family died. In these cases, are YOU doing something wrong? No, she is just in a state of which she is unable to respond positively to anybody, let alone a random guy like you. This is what we call an element of randomness.

The way I see it for myself is that as long as I'm on top of my game and I did everything I could at that moment of time, there is no reason to feel bad. I focus merely on what's in my control.

One of the great benefits of doing pickup is that you will become unreactive to bullshit. Whenever someone has an intent to bring you down and tries make you feel like shit, he will fail. By practising pickup, you will develop this emotional barrier that is pretty much unbreakable. You just don't get emotionally invested in their insults and just stop caring about what others think about you the better you become at game. This allows you to focus on endeavours that are important in your life like your career, health and such without letting bullshit be overwhelming and fear control the life you're living. Pickup makes you realize what really matters in life, what to focus on, who to listen and trust, and keeps you on the right course.

Have you ever rejected someone because of your insecurities?

Sometimes a woman will reject you because she is intimidated by you or thinks a guy like you wouldn't seriously be interested in a woman like her. So when you try to get her number or try set up a date with her she will reject you. She does this because she thinks she would not be able to keep you interested for the long term and that you will eventually stop seeing her. So in order for her to not have to face that rejection later down the line she rejects you before anything can happen between the two of you. What she will do sometimes is make up something in her mind that she sees wrong with you to justify why she rejected you.

This is kind of the same thing as when you stop yourself from talking to a really hot chick. You do this because you think that she won't like you. You're thinking about approaching her but then stop yourself because you think she wouldn't want you anyway. So you sort of reject her in your mind and don't bother approaching her and might try to find something wrong with her to rationalize why you didn't approach her.

"The girl was not nice to me!"

It's not that the girl is not nice. It's merely the lack of proper education, of understanding how our feelings and desires work. Since most of us have not even a clue on how and why something in our brain operates, then it's no wonder that some women are bitter after dealing with small discomforts through her day. If you catch her on a good day, she'll respond with positivity. If she's having a bad day, there's a good chance that she'll be bitter and push you away. A smart person, and I don't mean the people with PhD's or nuclear scientists, I mean those people who understand what life is and how one is supposed to live in order to reach the maximum potential in terms of happiness and success, both balanced together, that kind of a person would not be mad at every little disadvantage that comes onto our path every single day. The girl might be angry because of a mean text message she got few minutes ago, therefore your approaching her making her even more unstable and ready to blow up. Maybe the girl is thinking of her girlfriend who had her big break and got a small part in an acting gig, therefore feeling a bit jealous which can be seen from her nasty response towards you approach. The options for her rejecting you are almost limitless. As long as there are people who don't know how to successfully deal with their emotions and create a positive environment for themselves to be in at all times, there will be rejections. Some are simply because the guy that's learning pickup is a beginner, but most of them are because the girl rejects herself by being flawed. This is not just about girls, it's with all of us.

There are no nice people, nor any nasty women. There are just those who are able to understand life and those who aren't. You might catch the so called "nasty" woman on a good day and she'll respond with positivity, but same goes vice versa for the woman you had figured out to be nice.

For those of you who still believe so deeply in the concept of rejections and have trouble letting it go, I'll leave you with a quote that I came up with before I realized the truth about rejection.

"Rejections build the foundation of a successful career in pickup. The guy who's afraid to be rejected, will never experience success." Both definitions are equally correct and will help you through the pain of not reaching sex with every single girls you'd like to.

Self-sabotage

"The woman will always be into you if she sees that you're into you. Self-love is highly mandatory."

Another great way of eliminating the fear of talking to strangers is by realizing that every time you fail to take action, you see that cute girl and you don't talk to her purely out of fear disguised as rationality such as not having enough time, she not being attractive enough, you having a girlfriend already and so forth, you're rejecting yourself. Every time you fail to approach a girl, you're rejecting yourself. It's funny how we're trying to save us from the harsh truth, from not finding out that we're not being liked by everyone, from pain. We're not letting others create us pain by creating that pain to us ourselves. You'd rather destroy our best ally, yourself, instead of partnering up with it and actually enjoying the spoils of life that only come to the smart and bold.

The only way to remove rejection and have success in dating is to talk to the girls you find attractive and let them decide whether they want to see you again or not. If you don't, then the girl does not say no to you, but you, yourself, will. That's much worse. It's not the girl keeping you from being happy, it's yourself. Self-sabotage.

This is what happends when you take rejections personally

"Being challenged in life is inevitable, being defeated is optional."

- Roger Crawford

Let me give you an example of a guy who has some confidence, but also a weak mind. This guy wants to talk to the girl and has positive expectations such as her liking him back, getting her phone number and so on. Since we tend to condition certain habbits in our brain, here's what happends. He is fairly confident in his skills and goes up to the girl while being fairly certain that he's going to get the expected. She rejects him. What happends in his brain now is it begins to condition all the upcoming interactions and will make him belive every time he goes up to a girl - boom, another rejection, therefore this belief will be ingrained in the brain and the guy will expect that result every time he feels like taking action. It's called brain's mechanism of coping with our situation, finding answers without having the right tools, the right knowledge to do so. So in conclusion what this is doing is that since he is sure in his upcoming failure, it has a higher chance to actually happen. In result of that this idea will be ingrained even further into your brain. It's a self-fulfilling prophecy and the only way to avoid this is by being aware of it.

This is the natural cause of low self-esteem. To improve this area of your life I advise you to read The Six Pillars Of Self Esteem, but since you're a busy person I'll save you some time and have a quick summary on this subject.

High self-esteem is about taking 100% responsibility for your actions just as I explained in the first chapter. Every action you do is either a − or a + depending on your intention. With every minus your self-esteem goes down, with every plus it rises. All these pluses and minuses add up and create the level on which your self-esteem lies.

In cold approach the minus would be rejection, an interaction in which the girl is not in the mood to socialize with you. Get too many of these and your self-esteem will go down. However, if you accept that rejection is bound to happen at some point and you won't take it personality, you'll stop giving a shit about all these girls who push you away. Funny enough, having this mindset of not caring will skyrocket your game into great distances.

There is a fair line between a real rejection and the girl just playing hard to get. This is a concept I see guys struggling with all the time. They simply give up too quick after getting a few mean comments from the girl. Realize that girls use these things called shit tests, which revolve around testing you and seeing how much shit can you really take from them and how strong you are mentally. Shit tests mean this one thing – woman is interested in you, but she wants to see more of you and is not afraid to play with your emotions to tests your true colours. If you stay true to yourself and hold the frame of which you've chosen to have, then these shit tests will be passed relatively easily. So when can we know whether she is being real with us and when is it a shit test?

If she keeps talking to you, then she's obviously interested, this is rule number one. It has come to my attention that if a woman does not want to have anything to do with a certain guy, then she will simply not even respond to him. As long as she's talkative, you're golden. Also, be aware of her mental state and keep your eyes open since if she really doesn't want to talk to you, then it's quite clear to see. However if you see her trying to overpower you, humiliate you or is just making fun over you, then it's a shit test and nothing more.

Mustering the audacity talking with people who don't know you simply comes down to balancing the fear of embarrassment and the fear of repercussions. For me it's either being successful or not. Thinking in this certain way will make the fear of failure look much lighter next to the fear of losing your only chance for a great life. That fear always overrides my anxiety about rejection and being embarrassed.

Ask yourself, how you're going to fail. We all do at some point, so it's better to just accept it to get the upcoming mental debate with yourself out of the way. Failure is inevitable, fear is inevitable. How we react to these two occurences is however totally up to us and will determine the lives of each and every one of us.

Pickup lines

"The cool version of yourself, the cool personality that you'll use when it comes to talking to women – destroy it. Approach from the place of how you're feeling at the moment while either feeling or faking positive."

If you're one of those guys who believes in pickup lines, struggling to find the right ones that work and think this is something that creates attraction, then you need this paragraph more than anyone else in the world. First of all, let's start with an example. Let's say James Bond walks up to a woman in a high class bar, the one that all rich and famous people spend their weekends in. He walks up to a woman and says:

"Did it hurt?"

The girl asks: "What did?"

James responds: "When you fell from heaven."

Regardless of whether the girl likes James or not, let's take a look at some hypothetical situations such as the girl being attracted to James. First of all, what's the story behind this girl liking James after this pickup line? What actually creates attraction? Do you really think women are so stupid to fall for a guy who says these "magic" words? Do you really think the girl is going to fuck him after that pickup line? Do you really fucking think this exact line was the reason why James got laid that night? Absolutely not.

The reason why that particular woman liked James and gave a positive response is because the guy was James fucking Bond. The way this guy carries himself, the way he looks are her, his body language is giving away vibes of an alpha male all the fucking time. Deep and calm, low toned voice, you can sense that this man has a purpose in his life from just looking at him. Do you remember how I explained earlier how women love a guy who has a purpose? Mr. Bond with all his personality traits, body language, voice and overall characteristics is the definition of purpose.

To be completely honest, being James Bond in order to sleep with many women, surprisingly, will not be the most optimal thing to do. He is everything a guy should be, but he lacks of some principles that would make him not attract many women in a realistic situation. First of all, a guy like James only approaches women in high class bars and lounges, the places where you need a certain amount of prestige to get in. So if you're already inside, then so much work has already been done for you. The fact that you can get into this specific place is already a high value trait and women over there will take pretty much anyone who shows some initiative, since every choise is pretty much a win for them. However if James walked into a normal, maybe even a low class bar, his tactics would not be the best simply because he does not offer than much fun for the girl. Fun is an important component when it comes to attraction. James merely relies on confidence and on a sense of purpose. It can't also be denied that women in low end bars, clubs, pubs will react better to the "fun" type of guys simply because those types of girls are lower class, often see themselves as failures in life and take pretty much anyone who can take them out of their own reality. If it was possible, then they would have sex with alcohol and would not even need a man. Fun thought, eh?

Also be aware of your own preferences. If you're not a loud guy and hate clubs, then feel free to skip them and practise day game instead. It all comes down to knowing yourself and what you like. Why should you go to a club if you're not a loud and expressive person? I personally don't hate clubs, but definitely prefer other types of girls as well since the whole environment and club girls overall are exactly not what I'm attracted to. So you will have to ask yourself questions. What type of a person are you? Who are you attracted to and where can you find those girls?

Low end places are harder to pick girls up in, because in the eyes of a woman you're some random guy who needs to start from the bottom and work his way up to so-called "prove" his worth to her. Low end places are also full of women who really want to escape their day to day reality, escape their routine, and for that you need to stimulate her, which James' tactics simply won't do enough. Bond is all about making the girl feel his reality and experience who he is, but the woman will have to work a bit more than usual for this effect and does not get to party like no other. These types of women don't think ahead and must be approached by using the principle of offering stimulation, which to me is offering plain and simple fun.

High end places will do the work for you and already prove your worth since you were allowed into such high class space.

Coming back to the pickup line – the reason why it does not work is because one simple little line cannot change the person who you are. You can look at a pile of shit and stick one flower in it. How long does it take for the girl to see that it's just a flower in a pile of shit? Then there is also the fact that you trying to impress the girl with pickup line will implement that you're not worthy of her without it anyway and try to use some learned lines to get her attention, which will always be a low quality trait. This is pretty much the whole deal with pickup lines.

A pickup line will not change who you are in the eyes of a woman. If anything, it makes it more difficult for you to sparkle attraction. In other words – a pickup line is always a big "No".

How to open properly

"The girl who you really like will get fucked by some other guy tonight simply because you did not make up your mind and were caught up in dreams instead of facing the reality, therefore didn't approach her. This other guy could be you right now."

The most important part of the interaction is actually opening the girl to create the interaction in the first place, on which you can start building on. It does not necessarily mean you have to make the first move. You can create a social environment where she opens you or get introduced through friends. Regardless of these methods, if you're not either putting in the effort of opening a girl or at least create a possibility for her to open you, then you will not get anywhere in game. I myself advise all guys to make the first move themselves since it's the easiest, most optimal and also the least stressful way to get women. If you want the girl to open you, then just stand out by either wearing some unusual outfit, act a certain way to get that desired attention or just have really high status like a movie star or a rich businessman.

For an example a friend of mine who at that time was just few weeks into my pickup program came up with an idea that was doing push ups in the middle of a crowded street to break his social anxiety. While doing so he was getting tons of female attention and had constantly women approaching him. I'm not saying this method is great, I'm just sharing different possibilities and showing you how there are many ways of approaching this. A guy does not always have to be the one do make the first move, although doing so it will produce the most results and will make your confidence, self-esteem and skill grow much faster.

Here's a pointer for you guys when you decide to do the open yourself, which should be the case for all men. Hit her with your open the very same second you have that girl's attention. This means as soon as she notices you. This could mean looking at you, turning her head to observe who's in her environment or any other scenario where her attention is on you. Even if it's just for a second, this is the time to strike.

How to strike?

Worried about what you're going to say to her? I used to have severe troubles with this myself. Everything I could come up with was too much self-qualifing and needy for attention. Nowadays I go up first and right when I make eye contact I'll hit her up with a comment on her looks, her walking speed or the way she carries herself, basically anything I can come up with and that is not too much in terms of giving her validation. The idea is to say something to get her interested, but not something too nice so that she would think she's above you.

If you're approaching girls during the day then I advise you to start with a remark on the weirdness of this situation.

"I know this seems weird, but I just had to say hi." If

she's interested, she'll respond.

Make her feel like you're not just some any guy who wants her for her looks. The basic idea is to let her know her looks made you to approach her, but that's not what you're all about and would like to find out more about her before taking any vital steps. It doesn't matter if you're actually like that since most men never are, and mostly just want sex not even caring about her personality, but it's important to convey this trait of having options and not just choosing her for looks and more for who she is.

During nightgame it doesn't really matter what you say, sometimes it's better to not even say anything at all, gently grab her hand and pull her closer to you and start commenting her eyes, her lipstick, her hair or whatever you feel like making a remark on, or even do some roleplay.

Basically, during nightgame you can say and do pretty much anything, during daygame it's more important to empathize and acknowledge the weirdness of this situation, of you approaching her just like that, since it's not really a normal thing to do amongst most guys.

Keep in mind that by approaching her you're already higher in value than most guys in the world, because not many of us have the balls to approach strangers while being sober. Doesn't matter how it goes, just get the approach checked in, and then start building on this foundation.

The reason why I emphasize taking action so much is because the best way to learn is not by reading, seeing nor hearing about something. The best way to learn is through experience. None of these points will ever make complete sense to you, if you do not apply these in your own life.

The idea of something is not enough. An idea only holds value if it's being applied, if it's being lived.

The Great Opening

"The way to make your vibe smooth is by knowing who you are and what you want to do with your life without being too stuck up about it, and by being comfortable with letting the girls who are not interested in you, go. Funny enough, by being outcome independent and not caring about getting the specific girl, you'll start to attract the ones who would not like you otherwise."

There's a football game going on. The whole bar is filled with crazy drunk fans whose only ambition is to forget all their troubles and just let loose for this one night. Amongst them I find two girls sitting quietly in a corner while having the greatest table in the whole bar in their possession. I step up, sit down right next to those two beauties while creating the illusion of politeness by asking whether it's okay for me to sit down and have a chat, although I've already made the move of parking myself really close to them. This move is one of my favourite since it portrays confidence and leadership while making it looks like I'm being nice. The idea is all about asking if it's okay for you to sit down right next to her while already setting it up without caring about their answer. This makes the girls unable to say no since you're already there while also not seeming like a complete douchebag. It's the situation of the girl feeling the need to say no, but her body being drawn to you and therefore creating a conflict within her. While she's battling her emotions and thinking whether it was a good idea to not shoo you away, you'll be starting a conversation and taking her mind off your so-called "rude" open. In my eyes it's not rude, I call it demanding in a fun and playful way, which is a great combination at all times. This technique probably has the highest success rate in terms of rejections and will produce you amazing results, if you're not just some random boring guy and actually invest in that girl by using the same conversation principles that can be found in this book.

How to talk for hours and never run out of things to say

„Hey I'm … .“

Now what? When you meet a girl in a club, a bar or just on the street, what's the thing you have to do after saying hi? Talk. Altho there are forms of nonverbal conversations that are highly effective in game, I will not touch them here. Anyway, you have to talk. Guys always have a problem with this one.

„What should I talk about?

Will she find it interesting?

Maybe this is not what a man should say when he meets a woman?

I have no topics to talk about!“

All of these are common problems in a guy's dating world. Funny, the fix for this is quite easy. Are you ready for it? It does not matter what you say. For some guys who are with a technical point of view, this might be quite hard to understand.

„What do you mean by it does not matter? I can't just say anything that comes into my mind!“

This is where you're mistaken, my friend. You can pretty much say anything that comes up in your mind. Now you do need some common sence so you won't yell only curse words and warmonger praises for the whole conversation, but as far as topics go, it does not matter. You can talk about anything. Since now we have established the fact that it's okay to talk about anything, let's move on to the next part. Which topics to choose? There are so many of them! Well, why don't you pick the ones you like? Then you will be more energetic to talk about them, since you like them. Makes sense, right. The more you're invested in the topic, the more you will make it seem like it's relevant, important and interesting. You will show her a glimpse of your awesome world, your personality and style. The girl will also respect you for sharing things that you like and not just go for the typical „so where are you from“ type of talk. There is nothing wrong with that sentence other than it's just too damn played out. You can always use it, but it better not be the only tool in your arsenal. To sum it all up - If you're comfortable with the topic, then she will be too.

There are also some quick tips that about where you should have long conversations and where you should keep them short and focus on the physical part. Obviously, you will not be giving the girl your entire life story on the dance floor. In the club it's better to focus on saying more obnoxious things and keeping it short. Do not be the only one investing in the conversation. It's essential to give the girl a chance to say something back. It should be mutual investment, not just one sided like one guy talking for half an hour and the girl just nodding and pretending like she knows what you're talking about. In that case she is just too damn nice to make you leave. If the conversation is not mutual, she will feel like you're trying to qualify yourself to her, because you think of yourself as lower value. In this state you don't really care much about her interests and just want to fuck her because you don't really have any other options. Simple laws of charisma apply here tremendously well. If you're not familiar with these, then let me reveal you the most important one by far:

Charisma is not so much about yourself, it's about the effect you have on others and how you make them feel.

In nightgame – when you feel like the set/your conversation is boring or is about to be boring, then just move her to another location. You can also change the subject depending on your gut feeling.

Let's say you'll meet a girl on a street during daygame and in your mind you'll come up with literally nothing worth saying. It's important to understand that pretty much anything is worth saying, if you're passionate about it or you just find it funny. The easiest and most effective way to start a conversation in this situation is to make a remark about her appearance or activity such as waiting for the bus, smoking, looking worried or walking really fast. You'll just have to roll with the current situation and make the best of it. She wants you to succeed, trust me on this. Why wouldn't she? Girls dream of meeting a cool at least a few times every single day.

Once you'll get the conversation ball rolling by joking around together with her and giving her positive emotions, then you can ask her some quality questions about her job, school and passions. When your idea differs from her's, do not be afraid to disagree, but just don't do it in an unpleasant way nor try to make her change her beliefs. In this case it's more about quality conversation opposite to nightgame, where girls mostly just look for emotional stimulus.

The rules to be a good conversationalist say that you don't have to agree with everything the opposite party has to say, but you also don't have to disagree. A good conversationalist will always be on a neutral ground, he is very diplomatic, but in pickup, to get the most optimal results, this rule should be bent. Disagreeing with a girl can be really good in terms of you seeming a guy of high value, since it shows you having abundance of girls and not caring to make it work with this specific one that much. It's the idea of if we fit, we fuck. It's better to not change your frame for anyone and stay true to it for the rest of the conversation. Funny thing is by using these methods from this book you'll pretty much fit with any girl right off the bat and the pressure is on her whether she's ready to take that jump towards socialising with you or is she too caught up in her own excuses.

This works because girls actually like when a guy disagrees with them. The guy who agrees, is their friend since they get along just fine, but the guy who disagrees is a man and worthy of a fuck. This does not mean you should disagree with them even if it goes against your beliefs, not at all. This means women like a guy who's real and who is not hiding behind a mask. The trick lies in being comfortable with the guy who you are right now, whoever it might be. Girls ultimately don't give a shit about what you are, they care about whether you like yourself and are you comfortable with being who you are.

Another important tip I want to add here is to give women the chance to say something back by making playful and sometimes over the top assumptions that they can reply to, so they will feel like she's under the spotlight and being screened. This last point will especially show the girl that you don't settle for anyone and you're just giving her the chance, not the other way around. Remember –the vibe you're giving out should to be positive and fun which is achieved through yourself simply feeling that way about yourself. Some of us need to fake it at first to develop this, others have it naturally and both work just fine.

Still feel like you have no topics to talk about? You can always look at her clothes, bag, hair, nails, and eyebrows. Look at her shoes. Compliment them, ask about their trade mark. Even better – try to guess the trade mark. Compare them to something, anything, and be positive about it. You're not there to bring her mood down, you're there to lighten up her day. Ask her advice on your own style and what would suit you. Next, ask where she's going. Let's say she's going to school. Say something witty about your school experience like:

„Oh, school almost killed me, hope you'll do better."

The trick is to be cocky and funny to set off a playful yet confident vibe. This is where the book „How to win friends and influence people" really comes in handy, which is most definitely a masterpiece of the last century.

A good conversationalist and also a great pickup artist does not just talk. He is also a good listener and asks also those questions and show interest in them that will not so much offer yourself pleasure, but seem important to her. It's not all about you. It's a conversation. It's supposed to be mutual. If you genuinely show interest in the other person and ask questions about the topic she's interested in, then it feels to her like you two just had an amazing conversation and you both learned a lot about eachother even tho she did most of the talking.

The date

"Girls don't notice the overall emotions, they notice the change in the emotional state."

The longer I spend with this guy, the better I feel. We are getting closer with each minute. This is the kind of stuff you'll hear when purposely making the date boring at the beginning, but moving the state up progressively. Don't bring you're a game in the first half, instead build it up to be you're a game when it's time to pull.

Treat the date as if you were going out with your friends, so you wouldn't be very devastated when they're turning you down for some reason. Even if your game is on point, girls do flake, meaning they skip on meeting up with you for instance on the last minute, and there is nothing to really do about it. Think of her as a friend with who you're going to have sex with eventually.

The date does not need to be flashy, it can easily be something extremely casual, like going window shopping, giving each other challenges to pick different clothes and so forth. There is no need to pay, there's even no need to do something that requires money, since the girl is there for you and not the free meal or movie. Remember that the frame you set out at first will be the one that needs to be crossed in the long run while being on a date with her. If you're starting out with paying for her dinner and whatnot, she will feel like she's entitled to this every single time she meets you, therefore setting really high expectations for you and if for some reason you're unable to deliver this performance or even a better one next time, then the connection will be weakened tremendously.

Always go for the kiss on the first date. This act alone is going to show you tremendous amount of feedback and will show you the glimpse of what the next level in game is going to be like. The girl will not have much respect for you without you at least giving a shot at it. Without kissing her on the first date, the friend zone is pretty much imminent. Kiss is the absolute minimum you should go for on your first date. Accept the fact that if a girl is coming out to meet you, then she has already figured it out in your head you being a potential sex partner. There are millions of other things she could be doing instead, yet she chose to

meet up with you. That's the clearest sign right there that here's your shot, go on and take it. A date is also mutual, meaning you will be screening her as much as she's screening you. This concept can be played around a lot by making her chase you and some other scenarios, but the overall theme is still you both not just qualifing yourself, but also looking for traits of quality in the other.

Why words don't matter

"Girls love to talk. Let them."

In a famous recent study conducted by Albert Mehrabian, the results were ground-breaking. When you talk to someone, 55% of the entire conversation is carried by your psychology, your breathing, posture, muscle tonus, gesture, facial expressions and your movement. This is called reading our emotional states that we for some reason just cannot ignore.

Another 38% of your message is conveyed by your vocal qualities. The tone, speed, volume and inflections of your words convey more than five times as much as the actual words.

Finally we get to words. The overtake is only about 7% of the whole communication!

This all is just a reflection of our communication system. We do not care about the words so much, since we're built to prioritize body language, voice tonality and everything else. Even if we focus purely on words, we will miss the true message, because we definitely miss their subliminal messages that usually play a bigger role in every conversation.

This is also the main reason why people with high logical thinking pattern are unable to read social cues, they've been programming themselves to listen to the words and miss paying attention to other indicators of getting the point across.

Our words may contain only 7% of what we communicate, but they offer many opportunities to reduce differences and enhance similarities. Meaning with words you should only focus on being relatable and talk about stuff she would be interested in and would love to hear.

I play around with words a lot. The first rule is to be relatable. Second tweak that I've done is match the speed of my voice to hers or at least come close. The basic zest of it is to come across with same energy as she's in right now, so she would not be overstimulated by your fast talking or get bored when you talk too slow. It's all about reading her state of mind, seeing if she's already having lots of fun or did she just step out of a library. Energy levels differ a lot during the day. It's your duty to make yourself relatable by talking about stuff that she would have a say in it plus matching your energy to hers. It does not have to be a perfect fit nor copycat, but adjust yourself to be closer to her in the whole communication, so she would feel connection.

Results, not conversations

"Ask yourself: What do you want from the girl? Why are you there talking to her in the first place?"

That's as direct as it can be. Every time right before you go out there is a decision you need to make. What do you want to accomplish? If you're a beginner and just starting out, then your goal should be having conversations. However, if you're already in that phase and find yourself having the same type of interaction over and over again, then something needs to change. The key word here is progress. Improve yourself by moving out of your comfort zone.

One of my main wingmen back in the day had this problem constantly. He was literally an approaching machine being able to adapt to any situation, snake himself into any group and start a conversation that's not just one sided. This does not sound like a bad thing now does it? Well, to do this same routine day after day for over a year without having any results other than just conversations – not that productive. You see where I'm getting with this. Step it up, learn a new technique if you have to, put yourself to a test and do not be afraid to fuck up. Do not be afraid to fuck up. Do not be afraid to fuck up. Winning gives you feedback on what you're doing right, but losing will show you what you're doing wrong. Both are necessary parts of the game.

Whether you win or lose, are able to reach the level of sexual intercourse with a woman of your choosing, or get rejected by that same one – this should ultimately not even matter to you. The guy who keeps making progress is always considered to be a winner. The outcome might be not what you expected, but as long as you're moving closer to the result of your choise, you're winning. Keep battering through challenges, do not give up and expand your comfort zone every single time you go out. This is the recipe of becoming legendary in any endeavour and especially in pickup, since it's all about daily expansion and pushing your limits of what's possible and keep lowing your own mind by becoming that guy you set out to be, getting closer minute by minute. With every single push you'll discover something new and experience a massive growth in your skill almost without putting much effort into it at all, it's like your brain is learning these successful behaviours on its own without you even focusing on it. All we need to think about is putting ourselves in the situation, our brain will take care of everything else.

"Keep hitting the iron and see progress, but break the iron and you'll see instant change."

Contact

"Accept your current state, talk to her anyways, and allow your state to naturally be livened up. "

If the interaction between you and a girl does not turn out as you'd like and you're about to be left alone, make sure you'll get the girl's number so you two could hang out later. Although, do not make getting her number the last thing you'll do with her. That's almost a guaranteed flake, because you are not building enough leverage on her to come out with you. Get her number and keep talking, do something with her and don't leave right after getting the number. If you leave right after getting the number, she will view it as a tool to get rid of you, not always intentionally, but in her subconscious it's pretty much guaranteed. Number is not your goal, having fun with her however should be. If she can't really stay for long, then get the number for sure, but the idea is to stay in the set for as long as you can and end it on a positive and fun note and then text her up later and arrange a meetup instead of running away with your small little number like a beta male and then texting her without having any leverage over the whole interaction.

If the number is the last thing you'll get, then there will be little to no leverage, she will only remember giving you the number and not the conversation. If the conversation lasted for about one minute and ended by you getting a phone number, then the rate of flakes will be even bigger. The way you end the conversation is a key factor. Do you come from the frame of "I want to see you again as soon as possible" or "Thanks for the number, bye!" The first one will be optimal in every situation and is created by creating leverage, something she can hold on to.

Also, always make sure you tell her of your intentions while getting the number. She must know why you're getting it and that you're not just some next text buddy she's about to have. Make your intention clear, tell her what's up, that you want to see her again and even try to arrange a meetup while you're there talking to her in person, then later on just confirm via text. Asking someone out through texting does not spike the same amount of emotions in a girl whereas chatting her up on the street, getting the number and then implementing a date for the same day or the next will. Texting is a tool to arrange a date while you two have no way of meeting each other, real life conversation is to build attraction and in those moments you should also ask her out since she is a lot more inclined to say yes. A cool guy like you being there asking her out and confirming later through text versus a guy he knows nothing about or does, but has forgotten the emotion behind meeting him, texting her out of the blue asking her to meet up somewhere. You need to have leverage, since girls usually don't go out with random dude they don't know well. Building leverage will make it seem like she knows and can trust you.

Remember, women use emotions, men logic. The fact you two really hit it off on the street or in a club does not mean she is in a mood to talk to you the next day, maybe she won't even reply to your texts. Always keep this in mind and make your texts interesting and full of fun to bring out those same positive emotions she felt meeting you for the first time. Do not re-create the conversation, just keep moving and treat every single new girl you're texting for the first time like it's starting from scratch again despite the fact that you already met her once. The conversation does not keep going from where you left off, it starts from zero again, otherwise you'll make it tedious and boring.

Pro tip: The first text I send to the girls after I've gotten their number is asking if they remember what my name was. This works wonders, shows the girl massive high value on your part and makes her invested since she will feel like you're someone she should not lose.

Women who play hard to get

One reason why most women play hard to get is because vagina is their only bargaining chip. If they give you sex too soon they risk losing the money, time and/or attention that you would have given them. In some cases if a chick has no problem fucking you sooner rather than later that could indicate that she just either wants you for sex or that she has more to bring to the table than just vagina.

What your goal should be

"Girls just want to have a good time. That's it."

When I'm in the club, my main motivation is to improve of course and so should yours be. Not getting sex, not getting kisses or make outs, not getting positive reactions, just pure and simple progress in the right direction. Everything else is just a short term goal that will be reached very soon regardless of how my night goes. Your main goal should always be to evolve since that's all what it takes no matter what endeavour you choose to dominate, what job you're going to pick and so on. Progress, guys. I can't emphasize this enough.

Once you've established that you're out in the club or in a bar or just on the street to improve your skillset and be more advanced overall, only then you can start setting small term goals for yourself.

Being able to approach and introduce myself.

Agree to meet up with her the next day/exchange phone numbers.

Implementing a kiss/have a make out with her.

Reaching the level of sexual intercourse.

Always know why you're going out, but never forget to have **fun**. Even though progress will always be our number one goal, having fun is crucial and should be a natural side effect of our evolution. If you're feeling stretched and really tedious about this whole pickup thing and would just like to not change anything in your life, then go ahead, nobody will stop you. You need to do some serious thinking right now and make it perfectly clear to yourself, whether the lifestyle of a so-called player will improve your life quality and whether it will make you have more fun overall. Maybe you have different goals, maybe you want to take your life in a different direction which is totally fine. However, if your answer is yes to this specific lifestyle or at least would like to learn the traits of a successful dating life, then this temporary pain that you're going to feel when approaching a girl will all be worth it including huge bonuses that are different for all of us. Sometimes it's essential to suffer in order to reach the higher ground. A momentary pain will produce a lifetime of joy. Is this joy worth going through some painful experiences that you at some point will have to experience regardless of your choise right now? To me it's always worth it, for you maybe not yet, but I can assure you that taking action and facing whatever you have to face will satisfy your overall desires in the long run.

Someday regardless of your decision right now you'll be faced with a tough situation where you have to do something you feel fear towards. When that time comes, you'll wish you had started learning about pickup and women's psychology sooner to have the courage and the reference experiences backing you up in every endeavour. Will you immerse yourself into pickup and achieve the mindset of Steve Jobs, Arnold Schwarzenegger, Muhammad Ali and many more? Me and many other masters in this field will assure you this is not even an exaggeration and whether you choose to believe and taking action by following this belief to achieve the richness of your mind is, as always, totally up to you.

The Decision

"Women have this natural skill of being socially very adaptable, which turns your beliefs about them into a self-fulfilling prophecy."

There is a decision you'll have to make if you decide to truly live the life I'm advertising so freely in this book. The decision you'll have to make is to decide whether you want to have sex with a woman or be liked by her. Although these will seem like they'd be in alignment with each other, it's truly not the case. The guys a woman likes and the guys who she fucks are totally different. Main difference between these two types of guys is one guy has little to no congruence, which is an alignment in your thoughts, words and actions, and the other one is set out to have sex with the woman he decides to approach. If you go for being liked, then she will most likely like you, but will not sleep with you. If you decide that you'd rather get sex than be liked, then the best way to go about it is to be real, share your true personality and the type of guy who you are as a whole. The guy who wants to be liked, will betray his true indentity since human beings are not made to agree on every level. In order to be liked, you'll have to agree with her on anything. In order to be fucked, you'll have to stay true to yourself and your values while being respectful of hers and understand that their differing from each other is completely normal and just the way life is.

"Women fuck men who convey manly personality traits."

The guy who wants to be liked, will agree with the girl despite deep down having a different opinion. Women will like you for it, say that they'd wish they had a nice guy such as you, and complain about all their ex-boyfriends being assholes. Welcome to the friend zone. The only reason women are mad at their ex-boyfriends is because they're mad over still liking them for their honesty even though the guy does not like them back anymore. Women get mad over being attracted to guys who are assholes, they do not understand why it is so. Reason for this is because assholes are only assholes because they stay true to themselves and their belief system, therefore having higher value as a man than the guy who doesn't. Those so called assholes might believe a man should be able to sleep with multiple women at the time. Their woman has been grown up in a society where polygamy is condemned, therefore they have learned to hate it. But since the guy who is ruthlessly being himself is extremely attractive since that kind of attitude portrays manly personality traits, women can't help but to feel sexual tension towards him. It's biology versus learned thinking patterns.

We think we seem pleasing to the other person by agreeing with the other person even on things we don't agree on. The truth is that women and men most of the time do not even know what they agree on, so you'd both be agreeing on something none of you agrees at all. On some deep level the one who does not fully agree with the things he or she says, knows this perfectly. They also feel on a subconscious level from your energy that you do not agree with their stuff either. Since you're not standing up for your own values, you are not much of a respectful person, therefore they find it hard to respect you since there is no you, there's just the other person who you're talking to, you're just adopting his or her values during the interaction.

Being the guy who wants to be liked is actually counterintuitive and will produce you not being liked. Being the guy who's true to himself has people hating on him, but also those who love him. Now, being someone who stays true to himself, but also does not disagree with the other side, is the one that's most appealing to everyone and will be the best style of thinking for you to adopt.

The next time you go out with the intention of picking up women, ask yourself:

Do you want to be liked or do you want to be fucked? You're there to share your values and experience her's. You don't need to agree, but you don't need to disagree either. This is what creates true attraction.

Chances are your success rate will drastically increase.

How to have enough time to do anything

"If your priorities are in check, then you'll have time for everything."

I see this concept of not having enough time to do something constantly on my clients, but particularly on my friends. They have great life goals such as getting really fit and being healthy, making lots of money, reading many educational books, being good with girls and so forth. And guess what? Surprise surprise, they say they don't just have enough time to do any of it. Many of them even make valid points about why they are not learning game just like many of us have done so to improve our lives. Earning a living and looking after the family, according to some of my friends, is taking all their time away. And yet, I see them constantly on Facebook posting totally useless links that exist just for the sake of entertainment. They are totally right, they do not have the time to be successful, if it's being used to procrastinate.

Saying that you don't have time is also just being untruthful to yourself. It can make a really good excuse, because it seems acceptable on the outside lair of the thought process. But inside you'll know it's a lie even if you don't completely understand the concept of it. You will have the itchy feeling regardless of your ability to understand it. Deep down we all know what we must do. And as always, it's a lot easier to say than do. Here's what these excuses sound to me like:

"I don't have time to be successful, because I need to focus on the areas in my life that are worthless, but give me a short term satisfaction and a feeling that I'm not completely useless."

Don't ever say you do not have time to do something in the present of someone successful. You'll just lose all the respect they had for you right there, in the end of your sorry little excuse.

Let's move on to the technical part of this subject. Sure, some of you might not really have time to do practise game as much as some other guy, but every single person on this earth can find at least twenty minutes at minimum each day to devote themselves on something that will benefit their skill level. In the case of pickup, you can practise your game on the street while coming home from work, in the bus while driving to your parents' house, you can practise game literally in every single place, if there is at least one girl for you to talk to. You can also game every single woman that you walk past in the office, in the gym, just about anywhere. There is really no excuse for this. Twenty minutes a day is ten times better than nothing. Hell, even a hundred times.

It's highly inaccurate to say that you don't have time to do something. If a TV show is important to you, then you'll make the time. If reading a book a day is impotant to you, youl'll make the time. If being successful in game is important to you, you will make time. Let's make a deal with ourselves and be honest from now on. You can make time if needed, you just don't want to. It's the question of your desire.

This is your moment

"In game it's not just the early bird that gets the worm. Everyone who go out and take action will be handsomely rewarded."

After having countless thoughts on which one of these will hit us with more resistance – the beginning or breaking into different levels of success after taking the first step, I believe I finally found the answer. It's already known worldwide and is not really anything new, but to have a deep understanding of it is still something that I had not experienced untill now.

The beginning will always be the hardest part of any success story.

This is part of a famous quote by Henry Ford. Throughout time many smart individuals have always said that getting the ball rolling is always the hardest part in every story. In reality it just feels like it simply because our paradigm, the vibration on which our thoughts run does not accept change very kindly. Once our brain has adopted a new way to live by such as working out, writing a book, meditation for 30 minutes every morning and stuff like that, we begin to run on an autopilot not having to force ourselves every time and doing things more out of power rather than by force.

Having power means to understand what you're here for and what to do in a current situation. Power does not run on willpower, it's simply a way of life which just seems right. If you have been jogging every morning for the last three years, then your brain has taken in this idea of living healthy. Not much willpower is required to go for that run every morning, it's already a part of you. Same with brushing your teeth and many other. Power= a way of life

Force= applying willpower to do something we're not accustomed to.

Every single journey cannot exist if the main hero won't push the ball to get it rolling, meaning without beginning there cannot be an end, since the story simply does not exist. This is why every single motivational speaker puts so much pressure on the importance of starting out. All of us know that in order to do something, it's necessary to start. But how many of us actually understand it? We walk around wishing to be rich, to have all the women/men who we want in our lives, to be respected and famous, but what are we doing in terms of getting there? The answer is nothing for the majority of us on this planet. It's like beating ourselves for not being able to get up from the chair and walk to the fridge without realising that the beating takes more energy than actually getting up and getting to our destination.

Every story starts without power. Power can only be created by forcing ourselves to adapt new habits and change our paradigm. A book called Power vs Force has a debate on this subject and questions whether power can exist without force. My answer is no, it cannot. In order to create power, one needs force. In order to keep power, one needs to apply force every once and awhile.

We should not expect ourselves to have power to be the best right away while still having a great deal of years ahead. Did you know that Winston Churchill, one of the most famous British Prime ministers in our history, became a somebody after the age of 65? While still in his 50s he was considered to be a laughing-stock of politics and had no power what so ever, both figuratively and directly. Another example would be to look at the average age of US presidents. It's around 55 meaning they've had 55 years to study the craft of success in politics and how to win the crowd. So how could someone in their 30s expect so much from himself that he would know the same stuff or even more than the guy in his 50s does? It's possible and we should all aim for that, but if it does not work out, just remember the things I just talked about. I tend to feel bad when I don't accomplish the things I set out to do. Later on I find out that nobody in my age has done it before, at least no-one we know of. The point is to not beat ourselves up for something we're not meant to accomplish so soon and skipping important life lessons that come with experience, which comes with age.

Aim high while having your feet on the ground.

This is the moment when you go out and try these things out for yourself. You have all the knowledge you need in order to start. I really urge you to go out and try at least some of the things I've bene writing about untill now, approach at least one girl today on the street in a bar, in the club, in a coffee shop, doesn't matter where, just put in the effort and do it. See how you feel and make truthful conclusions, then you can come back and keep reading, there is a lot more to come that will skyrocket your results to the level of a complete master.

I know it's scary, for some of you it might even feel like suicide since that's how I felt for the first time. I was most likely even more scared than you are. The results however are phenomenal and worth going for.

It's important to know that everything will be fine no matter who or where you approach. We are designed to feel fear before every new situation that's about to happen, don't let it fool you. Sometimes this fear is justified, but pickup is definitely something not to be afraid of. Nobody is going to beat you up, you won't lose your head and fall into sudden death, all you'll do is having a chat with some girl about anything like a fully functional human being.

The brighter the glow you feel within yourself, the more it attracts people. This is exactly what people mean when they say someone has that "thing", the bright eyes, the glow, the nimbus, the glow or the force of being likeable, charismatic and makes other people inspired to hang out with you.

Outer game

Outer game is everything that's taking place outside of yourself. Your movements, your words, your actions. Learning the right moment when to take the girl you've been talking to back to your place, knowing how to deal with anoying girlfriends that the woman you're gaming might have etc. Outer game does not focus on your feelings, it focuses purely on what to do and when to do it to be able to get the most optimal response and reach sex in the fastest way possible.

Outer game is great because it is independent of state, meaning you don't need to feel good about yourself in order to get results and get the girl. I've gone out many times and felt like shit, but still managed to pull a girl and have a great night at the end.

Outer game is the tactics, techniques and technical behaviors you demonstrate to create attraction, build investment and comfort with her and solves logistics so you can take her home.

Outer game is the technical side of pickup.

Inner game

"Mind will always be over the body, but sometimes, to get the mind going in the right direction, action needs to be taken first."

Inner game is the mindset and beliefs you have about yourself and the environment that gives you high self-esteem and confidence to naturally attract women. Inner game is being comfortable with yourself in any situation, basically being the cool guy a girl would always want.

Inner game is all about who you are and how you feel.

Inner game is more valuable and is something that I focus on a lot more, but to maximize your results it's optimal to still need to know how to solve logistics and seal the deal.

Outer game vs Inner game

"The act of sleeping with hundred women in a year consists of having masculine traits and using these to play the odds. It's a big numbers game and the more masculine you are, the better odds you'll get."

Outer game trumps inner game in terms of getting the results, but inner game is better in terms of having fun, feeling good and being really comfortable with yourself while having these amazing nights and experience people from a whole new side.

Outer game is very mechanical while inner game more of a free flow of energy.

In conclusion:

The person who's focused on outer gam will eventually get more sex. The person who's focused on inner game will be of higher value, completely at ease with himself, his results and results despite what they might be.

As you see, sex is definitely not happiness. Being able to get sex however is an important part of it, but it is not "it".

In order to be a great pickup artist who enjoys his life while also getting amazing results, dates models and other people of high caliber, you'll need to know both, inner and outer game. Think of it as a coin. Really good game cannot be valuable without both sides existing and being in harmony with each other. Outer game does not work without inner game and inner game somewhat works without outer game, but could still use some knowledge to optimize results.

How to kill unworthiness

"You can't give other people good time, because you can't give yourself good time."

There is a friend of mine, whose name I'm not going to mention, and who is experiencing this problem to this date due to many reasons, especially low self-esteem and the lack of confidence. The guy I'm describing has this simple, yet very profound situation, where he does not believe in himself, has nothing to offer for the girl, and the only way he could ever attract a girl is by being fake, extremely manipulative and even if all that is in play, there is still the factor of luck involved. A guy like this has an extremely negative image of himself, is probably at the lowest point any person could ever reach and whenever he experiences success, the only explaination for this that he comes up with is luck.

Another thing this type of guy will think of is whenever he approaches a girl, a guy or just about anyone for that matter, he is taking something from them, he is being disrespectful and wasting their time since he believes he has absolutely nothing to offer, not even a nice ten second conversation. A guy like this does not want to oppose himself to the girl, he is coming from the taking mentality, and he believes he's taking something really valuable from the other person.

This is the imposter syndrome, which means despite external evidence of their competence, those exhibiting the syndrome remain convinced that they are frauds. It's like being afraid of being exposed of learning game. What if the girl finds out that you've not been born with the natural knowledge of knowing how to sleep with hundreds of women? What if the girl finds out that you have been learning about this and are not able to apply these skills naturally? What if they find out I had to learn the ways of becoming a cool guy?

I have an answer for you. The woman does not care about the fact of whether you naturally being a cool guy or having to learn this skill not one bit. All she cares about is whether you are the cool guy or not, the origins are not important at all. If anything, she will be more intrigued since you're the guy who has been working hard to learn these skills and is not just born naturally like the kid born in a rich family, who in most cases does not have to work a single day in his life. The person who has been through hell, has spectacular value to offer and in this case, that guy who's feeling like an imposter, most certainly does once he sorts this stuff out in his head.

Impostor syndrome – Proof of success is dismissed as luck, timing, or as a result of deceiving others into thinking they are more intelligent and competent than they believe themselves to be.

Despite the strong evidence of people liking you, hanging out with you, being able to take girls home and have sex with them, a guy with the imposter syndrome believes it's merely due to game and not him, because of the things he told her and the learned behaviours that many pick artists emphasize. A guy like this thinks he is getting laid thanks to the things he does rather than for who he is. A guy like this is overestimating game so much. Game is merely a tool to bring out the sexworthiness and successful mindset in you, it's not why you're actually getting laid. That reason is you being you.

How to sort this stuff out in your head?

The truth behind why you're feeling as an impostor, imposing on others, taking something away from others, wasting their time by approaching women is you believe you can't give them good time, because you're not able to give yourself a good time. Figuring out the answer for this specific concept and making yourself able to offer good time to yourself and to the girl is determined whether you're happy or not. You don't have to be at the end of your journey to be happy, you do not have to "make it" in order to be complete and enough for the girls, it is simply enough for you to be on that right path, which consists of game, living a healthy yet fun lifestyle and just enjoying your days as they are while also striving for more.

"The more beautiful a girl is, the more she'll project the perfect lifestyle regardless of it being true or not. Every person is flawed in one way or another and their perfection is just our interpretation."

We are all lacking in some areas. When I first started to take action and talk to girls in nightclubs, bars, streets, then I was totally broke, living in my mother's apartment not paying for anything, fallen off my healthy diet and lost the habit of working out and playing video games, yet I was moving in the direction of where I wanted to be in life, I was moving towards becoming that perfect guy who I always dreamed of being, but never had the right knowledge to be able to actually take action towards becoming. I knew I am making my life better, I'm in the very process of getting where I eventually want to be in my life. If you're saying this to yourself every day, reinforcing the fact that you are doing all that could be done towards making yourself better, you'll realize how valuable you really are. Then, you're finally able to share yourself, your personality, offer value and have fun with random strangers without actually paying, faking or manipulating anybody. Then, you'll have your mind straightened out. It does not take for you to achieve those goals, the only thing that matters is you giving your best effort towards moving there and enjoying the process.

The other part of eliminating the impostor syndrome is simple. It's foolish to overestimate other people. We don't realize how small the group of guys and girls who ate into self-development actuallty is. The chances of you bumping into someone whose time is actually valuable, like Albert Einstein, Michael Jordan or Steve Jobs, are really fucking slim to none.

I always saw other people as these perfect individuals who know what they want and who they are, they are probably working on something important, therefore their time, even if it's one single minute, is really valuable. We tend to think that we are the only ones with a problem out here, which is crazy. I used to think everybody's social, without anxieties and simply perfect. Even if people look really fucking perfect, in shape, wearing expensive nice clothes, they still have their problems in one way or another, that they're anxious about all the time. The more I spend time talking to strangers, women and guys, I realized how fucked up their lives actually are, how mediocre most of us actually are, how little do they know about how world actually works and most of all – how dellusional and afraid all of us really are. The reasons for us being this way are all different, but the outcome is the same - humanity. This was the first moment when I realized that we all have problems no matter how many cars we own, how many women we bang or how famous and good looking we are. The only thing that separates us from the masses is the road we've taken, not the fact where we are on it, but which one have we chosen, either growth, mediocrity or degeneration, and even more importantly – the way we see ourselves.

"If a cat truly sees herself as a lion and acts like a lion, then she obviously is a lion. Does not apply in biology, but it does apply with the human mind and the spoils of life are earned accordingly."

If you look at the people on any street, chances are most of them are really bored, frustrated and even anxious, so by you being that positive influence and by approaching them to spice up their day, to add a little bit of color to it, nobody in their right might is going to reject you. Even if you're not able to make something happen, even if she is not interested in hanging out with you in the future, you'll still be making her day, even if it's just by a little bit, better. The more you do it, the sooner you realize how happy you can actually make others by being unstifled yourself. Pickup is not just about getting laid, it's about changing you into a better, more likeable, charismatic and successful person, who offers positivity and is an inspiration to all of us.

The Law of State Transference

As human beings we have an energy that's constantly revolving around us. The energy is different for each and every one of us, in a way we're all unique. The chances of a person just like you, with the same mindset and experiences every existing again are slim to none. There is an element of randomness in life that prevents these sorts of occurences from happening. But the energy that we all have, hence the title, can be transferred to the other person by just using the method of a simple interaction. The more influencial and charismatic you are, the better it will work.

The main way state transfer occurs is through the mirror neurons humans have and social pinging. On one side, people naturally mirror each other's behavior, and ping to see how they should react in a specific environment. Who reacts to who comes down to who is more congruent in their state, actions, mood, emotions...

The basic idea of this is whatever you're feeling at this given time, the person who's talking to you will feel it also. The one who's more influencial will be sucked into the other ones reality, at least for the short period of time while talking to each other.

In game, it's all about whatever you feel, she feels. If you're angry and trying to provoke a fight, she will have her guard up and becomes really defensive. If to be like this in the presence of a male who gets heated quite easily, the fight is almost bound to happen. However, if talking a woman while believing that you two already had or are going to have sex, then you'll be giving off some extremely sexual energy, that will put her in the mood for sex. She'll be more open with you, happier with you, more experimental with you, she will respond to you kissing her with much more ease and will feel really fucking good hanging out with you overall. The idea of male and female energy coming together and expressing themselves freely without any barriers. The barriers are there for the man to remove through law of state transference. Whatever you want her to feel, you must feel first. This is why professional pickup artists emphasize congruence so highly. An alignment in your thoughts, words and actions all actively working together for a common purpose.

Logistics

Before we move any further, let me clarify the concept of logistics. You'll see me talk quite a lot about scanning for logistics and stuff around this L word. It's basically the woman's situation during the time you meet her, whether she's out with friends, has a boyfriend, owns a flat where she's living alone and does she have time to chat or even fuck with you. It's her current situation and is a must for you to find out during the conversation so you'd know whether she's just killing time and would love to hang with you right now, or if she's busy then get her contacts and text her later for a meetup.

Logistical questions presented in a funny way so it would not seem very formal:

Who are you here with? – Which one of these hippos you're here with?

What are you doing tomorrow? – Will you be bored tomorrow?

Who do you live with? – Does your boyfriend know you're out?

These three questions are the fundamentals of logistics and just must be found out at some point of the interaction. Of course you should try and throw some other topics between there so it would not be too formal, but this is what you should be trying to find out during the interaction while offering her loads of fun and being confident at the same time. If this seems too much, then just do the things you're capable of at the given time period and don't worry about confidence and fun. The more you'll do it, the more natural you will be and the easier it will be to work these concepts into your game.

If she has a friend with her, I tend to do my best and try to get rid of him or her in the funniest way possible, which can easily done by befriending her or him. You could either take the friend with you and the girl you just pulled and see what will happen, which can play out really nicely for you, or just use to simple idea of isolating the girl you're trying to pull. If she says no, play it off as a joke and keep talking to her untill you've got enough leverage meaning she likes you a lot more than before and then go for the pull again. The more leverage you have on her, the more is she inclined to come home with you. If logistics don't work out meaning you are not able to pull her to your house, then just get the number and implement a meetup on some other day or even later that night. You could always invite them to your place and create a so-called small party.

Loads of options, the trick is to be sure of yourself aka confident in your material and strongly believe in yourself. If you will, then she will too.

Law of State Transference

"You should be more interested in what you have to say and not what she has to say."

The first ever study of creepiness was done in 2016. It had a really interesting result. Men and women experience creepiness differently. To men, creepiness can be summed up by words such as taxidermy and supernatural. This means men are most likely to be creeped out when watching a scary horror movie. Women have those same associations, plus, one more. Men.

Somewhere in the course of every guy's life, he has done something creepy while flirting with a woman. The reason is because we don't have the same understanding of the word creepy that women do.

The first mistake guys make is eye contact. Creepiness with the concept of looking into someone's eyes comes out as doing it either too much or too little. The idea is to get it just right. We all know what too much eye contact looks like, it's basically unbreakable and will creep out not just the girl, but everyone else who see this occurrence. The guy who gets too much into the girls face, who's too much in her personal space, is being creepy. Too little though can be uncomfortable as well. That's when the guy comes up to the girl from behind and startles her. I see this from time and time again, especially on the dance floor when the guy starts to do all these moves being behind, next or even in front of the girl without her actually noticing him untill that one point where she freaks out and leaves, slaps or does something that can be defined as instant rejection.

The rule for eye contact is that she can sense you coming, but not too much that you hesitate. Meaning in the first few times, in my experiences maximum three, when you make an eye contact with her, you need to go and speak to her. I understand that this can be hard to do, especially for a beginner. Let me make this easy for you.

The first step is to feel comfortable looking into the eyes of another person. How? This is done by practise. Start making brief eye contact with the people you meet, walk past or see at the club. Don't be picky and do it to anyone. The more eye contact you provoke, the more comfortable you'll start to feel. It's a numbers game. If you've been practising this with 100 people, you'll feel like it's a part of your personality. Being done it for only two people will most likely make you still feel uncomfortable. Make these little micro actions of eye contact and you'll see the improvement in less than a day.

The main reason why couples go on so many dates before actually reaching the level of sex is not just because the woman needs to build her comfort, but because the man needs to do the same in order to implement sex. The guy can have sex with the woman on their first date, right then and there, but if the guy does not feel like it's right or that he is not enough for some personal reason, then she will not feel it either. The law of state transference.

By being okay with looking into a person's eyes you'll eliminate a lot of creepiness and head towards the right path. The second part is to be okay with interactions, being okay with talking to people. Same method as before, same system, a numbers game. The more people you talk to, the better you'll get. The more you'll do it, the more comfortable you'll feel socialising and feel like you're in your own element without just staring at your feet the whole time. If at the beginning you're able to only get one number out of ten approaches, then later on by becoming better, you'll increase it to 4 or even more. Love as in from the first sight does not exist, there's just people who are good at game and those who are not.

You can start with micro actions by making eye contact with the people you walk past, move on to waving people on a street and sending out positive vibes and then finally move on to actually going up and introducing yourself. Small, yet consistent steps will guide you to victory. Every woman who smiles at you, waves back and just gives off a positive vibe towards you in general, is sending out subliminal messages, for the most part without herself even realizing this, for you to go up to her and start a conversation. If you do not approach her, you're not just letting yourself down, but also her and destroying the reality of you two having an amazing time together. Every single girlfriend and romantic relationship I've ever had, the girl has been grateful to me for having the balls to step up and try to make that special spark happen. It's not just about you, it's about the two of you. One small simple step can provide a lifetime of wonderful daily emotions for the both of you. If not for a lifetime, then for that one day. Still worth the trouble, if you ask me.

The more fun you're having, the better each interaction whether its just eye contact, a random wave at someone or actual pickup, will go. If feeling like you're having the time of your life, people will be one hundred percent positively receptive towards you. It's the rule of bringing the party instead of being a value leech trying to feed from the fun emotions of others. You're the guy who has the bubble filled with fun around you at all times and whoever you decide to approach, will meet the coolest guy he could find on that day. If she's not receptive, it's her loss.

If you're comfortable with micro actions, then you can start focusing on the women you specifically like and not just practise on anyone you see.

The next step is an actual conversation. It has a million ways to be creepy, it has at least a million ways to go wrong, and the things that needs to be emphasized the most, are compliments. Guys have this belief that they need to compliment the girl's looks. Most of them have this idea ingrained in their brain, and since it seems to work in movies and society tells us it's nice to give compliments, guys tend to totally over the top with them by using the principle that more is good. When giving compliments, there is this same rule as with eye contact – not too much, but do not also go down to zero validation zone on your part. Don't say anything you don't believe in. If she's not beautiful to you, then do not call her beautiful. Authenticity is held in great value when it comes to dating. Also, you're not there to beg for her attention, you're there to offer her your attention. A big difference.

Every time you compliment someone, you'll increase the amount of tension they feel. If you've ever been overly complimented yourself, you'll know how weird it starts to be. Questions like it's all nice and all, but what does this person really want, are starting to take hold. What is this person buttering me up for?

You should still compliment women, the idea of this is not to cut this part of the interaction out completely. Complimenting a woman is one of the most effective ways in showing her that you like her. The solution?

The most effective compliment is the one that's combined with a joke to release tension. It can be either a neg, which concept I've explained in previous chapters, or it can just be a light joke that's not meant to be cocky at all. You can play around with this a lot, but keep in mind that plain and straight out compliment will destroy women's respect towards a man. You don't want to validate her too much so that she would feel superior, and you also don't want to show any intent at all. Find a middle ground, which in this case is a compliment hidden within a joke. Call negs compliments filled with fun.

A question that's been up in the air a lot is guys feeling arrogant when they're going for the neg. A neg is not supposed to be arrogant, the emotion that should be going through you at that given time, is self – amusement. The point of negging is to have a result of laugher and comfort. It has nothing to do with insulting somebody. Here's an example.

"Beautiful nails. Are the real?"

Imagine you being a girl and you're reading this neg on your message board. Take a moment to comprehend, and then compare them to the regular "hey beautiful". These lines that I just suggested, obviously hold much more value and create the need in a girl to respond. I recommend you to think of all your texts in such way, putting yourself into her shoes and imagining what emotions will come to surface, before sending them. Make sure the girl is inclined to answer and don't just offer random compliments that lead nowhere and she can easily ignore or even worse – acknowledge, therefore grow her hot girl persona also known as her ego.

Negs hold a lot more meaning than you might think. They exist to project yourself as a guy who likes to challenge girls and does not just go for anyone with a pretty face, or in many cases with any kind of face. A neg will show the girl that you're a high value guy who is going to fuck her, if she passes your shit tests, and not the other way around. Girls like to have sex and they like to have it with the most high prestige guy around, so by you playing it cool, not showing interest in her right off the bat, giving her hoops to jump through by using negs and other stuff such as this is going to project from you that you have standards and are also screening the girls you meet without being too outcome dependant and just going for any pussy that's being thrown at you. Negs also make you stand out from the other guys, especially the ones that are friend zoned and who can't stand up for themselves and are tremendously afraid to disagree with the girl since they think it will make them lose all chances that they might have with her. Any professional dating expert can tell you right off the bat, that if you sacrifice your own personal beliefs and opinions just to be liked by some girl, then you're not worthy of a fuck at all. The point is not to disagree with her, nor to agree with her either. The point lies in staying true to yourself and holding yourself to a higher standard, not being someone who gets just run over by others who in most cases are nothing special either.

The third piece- touching. Same principles again, too much ain't going to work and too little is not making you look confident nor letting her know that you like her. Physicality is one of the best ways of creating sexual tension between you and women. Guy who's really aggressive and furiously grabs girls will be awful and will definitely creep out not just the girl, but most likely everybody in the room, which is seen a lot with drunk guys especially. Too little though and you're wasting the girls time, including yours. You can just walk up to her and talk for hours and even if you two have the most amazing chemistry known to man, she will not make the first move. That is always the guy's job and the sooner you realize this, the more sex you're going to receive.

Creepiness comes from not understanding social ques. If you have a certain level of social equity, you can probably run up, give the woman a hug, drag her to a dance floor and make out right then and there without any problems. However, if you're unable to read social ques as well, then this action will definitely not be the best option. If you haven't developed a sense of social awareness, you might run into serious conflicts. My recommendation for anyone who's new to this type of interaction and pickup in general, would be this. You want to start off with small touches at the right moment, like when you're about to get a drink, check up on your friend or anything like that, put your arm on her shoulder. The goal here is not to make her attracted, although that will happen through this action, the goal is to receive information about her comfort level and how she responds to you being a bit physical with her. If she's really into you, she won't mind. If she's not into you or is just a bit shy about it, you'll sense it or if you don't, then you'll learn to soon enough. If she makes you laugh or went to the same school as you, high-five her. If I tell her to come to a bar with me and she accepts, grabs my hand and follows me there, she's obviously alright with physicality to some degree, so the next time I'll at least hug her or do something else that can be called next level. Always be sure to moving forward with the interaction in a direction of where you want it to go.

If the girl is not receptive and does not buy into your physicality tests and seems like is not interested in going anywhere with you, that's a pretty clear indication that she's not feeling comfortable enough with me to take it to the next level. Maybe you did something wrong, maybe she's just having a bad day, is not in the mood at all or maybe she just hates your look for whatever reason. If she does not want you to be touching her then the reasoning for this is simple. She's not comfortable enough with you. The best choise would be to go back to speaking with her with less intimacy, less escalation. If it does not work out, you two are definitely not a match for whatever reason, maybe she has mental blockages that prevent her from dating a guy of your type or maybe you just failed to project qualities of a high value guy. Either way, move on. This does not necessarily mean you're not able to sleep with her. The answer is never a no, it's just not right now. If she's isolated, responsibility taken off of her, and stimulated to a certain degree, she will sleep with you, a big majority of women will be up for that. How to get to that point of having major comfort with her, and she following you anywhere, is a completely different story.

Building comfort

If you're a guy, then you most likely don't fully realize that most women are smaller than you, they're going to lose in a fight to you, they weigh less, they're not as strong as you and so forth. All of these things make you a literal physical threat to women. This is why women over thousands of years have evolved this sense of creepiness, it's a visceral feeling of this might be not safe for me. So you can imagine the time when you're unknowingly trapping her in a space even if you're just talking to her and the conversation is going great, she will want to leave your company unless she has a high degree of comfort with you. The worst thing you could do as a guy is to trap her in a booth without having any comfort with her. She will not feel good and she will most certainly not feel safe.

Now is the time when you ask what's the best way of building comfort with any girl, and the answer is quite simple. Humor melts away resistance. Fun is the cure of every mental barrier. Stimulating the girl is a necessity to a successful pickup, and it can be done in various ways, from which the best one by far is making her have a fun time with you. It can be either talking, doing some physical activity like dancing, playing a game or anything else. The playground is big and the toys are limitless.

What to do with the girl before sex?

"In game and in with all interactions in general it's not about what we do. It's about who we are". Let's say a girl asks you to go dancing with her and you hate to dance. What will you do? My friends used to come up to me and ask such questions. My answer to them would always be the same, which is a simple question. Do you want to dance? It's as straightforward as it can be and works like a charm. Don't try to be fake and do something that's not your playground just for the girl, because the girl can sense the uneasiness on you. Not staying true to your core values means that you're not happy with the current situation and therefore creating a new identity for yourself, even if it's just for that brief moment. Not being real and pretending to be someone else to be accepted by the girl is certainly not attractive, especially if you're doing it to win her approval and not for your own amusement. Always be real with yourself and with the girl. Even if you happen to disagree with her and her ditching you for not agreeing to dance, it's totally fine, if you're okay with it. If you're not okay with dancing, then you will obviously be okay with not dancing since you got to be okay with something, and since you're okay, she will also be okay with it, plain and simple.

If a girl happens to ditch you for a reason such as this, not dancing with her or maybe even something smaller, then she probably did not like you in the first place. And if she does like you, then she will respect you for being you and will give you a chance to prove yourself in your own way. If the attraction between you two is real and the girl really likes you enough to spend her precious time with you instead of all those other gentleman callers whose messages arrive daily, then she, without any doupt, will.

Whether you have a question about game like should I do this or that, just ask yourself – Do you want to? It's really that simple!

There is also a fine line between realizing which actions benefit you and which don't. It's essential to move out of your comfort zone and keep expanding daily, but if you have a sense that you dancing with her would harm your relations with her, like having the effect of bringing your whole mood down for the entire night, then put your foot down and draw a line, at least for now.

Of course it's important to realize what the girl wants and what her interests are, but the basic idea comes down to your desires. Be aware of what she wants and be as nice about her wishes as possible, but do not do anything that you really don't feel like doing. Afterall, the man needs to be the leader of the group which in this case consist of a man and a woman. The man will need to take charge and make plans. Take her needs to account and use them to influence your game plan, but do not change the frame. The frame you've created is everything, do not let go. If you come off as an alpha at first, but after few hours start to give in to her and play nice, then she will lose the respect for you. See what I mean? Hold the frame you've created from the beginning of the interaction, it's the thing she's latched onto and changing it will destroy everything you have created with her so far.

At the same time do not be afraid to admit your mistakes, you can play around with the frame a lot by adjusting it throughout the interaction, just do not lose it completely since it equals to losing your character and your power you posess in her eyes.

Expansion vs Contraction

The idea of expansion vs contraction. Anything you venture in, you want to expand, you want to put your foot forward, but at the same time you want to contract and think about it. When talking to girls, you'll want to pressure on, have the formalities in check but at the same time, when you're constantly putting pressure forward, she will get discouraged and the whole interaction is starting to feel too one-sided. The most optimal thing to do is to keep yourself in the leader's role, but at the same time let her feel like she's also contributing to the relationship. You're the leader with a goal, she's the visionary with the vision to decorate your goal.

Overqualificating yourself

"Be relatable, that's the key of building comfort with the girl. She will most likely not be an overachiever since most of us never are. Play on the sides of where she can join in, but don't forget to share your value."

When you project yourself as "extremely cool" or as a someone who has his shit together, life well planned out and someone of really high value, and you keep subliminally bringing it to the girl through the content you talk about, which is in this case most likely not relatable, she will feel like she has lower value than you and at that moment she will start to lose respect for herself, at least untill she leaves your company. She is simply ashamed of herself, but makes compromises and says the guy is boring, creepy or just a douche. Funny how our minds work, eh? We do just about anything to save ourselves from the embarrassing truth. When a person is ashamed and feels she's not worthy, the biological reaction is to avoid the guy who's causing it. That guy is going to be you, if you're not relatable and don't give her the chance to shine at least a little bit.

Saving ourselves from the painful truth is just like taking antibiotics without getting any real treatment that would help us to fix the problem. All these lies we tell ourselves ever are, are just delaying the painful truth that we have to face at some point of our lives no matter how hard we try to makes comprimises.

Conversation is supposed to be mutual, otherwise it's not really a conversation. If you keep talking about all those things that put you above her, she will feel left out and most of all there is a high chance you'll look like you're desperately trying to qualify yourself to her. If you keep talking about the things that you're better at, she will sense you got nothing else to offer, otherwise you would not play on your strong sides so much. And if you're doing everything right, but still seem too high value for her, she will leave for not feeling important, needed and desired.

You should have your shit together and work towards having things that you could brag about to just about anyone, the point is obviously not telling you to not follow yours dreams. If you just happen to meet a girl about who you can sense she's definitely below your value level meaning her life and the level she's living at is not going to match your level, it does not mean you should stop trying to make something happen with her, since pickup is about letting both sides of the party experience positive and fun emotions, not about finding someone to match your value. The trick is to not make her uncomfortable about her insecurities and be unjudgemental while remaining awesome and not making a problem about her being lower value by bringing up all the things you're good at. You can even joke around and say you love her imperfection, which is not even a lie since we're all imperfect. Because you're already talking to her, you will probably have some interest in her despite her life being the way it is. This is why it's called game. It's not serious, it's playful and unexpected and full of positive experiences, not self-qualifing, seriously demanding nor value leeching to get something without having anything to offer.

We Love Masks

"The most important kind of freedom is to be what you really are. You trade in your reality for a role. You give up your ability to feel, and in exchange, put on a mask." - Jim Morrison

Every single guy who ever tries out pickup will be faking their personality at some point or other. This is definitely something we cannot get over or under and it has come to my attention that we benefit from such behaviour more than one might think, and it's not in terms of getting better results such as sleeping with more girls and improving your regular batting average, it's about becoming the guy of true masculinity and strenght.

Acting in a certain way to be someone we're not is something that most of the the guys do no matter how high their status is. We try to act cool, smart and sexy despite being even remotely close to it. Some use alcohol to bring out the true potential of this idea, some do it just by focusing on that type of bahaviour that they're obsessed over, but the end result for most guys will always be this „wannabe Bond" attitude, the act of being James Bond. There is not much wrong with the way James Bond acts to get girls, there is much to learn from him, since it can work really well. The problem lies in the fact that those guys, who put on a show in terms of acting as someone who they're not, are definitely not excellent at it and can always be seen as weird, insecure and most of all, fake. Acting as someone who you're not and making it look really obvious will just screams of insecurity and will do it extremely hard, because a guy like this is obviously not satisfied nor happy with himself, otherwise he would not try to act as someone who he is not. You may very well apply to an acting school if you find yourself to feel this certain way, since self-hatred is, in most cases, the very own recipe of a successful actor.

What does this type of behaviour exactly say about you? It just shows that you're looking for validation by trying to be someone you're not. You're looking for the girl's approval of you, you're looking for validation. It means that you are not sure in yourself and are trying to get the other person to validate you by liking or even loving you. For the most part it's backwards thinking and has the tenancy of not working out both mentally and also in your results with picking up women.

When does fake behaivour work? Only if you excel in outer game. It's like a method where you just need skills like knowing when to go for the kiss, when to pull the girl to come with you to the location where sex could happen and so on. In this case you can, at least in some situations, still have a cool time with the girl or maybe even a one night stand. Depends on the girl and most of all, depends on you. It's quite a sad place to be at mentally and it will not get you any long term relationships because no matter how blind that woman is, she will see the real you at some point and whether she likes it or not, is entirely up to her. Most of the time women can actually see that you're not a cool guy since they look for behavioral clues, not just visual. Visual clues will always be in the background untill you get really good with the behavioural ones. Since you're the only one who has the balls to do something crazy like going in for the kiss with a person who does not feel much for you, she will most likely take it. It can work temporary and just for these one-time hookups. Skill has the power to beat your insecurities, but only for a certain period of time. In the end, it's by no means an excuse to not work on yourself. If you're good at outer game, but you lack of inner game, then you should really put most of your focus on improving it. Having great outer game, but lacking of inner game just means you've watched enough masters doing work and remembered some certain activities and cues on what to do and say in conversations with women. Outer game is like the scientific part of game. People, who focus purely on this will miss the whole point of pickup and just gather the surface of this treasure that pickup is able to reward you with. There are so many elements of randomness in an interaction, so it's pretty impossible to fit them all into a hard cover manual. Besides, outer game only covers one area of pickup. The other half is done by learning the ways of a superior man and not just remember the right dance moves like a highly trained monkey.

This is why pickup books are mostly about self-development and becoming a better man, less about techniques on how to get a certain type of woman to do a specific type of things. Pickup is the best method to become more successful as a man, having more confidence in all your endeavours and being on top of your life in general. Knowing what to do and when to do it is ultimately just part of being cool. And in the end, there are no certain timelines for things like kisses and hugs. It's all about doing the things you want when you want them and being sure of yourself while doing it and not questioning whether it was good or bad or acceptable, unacceptable and so on. You're taking the stuff that you want without any limits. Of course there are some limits, one does not just run around the city putting women in bags and taking them to one's sex dungeon. The idea is to be calibrated and be aware of everything that's happening around you to be able to fully abuse the weakness of other males, the lack of social knowledge of everybody else in the room to get the women of your desire. Going after the things you want without hesitation like kisses, hugs, hot and steamy dances, sex and everything else in-between while also making others feel like it's the right time for it is what creates attraction. Being correctly calibrated to do these at the right time and putting others in the state of in which you want them to be in, which is done by being in the particular state yourself, is what makes you a successful pickup ART-ist, not a scientist. It's not about planning every situation to be ready for anything, it's about being free, spontaneous, being able to handle yourself amongst any crowd at any time and also do it successfully for yourself and for everybody else to make everyone have an amazing experience.

A big problem amongst successful guys is that they show off with their achievements, which will make them look like they're after validation and will be put by girls into the beta male box really damn fast while some other low life with the right characteristics will be having a threesome with those same girls on the very same night. Don't look for validation by trying to show her how awesome you are, that will most certainly push her away. Assume you're the shit, already assume you're awesome. It will be felt amongst the people who you're with and once they feel it, they'll also believe it. You do not need to prove anything to anybody. It's dysfunctional to show others what you are. Simply be what you are. A wise man once said: Dont just pursue. Attract.

Attracting the women you want does not mean bragging or trying to qualificate yourself to the girl of your desire. Much of this is about blind faith, knowing and truly embracing the idea of you being cool. It's not about what you own, how you look like, what type of music you listen to, who you spend time with or any of that since all this is just crap if we're speaking about being attractive. If you have a strong belief that you're cool, then you're cool. It's all about this simple mind shift, this decision, the way you tend to look at yourself. This is how guys who are terribly overweight, for an example also smell and have no way of offering a girl anything external can actually pull better than a guy with a full tuxedo and flawless hygiene. Those people have an idea about themselves being a certain way. Whether it's true has no value, what matters is their frame and how tightly are they able to hold on to it. Everything that portrays guy being attractive is created in the guy's mind and therefore will show in their eyes, energy and vibration, in their mood and in their body language. You don't need any external values like fancy and expensive cars, a lot of money nor stunning fame to be cool. It's all about your own mindset, your own personal beliefs, how strongly are you able to hold on to those beliefs and in the way you see yourself. People believe what they see and are being told. The guy who you truly believe you are is the guy who they believe you are. So many of us will argue that truly believing in being something or someone can viewed as being fake, but if you really think about it, true belief is actually the highest form of being.

The Ultimate Pickup Artist

One day I saw a daygamer, daygaming in the very center of Paris. Sounded English. From afar, I could feel the horribleness.

Firstly, he looked like he was having zero fun. He was aggressively and nervously pushing forward with his phone for the girl's number.

She didn't look happy. He
didn't look happy.

He looked stressed and kinda sad. Burned out and desperate, extremely needy and therefore low value.

She was urgently looking for her exit excuse.

It felt creepy to see. It felt disgusting as a whole. But, unfortunately, this otherwise good man, was doing what he was told to do by someone who calls themselves a dating coach, either on the internet or in person.

Men are completely unaware at how more and more unattractive to women he is becoming, because of the way he has been taught to relate.

It is very easy to see the HUGE difference between a guy who is gaming, and a guy who loves girls and is blatantly hitting on them with love. It's so visually and energetically different.

The regular pickup guy needs the specific outcome he has been programmed to achieve. The guy who loves girls...that is his outcome. Sharing his love with them. That's the ultimate pickup artist.

Good game works

There is this whole idea of manipulation and people saying that's what seduction is, lying and whatnot, since, according to the majority, no woman in their right mind would go home with a guy after the first date unless she is a complete slut. These people who believe in such ideas, have truly missed the lessons that life throws at us every single day to educate us on such matters. In reality, the girl who knows what she wants and is not ashamed to show and also live it, is actually considered to be one part of the culture of smart women in our world. It's useful to not show yourself as a slut, it's even mandatory for many women to their lives functionally. However, the people who live their lives to the fullest, explore the unexplored and understand how to receive the maximum out of this life of ours, those kinds of people are the ones that are an inspiration to all of us, including men.

The girl who truly likes you, will sleep with you very soon. Good game works. Cool guys and cool girls, when put into isolation, will eventually end up having sex. Cool girls usually hang out with cool guys, at some point will naturally get into isolation with those guys and end up having sex. This is just how it works. Hot girls end up naturally having sexual experiences, this is partly what makes them hot in the first place, if you really think about it.

It is what it is, we either deal with it or stay frustrated and bitter for the entire life. Accept it or not, feel free to choose to believe the lie to make you feel better, or accept the truth and rise from a sheep to a wolf and enjoy the big rewards in life.

As far as lying goes, there isn't really any point since girl is attracted to your frame and not to the truthfulness of your sentence. You can lie of course without having any consequences, but if you're not entirely excellent at it, then it will come off as owning a weak and insecure frame, plus, it will make you spend more energy on something that does not even matter in the first place, therefore doing more work for worse outcome. Lying should only be used to make fun of something, say jokes and shit, but not to make you seem like someone you're not. As you see, lying does not hold much use in game unless you're really good at it, which even then will not give you satisfaction since humans are simply not built to feel good through telling lies.

There is a fine line between flirting and lying. The methods of successful flirting do involve telling lies, but they come off as jokes, which should not be misinterpreted as manipulation, since they're totally different. One is playful and with the intention of creating fun, the other one is self qualifing and manipulative.

For those of you who believe the quality princess versus the dirty slut, the good girl versus bad girl, in my mind that's like the guy who will buy an expensive brand product truly believing it is the best decision ever just because some marketer told him that. There are always two sides of the coin, with all things in life. In the movie The Neon Demon, there was this brilliant line: people believe what they hear. We become what we think about, and we think about the things that we let in our brain. Choose your input information carefully. The fact that a product costs a lot does not make it the best right away, it will only increase the chances of it living up to the expectation. Don't just look at the brand, never forget to also look at the quality, look at it with your own eyes and make the decision despite what the marketers are trying to make you think just so you would buy their product. Ask yourself: Is it an item of quality? Sometimes it is, and sometimes it isn't. Exactly the same principle with women. If you're ever going to pick a girlfriend, pick a girl who likes you. The girl who likes you, probably slept with you really quickly. Let's leave the slut shaming for the ones who do not understand life that well and who will always have a pool of low quality women to choose from thanks to their own self-fulfilling prophecy, or in other words, their own shitty attitude.

Confidence

I'm sure you've heard many people say that if you want to get girls, then you need to be confident in yourself, but no one ever gives you an exact definition of what confidence really is about. One of my mentors had a great definition of how to describe confidence.

"Confidence is having positive expectations for favourable outcomes."
– Moe Abbassi

A perfect example about how important confidence really is, can be seen in the movie called Harry Potter and the half-blood prince. Ron thought of himself as a mediocre quidditch player, which was by far the most popular game in their fantasy universe. He did not belive in his ability to be good at it and was really scared of the upcoming ballgame that he had to participate in. Harry, seeing his friend in trouble, supposedly gives him the elixir called Liquid Luck, which is known to have the effect of destroying all your fear and giving you major confidence and drive. Generally in sports, when you get frightened, it's over. Ron goes off to win the game with with a feeling that he will beat everyone against him. In the end it's revealed that Harry did not use the elixir on Ron. He just thought Harry did. As we can already see, Ron won purely just because he belived in his abilities.

I'm sure we all have witnessed a similiar effect on ourselves, for an example, in sports. When we play to practise, we feel confident because we don't have much on stake and so we don't hesitate to try new methods. But when we play to win, especially when it's a championship game or just something that you need to win badly and you don't really have the freedom of outcome, then we appear to be much more scared to even try to do amazing plays and stick to the basic and solid stuff that we know the best and that has proven to be most effective in terms of minimalizing risks while achieving maximum results.

A great problem for all of you who are new to the dating world and especially those of you who have really low self-esteem, is the concept of self sabotage. For an example if you want to talk to a girl, if this is your first approach ever in your life, you will have positive expectations like she liking me back, me getting her phone number and all the movie magic that follows the idea of true love. The reason why this in the particular moment is not good, is because we tend to condition certain habbits in our brain. Let's say you're confident in your skills and you go up to the girl while being fairly certain that you will get everything you expect to get and despite your skill level, luck and everything else, she rejects you. What happends in our brain, especially for those of us who do not know any theory on game and neuroscience, is that it begins to condition all your interactions and will make you belive that every time you go up to a girl, you will get rejected, all this thanks to the false belief that your mind created after analysing your first approach by using false information or even more specifically, the lack of information. This belief is setting you up for failure already, therefore this belief is ingrained in your brain and you will expect that result everything you take action. So what this is doing is that since you are sure in your upcoming failure, it has a higher chance to actually happen. If you don't believe you can win, it will show in your communication such as voice tonality, body language, eye contact in particular. In result of that this idea will be ingrained even further into your brain with every rejection you're about to receive.

Past actions and outcomes will shape the idea of what will happen in certain situations. If you have positive feedback, you will start to belive in positivity. You will associate good things with taking action. If you get negative feedback, it will go in the other direction. The result is happening because of your expectation, your idea of what's going to happen, your ego's dysfunctional self-perception. This is why it's called self-sabotage. By feeling negative about the outcome and you approach a girl with that low and unattractive energy, she can see that you are not confident in yourself and just came to talk to her just to prove your own point that you'll get rejected. That's not attractive at all, losing never is, so she will reject you just like you expected it to go. However, if you go to her with positive thoughts then you will also seem more confident since you look like you know that positive actions will happen in result of you talking to her. She can sense the confidence, the positivity in you and will feel attracted. This does not mean that she will definetaly not reject you, but you have so much higher chance of she liking you. This is also the same principle that explains how winning streaks and losing streaks start. It's called self-sabotage, but it can also be turned around for our own benefit.

There is this idea, this mechanism of forming habits in our brain, that if the result isn't good, then we start to belive that action leads into bad results. Brain is making a connection, which is based on inaccurate information. Essentially it's short term thinking and will stop you from progressing especially when you're trying to get good with girls and finally get this area of your life covered. How do we fix this?

First of all, you got to start thinking long term and not look at the immediate results. Get feedback from it, learn from and and if it's negative, then think of how to make it better. What did I do wrong and how can I fix it.

For the second part, have a strong belief that with consistency you will start to progress and get results. By adapting this belief you'll start to think more long term wise and stop being so focused on the immediate results that are happening now at this very moment. Everything is setting you up for something greater, the stuff that we do right now and the decisions we make will shape our future. By thinking like this these short term small decisions whether you should approach or not start to make a lot more sense and answers will be much easier to generate.

Winners have a winning present. So in a perfect world you should be speaking, having the tonality, the body posture of someone who has confidence, of someone who is winning in life. In a perfect scenario you will start feeding into your sensations and your thoughts will be aligned with your body. You don't actually have to win in life like have luxury cars and houses that I mention so much in this book, you just have to feel like you're on the right path and that you'll get to the rich side eventually by just doing what's right for you. Pickup usually is that right path, can't really go wrong with this one.

Winning in life is not about what you own, it's about who you are. If you feel like you're winning, then you actually are.

Tony Robbins, the number one life coach on our planet, has once said that if you smile even if you're sad, if you keep a smile even just for 10 minutes, then you will actuallty start creating positive thoughts. Whatever happends, whatever thought we have, our body has a reaction to it. If you can control your body and start having a winning presence, you'll start controlling your thoughts. You will notice that you have a lot more confidence when you're about to take action.

What is one thing that you do not have confidence in right now and what are you going to do differently in order to create it? Find the answers to this question and you'll be set for life.

You're not the only one under the spotlight

Understand that the girl is not perfect and will make mistakes, and more than just a few. She not liking you the first time you two meet can very easily be a false interpretation. For an example I've found that most young women don't know how to act in the presence if a real man. The start to giggle, stay quiet for the most part and just seem socially retarded since they have no solid experiences. They are too young and haven't experienced any real interactions with men that are worth it, all they've come to know sofar are insecure guys from a high school football team who will fall off hard in the long run. When we're young the only currency we have is popularity. We haven't built a business, have strong charisma, don't know much about the world and think the path of degeneration is cool (smoking, drinking, drugs, chilling). So when a real man with real value comes up, they simply have no idea how they should act. They feel attracted for sure, but since they don't know how to respond, they giggle and give away so much with body language on how they're attracted to you.

I always take this to an account and try to have at least some level of empathy. Acknowledge that the situation of a random dude like you approaching her out of the blue sky is a bit weird and don't make her freak out over having higher expectations of herself in the current situation and not being able to feel fully at ease in this situation, but because of the lack of knowledge fail to comply right action.

A high value woman, and let me emphasize the word "woman", will realize that the guy who can approach women without alcohol or any other substances, ignores social norms to make his dreams happen by offering value to the woman he sees without hesitation, is most certainly worth her time. It's literally like she's just met the one that will have a major vote in world matters, in other words someone who's powerful and knows what it means to be a real man. This is what pickup, at least for the very best of us, is all about and this is what I teach you in this book.

If when you approach a woman, you're not there to prove your worth. You're there to offer value and see if she can respond with same. In other words you're screening her as much as she's screening you. It's all in the mindset, whether you go there to beg for her time, number, date, sex OR you're there to offer your personality and your time to make her life a least a little bit cooler and of course much more fun. Are you there to offer yourself, a cool and fun guy who would definitely improve her life or at least show her excellent time for just one night, or, are you there to get something from her and be a leech. I've toned the idea that it does not matter who you are and you can still get girls, but if you're a leech – disregard that message. It's the one and only form of which will not produce any great results. Only one of these behaviours comes from feeling happy, which is what we're all ultimately after.

It's a false assumption thinking that you must go up to a woman and beg for her attention, ask for her time or do anything that's trying to get something from her. It's all about what you're offering, which in the case of pickup will be yourself as a high value guy, who has the shit in his brain all sorted out. If you have, then you do not even need to worry about this concept since you will succeed naturally. You go up to her, make an offer she cannot refuse and even if she does, she's either having a bad day, other interests in life at this particular moment such as work problems or funeral planning, or is simply not interested due to having a husband or a boyfriend who she's not interested in putting to a risk. And of course there are those girls who will not like you no matter what you do or say or even are. It's inevitable to meet those kinds of women as well.

Always be thinking of what you could do better, maybe your approach was a bit off or your mood was not as positive as it could have been, but also recognize that you're not the only one on the spotlight. For an example when you get approached by a bible salesman, a club promoter or anyone like that, your mind will instantly start to worry about your own image, how your clothes look, is your hair cool and other shit like this, you barely have time to focus on the person who approached you untill later. People are so caught up in their own lives that for the most part it's not even that much your fault when you get rejected. Both parties could have been better in terms of your conversation, but since we cannot control others in this and can only focus on ourselves, then act on this concept - always improving your own game and strive to better, but also be aware of the situation that it's not always your fault. You are able to change yourself much better than someone else, so start with yourself even if the other person could do the same instead of You working hard on this. Someone has to put in the work and it might as well be you. Let

140

her follow her own path and you do the same, even if they're very different from each other. If she requires a bit more "getting your shit together" from you to get to her, then simply just do it and stop giving fucks about her attitude. It's about being a guy who she could benefit from having around and if she does not buy it, move on to the next one who can easily be much better than the first girl. Even if it's the girl's fault you two ain't getting along, you can fix it instead of her by just having great game. It's like looking past her dysfunctionalities and fixing them for her by just being better yourself. She will thank you for this later, for taking a chance on her.

Don't pursue. Attract

This is an amazing saying and could not be any truer. However, there are two ends of the spectrum. If you're very attractive in terms of how you act, carry yourself and look like, but you don't take action by talking to women, then it does not really matter. Women might really like you, but if you don't talk to them, then they are not gonna talk to you either. It does not hold any effect in dating to be just attractive and not pursue at all. Being persistent in putting yourself out there is a big part of pickup.

If you pursue women with great initiative, but you are also not that attractive (maybe you haven't had a wash in days, wear really shitty and lame clothes, look depressed and sad, feel very unsure of yourself etc.), then you're just going to get a bunch of bad reactions from people. Of course there are women, who would like you, but it's really a very small precentage and it's much easier to just fix the problems that are holding you back so you could experience women on a much larger scale. Like it's not that hard to take a shower every once in a while now is it? Same applies to being a cool and fun guy – it's not that complicated.

Main reasons why women will reject you are your terrible body language, voice tonality, lack of eye contact and being really unsure and indecisive with the way you speak. Some girls are okay with some of these, some are not, it all comes down to personal preference. But by removing these weak characteristics, you'll be playing on a larger scare and your pool of available women that want you will skyrocket. The world is full of great opportunities, great women, great experiences, but only for those, who work on themselves as an individual.

"Girls don't like the perfect guy. Girls like the guy who is perfectly fine with himself. Perfection does not exist, but being perfectly fine with your imperfectness is the closest we're able to get."

Cockblockers

"Women have sex with men who posess masculine traits. These traits are for the most part not considered to be nice. So if you're being a nice guy and are able to get a date with a girl, then she's obviously really fucking horny, even if she does not show it on the outside. Keep this in mind."

Ever tried to pick up a random girl who you've just met only to be ridiculed or stopped by her friend or another guy, who drags the girl away from you? It's something that all of us, professional pick up artists and the ones who are just starting out, will eventually face and not just once, but constantly throughout the career of becoming good with women. This is something that you definetaly need a strategy for or you'll better start packing your bags and move to a place of isolation. If you don't know how to deal with a cockblockers, then you will lose all of your value from the women point of view extremely quickly.

A big part of man's behaviour is projecting the characteristics of being able to defend himself when the shit goes down. Cockblockers, who can be either a girl or a guy, are this shit that's about to go down. This is the moment where you pretty much need to shine.

Women lose interest in guys who are not able to handle pressure, especially those woman who you're talking to at the very point. Good first impressions or in this case, first night impressions, matter a lot, and if you can't stand up for yourself in the same day when you talk to the girl, you'll be pretty much screwed from all the chances of ever being in an intimate relationship with that same girl.

In my opinion, there are three ways how you can deal with cockblockers. There is no best method since all guys and girls are different and will react to different styles based on their preference, that's been developed throughout their lives by random factors. Anyway, let's start with the first one.

Befriending the cockblocker.

I personally love this method the most. It's the easiest and also the most effective way to seem cool, confident, sociable, show the girl who you're interested in that you don't care that much if you get her or not, which shows that you're not needy and have other options if the interaction plays out in an unfavourable way. Basically, what this method consists of, is just acting friendly, welcoming the one we call a cockblocker, asking how he or she is doing, develop small chit chat, maybe talk a bit all together depending on the situation and your personal judgement on the current situation also known as gut feeling, and then turning the attention back to the girl while slowly moving her away from the blocker. This way you'll seem fun, friendly, and also dedicated to getting to know this girl you're focusing on. Since you're also friendly to the blocker, it will show that you're not trying to fight for her and you're totally okay with losing her since it's her loss, not yours. You are just screening her for her value and deciding whether she's a good fit for you, not trying to desperately defend that women and your five minute conversation with who you just met because you feel the fear of losing the only chance of getting laid. Besides, this will make others look at you as the guy who wants everyone to have fun and is not just picking his prey like a hunter in Amazon rainforest.

The guy who holds the frame and wins the mental standoff is the guy who in the end collects the reward, if he is persistent enough.

The second option is to ignore the blocker completely. In this particular case the blocker will feel automatically that you're superior to him/her because you won't even pay attention his/her provocations. This will work the best in a high stimulation environment like in a club or in a bar with really loud music, where you should not even start arguing since it will look more tryhard'ish than ever, but in a small crowd you cannot really ignore people simply because they're a big part of the so-called audience. In places where the social circles are small and most people know everybody, you'll have to win the crowd just like a gladiator, since they posess a big key that will determine the girls reaction towards you, which is social proof. Not being liked by people around you will hurt your chances of the girl coming home with you. If everyone out in the venue are despised of you, then the girl will in most cases not like you either.

This method of ignoring cockblockers is highly useful when, for an example, talking to an alpha female, the leader of her social circle. You can just ignore all her friends, since their opinion doesn't matter as much to the woman you've set out to seduce. This sort of woman is her own boss, has a strong character and is not used to take shit from anybody. Isolating her friends completely and focusing purely on her will work since the girl you wanna talk to is an authority to them, someone who they don't even feel like they have to protect unless the girl we call an alpha female is really disgusted by you, which won't be the case if you know game.

The last method that I will share here, is intimidation. It's not something you use to provoke a fight, don't even go in that direction. Physical fighting is by far the worst thing you could do in pickup. The point is to look like you could win a fight by just your body language and and verbal one, but never to fight for real. Fighting kills attraction completely. If you have to fight, then you're obviously not sure that you're going to win since you've got something to prove either to yourself or someone else. Intimidation is simply explaining the blocker the situation of what's happening at the moment. You're talking to this girl and you want some fucking privacy. Trick is to do it respectfully with a commanding, yet calm voice. A terrible example of this would be using this method during daygame, when everyone have their mask on and try to fit in and act normal. Nobody is going to appreciate the guy who loses his shit, being it playful or not. It's not the right energy type for daygame and therefore being just scary. Now it's essential that when you use this method in the club, you have to be a little bit playful with the way you talk. If you just alpha up against every single cockblocker with all the rage you have inside you, then it's just not going to work. Period. Remember – playful, commanding, sure of yourself and loud while also respectful.

There are many girls who are dieing to meet a cool guy and their friend that's with her is just fucking up the conversations by squeezing herself in. I see this almost every night when I go to clubs. We all have anoying friends who we just can't shoo away that easily even when the situation calls for it. Once again, the easiest way to come up with the solution is to take matters into your own hands and use these main methods in the war against people who are in your way, whether they're male or female. Everyone have their own way of dealing with this stuff, but no professional pick up artist fights for the girls with another guy. He will compete, yes, but fight, no, never. Even verbal fighting, name calling and everything like that is not worth it in any case. Fighting means that you're qualifing yourself by trying to be better than the blocker. Pick up artists don't fight over girls, instead, they attract girls and eliminate barriers that prevent them from having a great time with the girls.

Humor melts away resistance. – Bryan Casella

Which technique is the best?

"Being labled as a player is called having options because I'm a man in my prime."

I want to get one thing straight right now. Women get just as horny as men! They just don't want to initiative that shit all the time. They want to feel desired, shown some effort for. They want to feel like it was your idea to sleep with them. To give us, men, clues, they have all sorts of tactics that we completely miss. It can be as simple as touching her hair while talking to you or just giggling like a silly schoolgirl. These will seem like normal behaviours at first, yet all of these have hidden messages attached to them. The hidden vortex. I bet if you think about this for a while, you'll remember many times when a girl has done at least one of these behavioural cues that I just pointed out while having a chat with you. You might be thinking like „ Oh my god, I see this literally every day! It can't be so easy." Yes, it really is. Ultimately all women want to meet a cool guy, have sex and enjoy the entire aspect of this life of ours, in order to experience this they give men, mostly even unintentionally since these behaviours are written in our genetic code, social clues that only the best of us will pick up. Women are usually interested in a big number of men just like guys, but they need to give you a chance to prove yourself first and they give you clues so that you could approach them. This is why we as men will have to approach to show courage, talk to them to show you're comfortable with her and lead the way so that she could feel safe with you. These sorts of actions are the things that trigger attraction in women. Many guys see it as something that's really unfair, being mad at women for not doing any approaches and not asking any guys out themselves to find a life partner is totally wrong and is caused by the lack of right information and the dysfunctional understanding of attraction laws regarding dating. It's like asking a guy why he does not approach a woman he's not interested in. Well, he is simply not interested in her! Same goes for the woman, she is not interested in a guy who is not able to approach and put himself out there. The whole concept of dating amongst men is entirely misunderstood. As far as technique goes…

Small tweaks, tips and tricks and such do exist and will be optimal to apply in your game, but overall - a certain technique, something that can be described as the best does not exist. Small behavioural patterns here and there, but it's far away from having a special technique that will unlock every woman. The one and only ultimate guide that will be your best bet to focus on, is being the best you can be every single day and when you meet a woman you like, which will happen every single day, you'll be confident in yourself because you're improving, smart because you're learning and will portray yourself, not some fake James Bond'ish type fellow. You'll create your own brand just like entertainment business created Bond, the superspy who gets any woman of his desire. This is what women ultimetaly want in a guy – someone who is sure of himself and his abilities to succeed. Everything else is circumstantial. You don't need any pickup lines. You don't need to study some certain lines and have very specific replies all figured out in your head over the course of years to always have something witty to say for every single reaction possible to get. Would you like to have every single answer for every single interaction and life situation already figured out in your head, or would you rather become a funny confident and a witty guy instead who can just come up with his own material whenever he wants to? Being the guy every girl wants to be with and who every guy wants to be versus being well prepared to make it look like you're that guy, when you're actually not. You may be good at faking that special and cool personality, but it will never be real and it will never be satisfying as long as you know it's fake. Inner game versus outer game. In the case of pickup, having inner game all sorted out in your head will take care of your outer game on its own.

Pro tip: If you have the line of what you're going to say ready in your head, then it will make you seem needy and especially fake. You will lose a portion of confidence and you'll be just like a machine with no soul.

How to notice in a club if a guy is into pickup or not? Just look for guys who just stand there not having fun, that's like half the pickup community right there. They are quite easy to pick up with your eyes. Those are the guys who are scanning the room looking for potential prey just as hunters back in the day used to do. They are not original, looking for things to do instead of working on who they are, and not being part of the vibe, they come off as extremely creepy, desperate and needy. They have no soul in their interactions. It's like a machine has learned our language and now is trying to fit into the club society. It might say the right things, but you'll still see it's a machine, not a real person just like in game the girls are able to spot a cool guy who is sure of himself from the crowd full of admirers. A guy who is not thinking about what to say and does not care enough to be liked for expressing his true personality, is being natural and most likely having fun. He does not care about some fucking opening sentence. No woman ever has told a guy no to sex after they had talked for hours just because he had a bad opening line.

When you're real with the girl, then you will be successful one way or the other. You either get the girl or she rejects you for being you – that means she would have not liked you anyway. If you feel like you're not successful because you're natural state, your „realness" is not cool, then you need to learn how to bring out the best in your personality, lose the small petty insecurities by either not caring about or just removing them (getting in shape etc.). Most importantly - read about game. Get yourself some self-help books, copy the knowledge into your brain and then apply it in your everyday life. This is what my book is for. To help those who seek it. The point is to get as much information as you can, but to not overthink it, because that, my friend, leads to discouragement.

Number one rule is always taking action. Guys have different personalities, they have different attitudes, movement gestures, facial expressions, color, body sizes and accents. Pickup artists don't have some universal outfit, body type or a personality, they're all different people with different styles and preferences. What can we learn from this? Your style, your looks and the status you have accumulated throughout the years does not matter, every life situation you can think of and every single person on this earth no matter what his life might look like is able to attract many beautiful women, if he takes action and does the approach. So just jump in and stay on the course. Your mind will take care of the rest, which I can promise you. We can either be complaining at home or we can be out there doing the stuff that will get us the life we want, work for what we'd love to have, giving all our energy we have and at the same time fully valuing this kind of productive lifestyle that will lead to earning extreme value and will make our journey epic.

At the end of the day the women want you to succeed with her. Why wouldn't they? Why the fuck would women not want to meet a cool guy who shows them a good time and could be a potential partner who they could love for the rest of their life? Our genetic code has been built this way, we feel love and happiness and all kinds of satisfaction when we find that special someone. All women would love to find a man that can satisfy their needs. Besides our evolution and the traits and our biological needs that follow with it, our society has really done a great job by printing this idea of finding a great guy into a woman's mind. Entertainment business such as movies has the idea of love written all over it, there is literally no escape from the pressure of finding a man eventually. Sex sells, no doupt about it. This concept that can seem as a brainwash at times, actually benefits all guys tremendously and will make women much more receptive to a man's attempt to get laid. World is actually working for, not against us.

Pickup is sharing your personality the best way you can. In result of that you'll find more than just one woman, who is attracted to you, who will message you, text you, call you out, on which point you'll be totally in charge of the conversation since you're the one being chased. Looking for the secret technique for manipulating girls into liking and sleeping with you is totally the wrong way of seeing this whole side of life. Manipulation will not work in love, since women are all programmed to love the person for who the guy is, not for what he say or do. Manipulation comes from the state of negativity, unhappiness and desire to achieve something without giving much back, it's the opposite of love.

The so-called "best" technique probably does exist, but finding it and adjusting yourself to the principles of it will take longer than any of us are able to live. Pickup offers you the majority of behaviours and personality traits from this "perfection" pool, and that's ultimately all what you'll need. Even if you had the power of possessing the best technique to make yourself attractive to the most amount of women, you'd still get those who do not like you. Some women will not like you no matter what you say or who you are. This is why, in game, you'll have losses and you will have victories. Game is about creating options for the the victories, which is done by being the guy who girls would fuck, and then creating the oppurtunity for them to fuck you.

I want you really put yourself in the shoes of a highly demanded girl. Most girls are constantly bombarded with text messages from guys who's sole purpose is to ask them out. Girls have abundance. Put yourself in their situation and think about what's the best type of guy they would even respond to? Obviously it's the one that's positive, friendly and fun, just like the way we choose friends. Why would anybody go out with a friend who's tremendously negative, not relatable, always blaming something for his own misery and offers no fun at all? There is simply no point. Think of yourself as someone with high level of abundance and think hard towards understanding who would a girl like this want to date? Who would she enjoy spending her time with? The fact that I've eliminated the misconception of money, looking good and fame, and focusing merely on the other person's personality, I believe the answer will be quite easy for you to find.

Why is approaching so important

The reason why I got good at game so freaking fast was thanks to the fire that I was running from. My social life, regarding both friendships and relationships, used to be a complete disaster and when I found pickup and realized you can do this to get laid without having to go through all this other bullshit like getting a job at a coffee shop just to expand your social circle, knowing the co-worker girl for years, then finally asking her out and maybe after marriage get laid, maybe. Looking back at it now I realize how socially retarded I really was, how little common sense I had and how well my sober thinking was being blocked by every day anxieties and constant fears.

When your anxiety levels are high, then the brain won't function effectively since all this mental energy is spent on processing the fears and trying to avoid uncomfortable situations. This is exactly what was going in my head. I was even unable to realize if it was a push or a pull door for at least five seconds after yanking the door in one direction and just standing there like an idiot simply because my mind was not working as it should. It was clogged with bullshit.

A great majority of us spend so much mental energy on our anxieties every single day, like how we look, how we act, who should we avoid and so forth. If all our fears would suddenly dissapear, this society would be so entirely different and the amount of ambition that we have in our world all put together would instantly skyrocket.

When I finally realized how easy it is to meet girls, which happened after reading about game, doing few approaches myself and spending some nights in social environments such as bars and clubs, I felt this sudden urge to make up for the lost time, therefore I emerged myself into the world of pickup almost overnight. My life got to the point where I was approaching literally any girl I saw on a street, even if she was twenty years older than me. No exeptions, just full on go mode. I don't remember my success/rejection rate and frankly it does not even matter. The fact that I don't remember almost any of it is a sign of me having an amazing time without judging or needing anything from the girl and just enjoyed expressing my true personality. I was tremendously satisfied and really damn happy to be able to be free and talk to all these beautiful women that I used to only dream of. The more I put myself out there, the more women I was able to attract, soon enough the dates came, one night stands, relationships and much more. I was in a constant state of progression, instead of coping with life trying to get through it somehow, I was thriving and loving every single minute of it.

It has come to my attention that 50% of the entire game, the pickup industry if you will, is about getting out of the house, sucking up the excuses that your mind creates to keep you from exposing yourself and avoid possible harm that might be caused by new situations, and doing the approaches. The girls are ultimately not that picky despite what many people say. The truth is that a woman will accept the guy in any shape or form as long as the guy has his shit together meaning his mind is shaped with the very same ways I'm teaching you here today. There are tons of small nuances, there are many different techniques and behavioural ques that is really beneficial for any aspiring pickup artist to learn, but in the end all what matters is you approaching with the right intention.

Girls are designed to follow guys meaning they're attractive to this function, this leadership like personality. They care a lot more about man's ability to lead and be cool, looks and money and fame will always be secondary and viewed as a bonus, not the actual reason why to sleep with you. If you have the first level of attractiveness cleared up in your own head and you fall into the category of having your shit together, then these secondary traits will not be necessary at all.

Back in the day I was able to attract tons of women by being broke, without a job, living with my mother, having no particular style or a sense of fashion and literally looking like a low class poor and young high school student. I did not see any future for myself and had no idea what I could be doing. Despite all this there were hundreds of women who found me attractive and that were also really high class in terms of their looks and social circles. It's funny how a 32 year old successful and tremendously hot woman wearing clothes that can attract any successful business leader, can find a 19 year old attractive and is ready to sleep with him. This is a literal demonstration and the power of having good game. I could of just sit at home and play video games all day and I would have no insights on a woman's mind, I would have no idea that a guy like me could have some of the best fruits on the market. Instead I chose to put myself out there, do the approaches, read about becoming a superior man and attract women, even though most of my friends found this sort of inclination weird, creepy, anti-fun and certainly not necessary.

The fact that a guy like me made an effort to approach high class women with the intention of having sex with them was so fucking absurd that women actually found my optimism and self-esteem very attractive. Everyone could see I was definitely below those women's league with my external values, yet I did not show any signs of backing down and continued hitting the iron despite all this social pressure. Now I realize that it was simply jealousy and sensing the presence of a man that's superior to everyone else in that bar, it was never about me actually being too young, too broke or just too weird. Guys think you need a certain life to be able to get such women, but in reality it's all the matter of approaching and doing with an intent of offering your personality, trying to reach somewhere, for an example make out or have sex to make the girl's day memorable and better, to offer her a great time instead of going up to her with the intention of taking or getting something.

A big difference is also between begging and offering, taking and giving. Sort this stuff out in your head. You're there to experience, to offer good time for the girl and not beg for sex. You don't ask a woman for more sex but encourage her to have more sex with you because is fun and pleasurable.

Begging can be literal and also subliminal. You are there to offer and not take. If you offer, you'll be getting something in return without a doupt. This principle only applies to mental state, since you can buy drinks for the girl and still get nothing back simply because the drinks where a payoff so to speak, you were trying to buy her off, to gain leverage, but using a method that's never part of the attraction. A successful buyoff happens through emotions and communication whether it's verbal or not, never through money unless you're paying an escort.

In many ways, women are like escorts. They require something from you to give you sex. Real escorts ask for money, but every other woman trades in different currency – in positive emotions and in her desires.

50% of the entire game is the matter of doing the approach. When you get yourself to the point of doing this constantly and exposing yourself to different social situations, then you're setting up a foundation on which you can build your upcoming skills. You will achieve the first 50% right when you take the first step and say hi to some random stranger on a street. Being a pickup artist seems pretty damn easy when you think of it. In reality it really is, once you get the mind straight. Game is mostly about your mindset and how you view life. Game opens up a fun and a positive world that will let you in on a few universal secrets to success in all areas of life, including finding true happiness and fulfilling all your desires. Learning game and becoming something you always thought you could never be is becoming more and more real, isn't it?

The Key

"This can work like magic."

One of the biggest realizations I have ever made is realising that the reality is subjective. Your perception is the reality. There probably is a truth to everything, but nobody will ever know what it is. Ultimately it's all subjective. For an example the way how I look at this book that you're reading right now is a lot different from how you see it. Depending on when you're reading this, to me it might be the best product I've ever produced and I would encourage everyone to buy it simply because there is no other as informative and funny at the same time such as this one. To you however it might be just a regular book that you picked up just because it seemed intriguing and you're new to this kind of subject and you're reading it only to kill some time during lunch breaks at work. See how our realities already differ? With this example I look at it as some kind of a new age bible while to you it's just some "mental afternoon snack". It all depends on your perception which creates your reality. This is especially true with different religions. It's not like the guy who believes religion A is completely retarded and a guy who believes religion B is extremely smart and an inspiration to all of us. Your reality is king. The way you see the world determines how you feel in any situation, how your emotions will be and how far you'll get in terms of success in general, especially in success with women.

Your yellow could very easily be my red. If you see yellow and I tell you it's actually red, then of course you'll disagree with me. Same will happen vice versa. This is exactly how it is with pretty much everything that we have in our world. Religion, politics, ideas of utopia, favourite actors, soccer players and singers.

Think of the last time you went out to a nightclub. Some of us see girls in a nightclub, will be overwhelmed and literally can't handle this kind of situation without alcohol. Then there are those other guys who get pumped when they see girls, get so-called happily electrified and head up to talk to them. The interpretation is different, but the reality and the truth behind it is the same. None of us will probably ever know the truth. All you will ever know is how you interpret the situation and life in general.

"The only true wisdom is in knowing you know nothing. "

-Socrates

There is no right way of viewing the world. Once we realize that reality is subjective, we're able to create any reality that we want. There is no right answer. There are just answers that help you and then ones that don't. Lies can be extremely helpful just as truth.

Pickup is viewed as some evil hobby in our world. The amount of guys and girls, who call pickup artists with really voulgar words is quite high. If you really take a step back and think about it, then it's never about whether they're right or not, it's about why they're coming up with such conclusions. Are those hateful ideas coming out of the state of love or are they coming from a darker place like jealousy, pain and anger?

Let's not get caught up in what's right and what's wrong, everybody have a different view on this no matter what the truth is and changing their ideas is a waste of energy. Instead, let's look at what's beneficial for you. A reality that makes you feel massively good, tremendously confident and gets you ahead in life by for an example making you millions of dollars, having tons of women who want to date you and makes you really happy about life. The kind of reality that makes you get friends, girls, jobs that you want to have - Is something like this beneficial? Most definitely yes. It's much like lucid dreaming, having the freedom to do anything.

How does this concept translate into pickup?

When you go out with the intention to pick up women, you'll probably be a bit anxious and scared at the beginning of the night. But once you get a few approaches under your belt, you'll get more confident and begin to have a lot more fun. Think about it. Same night, different mentality created by forcing yourself to approach. Why do you feel more confident? Why are you having more fun now compared to the before? Why is it easier to approach girls after you've done your so-called warm up?

In the beginning of the night you'll see a girl talking to a guy and you're thinking: "It's her boyfriend, he'll probably beat me up when I approach her." After few approaches, once you're warm and mentally in the zone you'll be thinking "It's probably her brother or gay best friend."

Same reality, different perception.

A big part of pickup is first of all realising that reality is subjective, letting go of trying to find the right way of viewing the world (looking for answers, guidance, following the majority etc.) and finally creating your own reality, choose your own selective blind spots and just change the way you see the world in a way that's beneficial to you. This is a big part of the entire game and success within it.

Let's go over these sticking points once more.

1. Let go of trying to find the truth, the right way of viewing the world and adapting to other people's perception

A lot of us are so insecure that we don't want to take the responsibility, we're looking elsewhere. It's like comparing answers back in school during a test. When we see our classmate writing down an answer, we feel confident enough that it's the right one and just plain copy him. You can either call it being smart and using up all the available resources, or, you could say it's you just not being sure in your own answer and therefore needing some insurance to confirm your own thought. Both are true, but in pickup, the truth does not matter. What matters is how strong of a frame you have to get away with your answer, whatever it might be. The stronger the frame, the more attractive you'll be. Most of us are not confident enough to call you out on your theories, whether they're bullshit or not, therefore the only option left for them is to doupt their own story. It's funny how you can say the most absurd thing and if you have a strong frame, then the people will start to rethink their own ideas just out of the pressure of your strenght.

How do most people view pickup? The majority is negative towards it thinking game is all about manipulation and having loads of sex. Now the sex part is true, the meaning behind it certainly is not. If you think this way yourself, then your choise is to either follow the masses, be ordinary and not achieve success on any level simply because if you're a follower, then you're not a leader. If you're a follower, then you follow the laid out path instead of cutting through the grass and creating another. We are created to be creative, it's been proven we're all natural born creators, we just lose our way thanks to the wrong information that is being shared to keep our flawed society on float. Wrong ideas have penetrated our thought process and shape our world, definitely not in the most optimal direction. We sacrifice our wellbeing for evolutionary growth, which should never be the case and both of these concepts would, in a perfect world, go hand in hand. We've been poisoned, some less, some more. However, if you let go of your current perceptions and actually pay attention to my teachings, you'll develop a new way of seeing the world and also feel a lot happier since the bullshit belief that's holding most of us back, will finally be gone.

2. Think of the ways how viewing the world might be beneficial for you.

Women love sex just like men. We tend to forget that. Pickup artist is not some kind of a manipulator who tricks girls into sleeping with him. Most of it is done by the girl herself, a pickup artist just opens up the possibility by removing the responsibility, and makes it very easy for her to express her true self. Despite this fact, most of women are probably not walking around thinking about sex all the time. If you look at the girl who passes you on a street, then what are the chances of her thinking about wanting to rip your clothes off and dragging you to her room and proceed to have hot and steamy sex with you? Probably not that great. She is having many other countless thoughts about school, work, parents, old relationships. Assuming the fact that every single women wants you badly and can't stop thinking about you, however, makes your game and your frame a lot stronger. This is a blind spot that you want to have. Even though this is not true with most cases, truly believing this will make it into your reality.

Pickup is a lot about sucking the girl into your reality. If in your reality she's some kind of a crazy sex maniac, then she will start to get that vibe from talking to you and will also bring her sexual desires more to the surface. It's somewhat like hypnotizing that will require you to only believe in her being what you want her to be. It's also a lot about where this all is coming from, which should always be from a positive state of mind. This type of belief will also make you and her more relaxed, much more fun to be around and will easily surround yourself with positive and confident male energy that is attractive by itself.

If you know that by the end of the night you're going to have sex with someone no matter what, if you truly believe in it, then you'll be more chilled around the girl. This type of belief also eliminates the neediness. What does this behaviour tell about you? The most important trait it projects on you is being an alpha male. An alpha male takes his time, is definitely not nervous nor anxious and knows that whatever he'll do, the night will end well for him, which in your situation probably means with sex. Another reason why false belief or in this case, extremely optimistic idea of how things will work out even though you have no insurance nor proof, is something that will help you get laid much more. Have high expectations.

3. Experiment.

No idea is worth much if there is no action behind it. Remember – winning is important and should be focused on, but failures during the journey to victory is inevitable. Expect to succeed on your first try, but do not get discouraged if it does not work. It's like with basketball trick shots. It might take you a hundred tries to succeed and when you do, you'll feel like it was all worth it. Another keyword here is consistency. Do not give up. By taking action you have nothing to lose, but you have your whole life to win.

Conclusion – applying the belief that all women deep down want to have sex with you will help and is a lie you want to belive in, so your game and your comfort level around a girl will improve from the very moment you adapt this belief into your core thinking pattern. Since it will become a part of your reality, and the girl is always sucked into your reality, she will, more or less, depending on her type, adapt it at some point as well and begins to loosen herself up, removing the social mask she wears every day and her true personality that's most likely freaky and sexual, because she's also a human, will naturally show itself when she spends time with you.

Pickup is all about controlling the frame of which is yours to create and does not care about the real answers. Getting good with girls means that you're creating a personal universe that you love. Creating a world that you love is done so from within and not by accomplishing goals that are external. Everything external is a bonus, but the real deal, the real battle however only lies within us. It's our interpretation that is happening around us right now at this very moment. Finding the universal truth does not hold any value here, everything that we see, hear, do and think is the product of how we think the world works, how we interpret everything. There is no one way of seeing things or if there is, we won't be able to find it, we all have our separate visions of what is going on. Some say a certain presidental candidate is totally incompetent while others say he is the best choise we've got. It's not that one side is stupid and the other side is, everything is just our interpretion, our vision of the world that has been formed through our past experiences and the people we've spent time with. To be able to realize this concept, create a world for ourselves on our own that makes us attractive and able to sleep with many different women from every single point of the world is what gets you the results.

You disagreeing with me, saying everything I write here is bullshit, is also your way of seeing the world. It does not make you right nor it does not make me right either. All I really know for sure is the method that makes you really attractive to the opposite sex, man to woman, and how you're able to optimize this system. Truth is impossible to find and our reality is subjective. Change your reality into something that helps you as a human be happy, successful and really satisfied with your life is the best option we've got. It does not have to be rational. It's a way for a human mind to simplify it to cope with the reality that you're navigating through.

Fundamentals of Game/The Deadly Combo

Ain't this the paragraph we've all been waiting for? This is the moment where I'm supposed to lay out everything I know about attraction in short few sentences. Well, your wish has just been delivered. Here are the most important points that are optimal for every single interaction, with anyone at any place. There is no lay percentage, no win percentage, none of that bullshit, but if there were, this is the technique that will work the best take every type of woman in the modern world into consideration.

- Hold the frame. Don't be pushed over, stay true to your ideas and beliefs.

- Create as much fun as you're able to. Stimulate her in ways that are aligned with your personality and be alright with having a few laughs on yourself and make her feel like she's having a great time.

- Understand that women love sex as much as men do. It's just shameful for many of them to admit that thanks to social conditioning.

- Be persistent. If she does not respond, dance or kiss you on the first try, keep trying, but have some common sense to not just storm on her in every ten seconds like an idiot. Nonetheless, persistence and not giving up is sexy. The girl will see you being determined in your choise, which will show confidence and strong character.

By understanding these principles and keeping them in mind at all times you'll develop a great foundation on which you can build your style on. Think of it as a car. The mechanics, goals and principles are the same, only looks, speed and quality differ.

In this analogue an electric car would be for vegans.

The Recipe for Sex

You're at a party. Suddenly all people mysteriously dissapear to watch the asteroid falling down to earth or whatever the case might be, they won't come back for at least 20 minutes and you're completely one hundred percent assure of this. Then suddenly, a really hot girl appears in front of you, walks towards you and offers sex while repeating that nobody will notice nor find out under any circumstances since they're all busy with the thing that flushed them out in the first place. Basically what this is, is a free pass, sex without any effort and without any responsabilities nor consequences. A grand majority of men, also women, will take it without hesitation once the responsibility has been taken off.

Imagine if there was a woman instead of a guy in this same situation. It's not much different with women, they just have one more rule in this whole shebang, which is stimulation.

This is the principle of merely playing on the two most important components of how to have sex with just about anyone. Girls all have different personalities, some scientific theories say there are none, some say there's 5, some say there's even as much as 20, but in the case of having sex with the opposite sex, it does not matter not even just one bit. Women can all have the same personality or be all completely different, the one thing we cannot deny is women being attracted to men purely because evolution has made us this way, everything else such as being cool or funny is purely secondary. Men are naturally attracted to women and women are naturally attracted to men despite our personal preference.

This concept is the core principle of everything that you'll need to know about how to reach the level of sex with a girl. The notion is simple and consists of just two rules in this game of reaching sexual freedom.

- Isolate
- Stimulate

It does not really matter for the girl who you are at this given moment. If she's isolated meaning feels no pressure and the act of sex has no consequences or just feels like it doesn't at the given time, and you're able to provide some kind of fun context to her and then move on to implement sex, she'll take it. It's a decision done in the moment when there are no responsibilities, no judgement, no further consequences and just pure freedom to surrender to the emotional desires.

Women love sex. They really do. Just as men are able to sleep with pretty much anyone if there is no work involved, no shame in the face of others and the scale of horniness is high. We don't really care who we penetrate, since our emotions tend to take a hold of us, meaning we do not care who we fuck and the main priority is to just so to say bust a nut. Female mind works in the same pattern. If you'd take two people, a male and a female, and put them on a deserted island, they'd end up having sex sooner or later. It's just bound to happen since we all have needs and desires, and letting them out is our main priority instead of finding the right potential partner. The idea of saving yourself for that special someone is totally against our own nature and is nothing more but a limit set on us by ourselves to limit our freedom. We all love to have sex, and we want to have lots of it. So if there is a guy who knows how to create these certain circumstances for the girl and takes away the social pressure of slut shaming and promises carefree sex just to fulfil both of your desires, why in the hell would a girl not want to accept this offer.

Following this principle you probably cannot help to make a few implications of your own. Let me help you to plant this concept into some more realistic occurences. For instance getting a girl to follow you or meet you in your apartment already means she's down for sex, it's your duty to not fail both of you and implement the deed. If you don't, then you'll be disappointing both you and her. If she agrees to be isolated with you like in this situation, then she's probably, most likely down for sex and not just there to see your comic book collection. Now you'll have a better understanding why being ready to do anything in order to get her to your apartment also known as the sex location is so important. Once she is there, it's time to escalate after a short period of stimulation that's basically just talking with a fun vibe and intention behind it.

I believe you got the idea already. Isolation and stimulation are the key components and the recipe for sexual intercourse. The shortest answer anyone will be able to give you apart from paying for sex, which actually is just a cheap way to get her to sex location without much trouble. Plus it does not work as much as people think. Money does make the world go around, but certainly not a woman's heart, even if we're decoding one night stands.

Why You Should be "Normal"

The word "normal" has been thrown around a lot in movies, love stories, I'm sure your own friends have even told you this every time you ask for dating advice and how to be attractive to girls.

"Just be normal."

"Be yourself."

Very easy to say and there be also a lot of truth in this, but once again we need to focus on the context, to who it's being said to and whether it's something he needs to hear at this point of his life career.

This advice is something that's pretty much what a guy who's really good at game also known as intermediate, yet strives to be even better, should hear. It's something that will reward you with massive satisfaction, but can also destroy you depending on where you are in life. For an example if a guy is insecure, afraid to even go out of his apartment and plays video games all day, then that's his reality, his personality, that's who he is, at least at the given time. To command this type of guy to be himself is not a good advice for him since he is stuck in that paradigm.

If a guy's results are being held back by him being a complete asshole to everyone he meets, then telling that guy to just be himself will simply not help much.

Telling someone to just be himself despite everything I just said, is actually a truthful advice that will help in the long run, but not for all guys since the helpfulness of this advice highly depends on where a guy is in his life. The problem lies in a fact that the person who most of us are is something really sad and unattractive. Most of us are without goals, without vision, without the winner mindset and therefore just float through life being dependant on alcohol and other subliminal substances.

The first goal should be to fix your life situation meaning to find the road of improvement, joy and the balance between ambition and creativity. After taking care of this, which is done by just switching a gear in your mind by the way, we're able to relax and be ourselves instead of paining on our social mask and pretending to be someone else. The idea of game, picking up women, whatever you like to call it, is to be fun and confident without getting mad at petty little things while also staying true to yourself. The true self just needs to be something the girls could love, which should never be taken too seriously by you. Know who you are, but do not identify too hard with who you are. That's the foundation for any happiness.

Whether you have confidence or you're just a fun guy in general, only one good trait is needed in order to get started. If you're insecure, then at least learn to laugh at yourself and make others feel great around you. The idea is to have something that you're able to offer and not just be someone who's a value leech. An interaction is always an exchange of values. If they guy is able to provide, but lacks in other areas, then the girl will accept that in exchange for sex. If the guy is fun and confident, but also broke as hell, then the girl will accept that in exchange for sex. If the guy is able to isolate and stimulate the girl and offer her an easy way to satisfy her desires, then she will also accept it in exchange for sex. It sounds a lot like prostitution to be honest.

Interaction is a value exchange

Let's have another example. I used to work out with mad intensity and diet like crazy, which got me to be at 6% body fat. I was extremely skinny and muscular at the same time. In other words I was totally shredded, ripped, whatever you want to call it and had the fitness part of my life in check by having an amazing body that people believe is something that girls truly love and by having this will make or break the relationship. I was already into self development, reading books and on my way to master social interactions. One day when I went to a beach with my soon-to-be girlfriend, took off my shirt and all the sexy abs were revealed. She looked at me in awe and said I was too good for her. I was supposedly already smarter than her, stronger than her, a better earner than her and now also hotter than her. She found this extremely uncomfortable for not being able to offer me something back. This was the first moment I realized about value exchange rule and the first step towards understanding how social interactions really work.

I'm always asking people:

"What are you willing to give in order to get this?"

People are really confused about this. So many of us come from this "taking" mentality, to get rich we must make money, to get a girl we must take her and so on. The only people who make money are the mint workers. The rest of us have to earn money. Same goes with seducing girls with achieving success, with reaching fame and with literally everything. You can't just keep taking since everything is an exchange and at some point in order to not lose everything, you need to give something back from your part.

We are conditioned to preserve recourses, to not waste time nor money, basically to conserve the output and maximize the input. If we're dealing with an emergency, the reserve will come in handy. What this is really doing is reinforcing the reality of scarcity, of worry and anxiety and this is certainly not the way how to maximize your input. Maximizing your input comes from maximizing your output, the question of how much are you willing to give, how much value you are willing to offer is how much you will be paid. We don't get paid for nothing you know, we get paid exactly how much we're worth at this given time. By creating more value you'll create more value for yourself such as an abundance with woman, regular sex and all that good stuff.

In order to get sex from a girl you must offer her value, which in this case are emotions such as fun and yourself being a high value guy which can be easily projected by your self-confidence. In order to chat the girl up you can't just bombard her with the mentality of taking, you must offer something back. There is a big difference in your intent and this is what can be really critical. If you want to take her for sex or get her number, then it's going to work badly, if you do not come from the frame of offering your personality and good time to the girl. You see me saying that it does not matter what you say, since it's all in the sub-communication. I'm not joking with this you know, words do not matter if your intent is negative and not offering value.

I focus on what can I give her, what can I cultivate so that she would be attracted to be as a byproduct of me giving her that. In reality I'm not even giving it to her to get something in return, I'm doing it because it makes the experience simply more enjoyable. Giving comes from the state of love, taking from the state of fear.

By the way, by giving I do not mean acting like a beta male buying drinks to the girl who you just met without finding out whether she's worth your money or not and other actions such as this. If you use your money on the first meetup or a date, then you've already fucked up since you're enforcing the idea that you're not good enough so money will make a difference. Doesn't even matter what you say at this point, since the subliminal message is received just like this.

What will you give her?

Emotions, fun, her talking to a cool guy aka you, making her have a great time with you. This is true value.

Girls want to feel safe

This idea will take us back to the old days when we were living in a jungle, hunting animals, gathering food. Men have always played the role of the protector that will keep the woman safe. Even in most of our Hollywood movies, books and just simply history, men have always been there for the woman to protect her from harm. In return, woman will devote her life to support her man by giving him anything he needs.

Laws of the jungle have not escaped us, there're very much still inside us. For an example, we still feel fear amongst many other ancient genetic traits. We do not run away from lions anymore, in these days escaping from a predator transforms into coming up with rent money or defeating competition at your job. Fear of death is still within us, it just appears at times that are not so significant compared to our history.

Whether the fear is tigers or taxes, the same principles still apply even after thousands of years. Women desire safety. The girl needs to know that the guy she spends time with is able to take care of her whenever threat occurs. I'm not talking about the crazy fantasies that many girls have, such as the fantasy of rape, choking, several other daddy issues and much more. These do not hold any effect on this matter simply because those are the "in heat of the moment" kind of emotions that many girls will have, but in the end the guy who keeps fulfilling their fantasies is not the right kind of material for any long term relationship. They're just kept around for fun. They are just fantasies and that's what they'll remain to be. Dangerous situations like this are something something that most girls on Tinder and in fact everywhere are looking for, but in the end the girl will stay with a guy who is able to provide and who she trusts. I'm not just talking about the language of money here, I'm talking about a guy who will provide safety, care and has many "friend" -like traits. It's a deadly combo to have it all – confidence, being able to stimulate the girl aka have fun while also being in the provider role. Those kind of guys are the keepers and should look out for desperate women, who in my experience are willing to do almost anything to keep them (fake pregnancies, real pregnancies etc.).

When to have sex, go for a kiss, hold her hand, implement a hug...

"A high value guy is someone who owns a strong sense of reality. He knows who he is, he values his own beliefs and boundaries by disagreeing with others whenever the case necessitates."

I'm sure you've all, at some point, experienced the feeling of frustration, fear, anxiety or temptation when talking to women. An important fact here to point out is that these negative feelings that you're having are the result of you at some point failing to step up as a man. I've been on countless dates that end with me just sending the girl home and not even getting a good night kiss. After this sort of experience I feel angry, frustrated and just plain sad. I've found that we should let those feelings run free and do whatever we desire to do with the girl, just simply not from anger nor any of these negative feelings, but right then when we feel like it.

We've all felt like a certain moment is the right moment to go in for the kiss or go for sex, but we hold ourselves back because of the laws that are stuck in our head like a plague. My philosophy is that we should be able to take on whatever we want, whenever we want. The trick here is for it to come from a place of love and joy and most definitely not from negativity. We should not try to get even with the girl or even prove to her that we are worth something, not at all. The idea is to make her have a good time by letting go of our own fears and create comfort with your decisions and desires you want her to fulfil. Living by this philosophy and applying it as a dating principle will boost your results phenomenally.

The physical guide for this part does not exist. It's all about adopting the belief that you're able to do whatever you want, whenever you want, but only if it's coming from positivity. In my case, when I feel like I want to kiss the girl I'm hanging around with, even if we know each other for only twenty minutes, I'll go in for it and risk everything I've created so far. If my act is coming from a positive state, then it does not even matter whether she responds well or not, since I'm here to give and make her have an amazing time felling with great emotions. If she rejects me for offering her great time, it's her own problem. If it works out, you'll both have wonderful time. If not, if she rejects your move whatever it might be, play it off as a joke, certainly do not make a big deal out of it, quickly change the subject and then at some point make your move again. No does not mean no, it just means not now. Keep hitting the limits every now and then, and at some point you'll break through.

Why do I have to approach and not the other way around?

Laws of the jungle, my friend. The guy who's willing to act will receive tremendous rewards. A man will always have to be the leader whereas the girl will always be the number one supporter for the guy. That's how it has been set right from the ancient times. This is the system that has been built inside us and will influence our every move.

Why do you see men being dominant in almost every single field?

Why are men always leading our countries?

This is the only thing that I have our genes to blame on. We're simply more dominant whereas women tend to focus more on supporting rather than ambitious decisions that are essential for a leader to adopt. It is my true belief that women would be better leaders if our whole race would evolve and escape this rat race of insecurities and external value systems. Women are built better than men, but in our society and in every society throughout the the world men simply work better. Why? We're dumber, but more ambitious, goal focused and can look past distractions with much more ease. In this crazy world of ours that we're currently living in, the activist gets the reward instead of an analyst who sits at home and doesn't show up.

Despite all this, so many of us, men, get really frustrated and mad when the girl does not pay attention nor validate us. It often makes us think like what rights does she have to put herself higher than us? This is caused by somewhat high self-esteem, but low level of knowledge. We must realize that women mostly don't see themselves higher than us. The fault lies in both parties, but mostly in us for being uncalibrated and making her uncomfortable, then blaming the woman for not responding to our insecure bullshit. Think of it like this: the woman is the scared little cat that you want to pet, but who always jumps away when you try to approach it. In order to win her trust, build comfort and baby step it all the way to your goal, which is usually sex. This is part of our evolution.

Assume that your values are equally fine as the ones that girls have even if they're not. Do not assume your value is higher than the girls, do not assume her values are higher than yours. The only healthy thing that will get you laid is to assume both of your values are equal. You are just two people experiencing each other and not in a competition with each other.

"If that's true and this is the right mindset to have, then why is the girl bitchy when she meets me? Why doesn't the girl respond to my texts and my attention? Why is she so cold towards me? This does not look equal to me!"

The guy who asks such questions and sees the world through such frames needs to understand this one thing. That specific girl who has so-called "wronged" you, has been growing up for 18, 20, 30 years depending on her age and during that time has never seen you, has never experienced you. She does not know who you are. Are you going to harm her? Are you going to rape her or are you there to simply to get to know her? Are you weird or are you the coolest guy ever? Are you funny or are you totally boring and a waste of her time? She does not know and will act accordingly, which in most cases is a bit fake'ish friendly, sometimes cocky and unpleasant, and sometimes is just totally closed for an interaction. This does not matter though, you should be happy if she responds at all, since that's literally all you need to work your magic. All you need is some time with her to move out of the stranger zone. You could not ask for a better situation other than her just responding to you and staying to wait for your "pickup line". Anything above that is just unrealistic. Will she jump on your dick right after the first sentence? I wish! Will she kiss you right away? Dude please... Just get her attention and work your magic.

The exact same can be said about you. You've probably never seen this girl before, and even if you have, then the two of you probably don't know much about each other. Can you wait for this conversation to be smooth, easy and relaxed? One can only hope. Luckily it can be depending on your skill level and the girl's comfort level that is shaped by you and her past experiences plus the happenings of her current day untill this point, and for a relatively big percentage too.

I've found that on a larger scale, out of three girls one of them will simply ignore you and just keep moving on, the other one will stay and experience you for a while, but will move on at some point since she's just there to be polite and friendly, maybe even likes you a little bit, and then there's the third girl who will like you back a lot. The third one is who I'm always putting my focus on to find. In terms of cosmic theory the chances of me finding the third girl are around 33%. This means I'm bound to get rejected much more compared to having a meaningful interaction. The law has been set. We cannot go through the journey of pickup or any journey for that matter without being rejected at some point. The trick is to keep going, that's all. Simple, eh?

How to break out of black and white thinking

"Once we lose everything, we become free to do anything."

There is a lot of dating advice out there, which differ a lot, some even have an entire concept of how you should approach pickup. This kind of of confusion makes beginners and even advanced guys rethink everything, because they're seeing it as black and white. People are looking for that one method that's the right one and seeing this sort of split in the pickup community makes us simply feel lost and the whole game theory, these methods and this way of life in general loses its solidness.

If you recognize yourself in this group of guys who have trouble with finding the right method to approach this matter, seeing advice from professional pickup artists differ, not sure who's telling the truth, from who take advice and just confused about from which exact angle should you approach this, then you fall into the category of seeing things only black and white.

This type of BW thinking is one of the main issues guys have in terms of their game. It's not your looks nor your bank account that's holding you back, it's your own failure to see the nuances.

The key to understand here is the importance of seeing the context behind actions. Let's take the opener for an example also known as pickup line. I've always highlighted the idea that it does not matter what your pickup line nor how you approach the girl while some other instructor will say exactly the opposite. For an example if the guy is afraid to approach at all and focuses a lot on what he should say to get her attention in the first place, then for him learning the idea that it does not matter what you say will produce results and is tremendously helpful. But for someone who takes this concept to heart too deeply and walks around opening girls so badly like just saying "fuck your stupid dress, bitch" to every single girl, then he needs to tone it down for sure. Not saying it would not work, because it does, but it only works on a very specific set of girls and since that group is so small and hard to find, for the most optimal results as well as developing a healthy mindset, it's better to not be that extreme at all. It's all about optimizing your results and not finding that one girl out of a million who will like your bullshit. That type of girl will come, but by following the rule of optimization you will also get many other girls in the process. Is it manipulation? No. Is it fake and putting on a mask? Somewhat. The idea is to be playful and fun, not fake, lying and manipulative. It's either a lie or a joke depending on the context and the way you say it. The idea is to make the girl interpret your lines in a way that's beneficial for you, which is pretty much always having a fun vibe behind these words. Doesn't matter what you say, what matters is how and when it's said and where it's coming from, from the state of love or hate.

It's actually possible to get great results by being hateful, extremely cocky and just plain arrogant. I call that the dark side of the game. In fact if you think about Star Wars movies, then the game is not that much different from the principle standpoint. Luke Skywalker was a Jedi, who operates merely with the light side of the force, but in order to defeat Darth Vader, Luke had to mix it up by adding hate to his style, mix the light with the dark, and by doing so also defeated the most powerful man in the galaxy. Dark side and the light side, both can create a powerful individual, but only by uniting both sides you can be fully effective. Still, guys come up to me and ask: "Well, which one is it?" They want clear instructions and are too lazy to think for themselves. Not judging, only describing since I was right there in the same boat with you.

The answer - it's both. What works with one girl, may not work with the next one. Same with teaching guys game or just about anything, even fitness and business. One guy might need some tough love whereas some other guy will completely crumble in face of pressure. The guy who does not have courage to approach at all will need to hear things like opening does not matter and your words do not hold that much effect in the interaction whereas the guy who is too obnoxious will need to hear the exact opposite. If you don't approach, nothing will ever happen. If you do approach and act too "weird", have a really shitty vibe and can't hold your frame, you might not even get a second sentence with that girl. It's all about calibrating yourself to the current situation.

Clearly somewhere in there the opening sentence does and does not matter. It's neither black nor white, it's somewhere in-between depending on the situation and the people in this interaction, including you.

Ego

"Why Should I approach? Why should I prove my worth to the girl? I'm the prize here. I've been doing pickup for years now, I'm facing my biggest fears every day. What makes her so special for me to chase?"

One day, if you decide to stick to the teachings in this book, you'll be really good at game, you'll be able to pick up chicks left and right, talk to pretty much anybody without hesitation and feel the sense of freedom in the air. You'll be able to approach any woman, you're able to make her be attracted to you and you'll be able to get sex any day you want. One day you'll be this die hard self-development guy who's making stuff happen in this life. This is the point where we'll encounter a new set of problems, the biggest one of them being our ego.

I've been through this more than once. Just because we're into self-development doesn't mean the girl is forced to rip our clothes off and fuck us. This does not even mean the girl is supposed to even approach us. The problem we have here is we expect the girl to know how awesome we are right away and merely because of our ego. A big part of seeing whether the guy is valuable or not is his ability to step up and put himself out there. If a guy is not able to approach, then it's already a screaming indicator of either not being interested or just having low confidence, both traits not getting you anywhere.

Our ego makes us believe we're someone. It gives us an identity and holds on to it tightly as if our life depended on it. This is extremely bad and will influence us in a negative way on so many levels. To have high expectations for yourself such as being able to pick up every single girl makes us not want to practise anymore, because we believe we've mastered this topic, thus we being too much of high value to be chasing her since we've already done our part. Of course our ego could not be any more fucking wrong. The girl will not know who you are, if you two do not talk to each other. She can have a fuzzy picture of who you are, but she will never know for sure unless you two talk. No matter how good your game is, you'll still need to make the first move, without it your game means literally nothing.

Women are attracted to who the guy is, which can be found out during getting to know the guy, while men are attracted to looks and would bang the girl despite her personality being whatever it might be.

It's important to let go of your ego and realize that you're not your car, your house, your money or your girls. You are not anything external. You're you, everything else that's outside of yourself is just a reflection of you. It's not you, it's just where you're at. Your things, your posessions, even your skills are not you and will diminish if not maintained through practise.

I stopped going out and expected women to just approach me through social circles. Needless to say, it didn't work at all. This mindset was the outcome of feeling bitter and unsatisfied with the way how my life was going. It's the feeling of being a superman in chains, able to break out of them at any given time, but waiting for someone else to do it for you. When it came to realizing that we're the only problem in our own story, we're really damn stupid. I did not realize that if I'm not happy right now, then I never will be no matter what I achieve or who I drag to my bed. Happiness and any sort of satisfaction can only be internal, meaning it comes from inside and not outside. Everything outside of us is just a bonus and part of the fun ride that we're having. I think of life as a safari. Doesn't matter what car I'm driving, I still see the magnificent beauty that's outside. This is what happiness looks like, being able to appreciate everything and realize what life is really about.

Going back to the ego and its conflict with pickup, the girl has no way of knowing who you really are just as we cannot see her personality without talking to her. Men value looks more than woman meaning we already see her offering value from the first moment we lay our eyes on a good looking girl while she cannot feel the same so easily, unless she's gets to talk to you and learn about your personality. For a woman we're all just random guys, and very rarely women actually see someone towards who they absolutely feel the need to approach while guys see girls we'd like to date almost every single time we go out to the store. Even if the woman did see someone she likes just based off his looks, there is this social barrier, the rule of normality, men having the responsibility to approach women and not the other way around just because it's how we're made to believe, plus, for a woman to approach a man, slut shaming is something that most definitely comes to mind whenever you see something like this. There are so many of us who literally come up with the word "slut" as soon as they see a woman make the first move instead of the guy, and this is something that most women most definitely do not risk with since their appearance is extremely important to them. All women want to seem of high value and having ignominious lables on their persona will hurt the ability to find and also attract a high class guy. The society has fucked with our minds in every way possible, including the vision we have of pickup and dating in general, it's no wonder women are scared to make the first move. So as you see, it makes more sense for men to approach girls. Even if it did not make any sense what so ever, even if women were just lazy and men had to do the work all for them just because we're tail begging low class compared to all women in the world, what's the alternative? No interactions with the opposite sex at all? No sexual encounters for the rest of our life? It's either us stepping up as a man or not getting any results at all. So what if women don't approach men themselves and let us do most of the work, a high value man does not wait for opportunities, he creates them and that's what makes him someone of high value in the first place. Men having to approach women and not the other way around is a method for weeding out the weak and undeserving. In order to deserve any girl in the world, we must be able to approach any girl in the world with ease and having the sense of capability. All of us literally get what we deserve every single time. The universe might not always give us what we want, but it will always give us what we need. If men, me and you, are not able to pick ourselves up and go for the women we truly desire, then we are not able to get any woman, therefore by following the formula of getting what we deserve, we obviously do not deserve anyone. Plain and simple.

The importance of not waiting for the perfect girl is something I emphasize a lot, but the rule that's of same weight in importance is also to not wait for the women to approach you either. Develop the right mindset to be deserving and do it yourself, go for women to who you find yourself to be attracted. There is nothing for us nor the girl to lose, but we both have our whole life to win. The decision of whether you end up as a winner or as a loser, is once again in our own hands just as it has always been. The mind is literally everything.

This book is not just focused on explanations nor on hundreds of descriptions of encounters with women to brag over my own achievements over the years of taking action. This book's mere focus are solutions to get many other guys just like me back in the day to get out of their sad and tough situation, and make life more fun and enjoyable for all of us by pushing the boundaries and practising this thing of ours, that I love to call mental alchemy – creating gold from the shit we've accumulated. In this context, finding the reason why girls don't approach men does not even hold any value and is simply a waste of useful mental energy.

The fact that you're into self-development that you value self-improvement and desire to become better in any endeavors of your choice, does not in any way mean that the woman holds the same values strongly against her heart. This is where being non-judgmental comes into play, since it's an important part of being that cool guy who is able to sleep with many women. The idea is to have high standards, but not to shoo anybody away simply because they're not on the same level as you. A successful communicator and also a pickup artist knows that you will not make many friends by being negative and overly critical. People, especially women want to be around guys that are fun, confident and driven by something, but do not let it come between their good time during the moment of which women met them. Accept everyone, understand that every single person in the world is on their own path, struggling with their own problems and have a different style of learning, when it comes to speed and efficiency. Ultimately, all people learn the best through their own experiences, some even need to experience certain things more than just once to be able to fully understand the gravity of the situation. We're all on a different level, if you really go deep into the mind of anyone. Someone might be on the level of 3,21 whereas the other guy can be a 3,45. On the outside, they look the same, they talk the same and seem to share the same values, but in terms of getting to the next level, one of them will get there quicker thanks to all the experiences he or she has accumulated throughout years.

We are the sum of experiences that we've gone through, people we've talked to, movies we've seen, and books we've read. If someone is on a lower level than you, then it's not necessarily his or her fault. It's just how it's turned out. We should not condemn anyone, since we all have different bridges of resistance to cross. If you're better than someone, then simply consider yourself to be ahead of him or her, nothing else. Accept people the way they are, but always be aware of them, their flaws and choose your social circle accordingly depending on where you want to go in life, since the people we spend our time with, ultimately either make or break us.

How to know which girl likes you and which despise you

I'd love to have a sensor like the one in the movie called Terminator, which would show exactly which women want to date a guy like me, who will give a positive response and who is down for sex right away. Unfortunately, this kind of privilege does not exist for any of us. The only thing remotely close to this is stepping up to the women you find yourself guessing whether she's down for whatever you're looking for, and finding the answer out for yourself through the oldest method in any book – trial and error.

As far as dates go and how to know if the girl likes you or not…we could look for visual clues such as her making consistent eye contact, blushing, giggling, see if she's making certain movements that you've read about in some "Mystery Method" book, but it's all too mechanic, overly complicated, unreliable and will take away the soul of pickup by making it mostly technical and "sciency". Purely even just reading about this kind of stuff has a high chance to make you totally bored and dump the whole concept of pickup all together. What I advise you to do is something really simple and effective.

Whenever you're trying to figure out whether the girl who you're with, likes you, simply kiss her, put everything on the line and see how it plays out.

It won't go any easier than this. Just simply go for the next step, whatever it might be. If you haven't asked her out yet and are wondering if she likes you or not, then ask her out. If you've already kissed her, but are not sure if she wants to have sex with you, well…she is most likely already looking forward to having sex with you, otherwise she would not have kissed you in the first place since it's a clear sign of her having feelings for you, therefore start building comfort and make it logistically happen.

If the girl who you're having feelings for, is attracted to you, she'll love you taking initiative and going for the next step, base or whatever you want to call it, and was probably already waiting for you to do this. If she was not, she'll respect you for being a man and stepping up to "try your luck". It's not about getting lucky, it's about going after the thing that you want and giving the girl a chance, showing her why you're chatting her up in the first place and demonstrating your value as a man. If you get the expected result, cool. If you don't, cool, there's plenty of more out there, here, literally everywhere. There is also a big chance that if she did not like you before, then after this she'll be more attracted to you for you stepping up as a man and putting a stop to other fake nonsense. Men and women are naturally attracted to each other, this is ultimately why they all socialize. Being in the friend zone is embarrassing and uncomfortable for both sides. Girls don't like every guy, but every girl is able to feel attraction after such act. You can compare it to getting boners. Men get a hard on even with the girls we don't like, especially when they do something that tickles our sensors. Sounds cringe but hey, it's true.

Ultimately everything we have to discover in the life, everything is only behind taking action, meaning we are the problem of our own misery. Once we get the ball rolling by achieving a successful mindset, every problem in our life will sort out by itself just as history has shown us with every great individual who has ever lived on this planet. The biggest lesson I've learned from every single great man and woman before me is that theory is nothing compared to action.

This book is designed just to serve this one point – taking action. You can complain about the lack of information, the accuracy of my teachings and much more, but at the end of the day me being right or wrong does not even matter, if I've gotten you to join me and many others on this path of self-discovery through picking up hot and beautiful women. Even if everything I just wrote about turns out to be hundred percent bullshit, but you went out and destroyed your fear of talking to women, it's already more than the majority of books ever do. The point of this book is to be of service and not just for mental masturbation that makes you procrastinate and will get you nowhere.

Text Game

For those occurences where you're not able to sleep with the girl on the first meetup…

The age of technology is upon us. Girls are addicted to Instagram, Snapchat, Facebook and many other social platforms. Those are the main places where the majority of her attention throughout the day goes. The caveman days are over and texting is a big part of getting the girl to actually meet you. Let's say you've gone out on few nights and had the liberty of getting phone numbers from three girls in total. Depending on your first impression, how you carried yourself and how they received your energy, you'll either get flaked or go on a date. Although, even if you left a really good impression, it does not always mean you're able to see her again. A lot of it is luck and your ability to text her by giving the right amount of information, intent and being overall calibrated. If you truly understand the word calibration in pickup, then you'll know exactly what needs to be done.

Right off the bat, text game starts before you even get the girl's number. Text game starts with good in-person game. If you do a great job in person, then text game gets much easier.

Online game is different from the face to face conversation since you can't actually see eachother. You do not know which type of facial expressions she's making and the whole concept of looking for signs of attraction from her body language is totally out of the picture. So how do you talk to her? On what should we put our focus on? Most importantly, how are we able to make her be attracted to us by just purely using our words?

Text game is not meant to be a real conversation, its only purpose is to give her just a glimpse of you and not your entire life story, so she could see if you're a cool guy or not. Real attraction is built in real life.

How to know if she likes you or not? As long as she replies, you have a fairly good chance.

"If you win her over with your first impression, you'll drastically increase the chances of being on her top list at all times."

While texting, do not be afraid of silence. It's not a bad signal. If you know she likes you, then she will respond. Give it some time. She gave you the number, therefore she likes you. She responded the first time, so she likes you, which means it's likely that she'll respond again. Most of the time the girl is simply busy and won't have time answering your texts, which is not a bad thing, but more of a long term thingy meaning pulling her will just take a big longer than usually. By texting her with questions regarding her absence you'll destroy attraction.

Safety

There was a survey that explored the deepest fears of women and men in online dating. Men's biggest fear was that the girl will be fat in real life while women were scared that the guy will kill her. As you see, no matter what the woman's fantasies and deepest desires might be, she will not reveal them so easily and still has some logical sense left in her, call it the will to survive. It is really important to make her feel like you're not some kind of a mass murderer, because that's what she's afraid of the most. This is done by just sharing your personality in a fun way, but not being overly attached to the chat. After you've proven yourself to be a guy who she can trust, then she will want to push it to the limit and experiment with you. Making her feel safe should be your priority and is a big key at any point of you dating her.

It's just like chess

Think of text game as a game of chess. You make your move, then she will make hers, one by one. If she fails to make a move, you'll keep making your move, still texting her, but by keeping the same distance as you two left it, staying pretty much in the same place, and not moving the comfort level of the conversation forward without her. For instance, if both of you only send one text to each other per day and she suddenly stops sending you hers, then you will keep sending yours every single day to convey value on your part untill she responds. Keep in mind that every single text should usually have a certain degree of flirtation in it, unless she's chasing you super hard.

"It's not that she does not like you, it's that you're just not a priority, yet."

I personally like the tactic of only asking the girl out once a month, maximum twise depending on the situation. If she does not follow up, I will not ask again untill next month or sometimes wait even longer. Although, it has come to my attention that for a beginner it's important to go straight to the end of the spectrum, meaning to keep asking any girl who's phone number you're able to get, out multiple times even if she does not respond well the first, second or even the third time. The reason for this is that a guy who has no solid knowledge of text game, will desperately need these "over the top" experiences to be able to understand the dynamics of a social interaction though text. It's essential for a guy like this to learn what it really means to be extremely needy and also not dependent on the outcome and give little to no fuck at all.

"If your texts get negative, you're done, failed."

If you're past the beginners process, had some success and also at the same time failed miserably with some other girl, then what I advise you to do is always ask the girl out, whose contact information you're able to get, but when she does not respond well and flakes on you meaning either cancels or does not want to meet you at all, then do not give up, but throw her out of your mind for some time, at least for a week. If she flaked you on Friday night, then simply message her next Thursday to arrange a new meetup for the next Friday. You can still send her messages from time to time, funny texts, status updates and whatever you feel suits to the situation, but do not ask her again for at least a week. This will convey your value and shows her you're a man with options, who does not need her that badly to ask for extra free time from your boss on a workday, ditch other cool plans to meet a girl who you don't know much about, and doesn't really care if she responds back or not, since you've got tons of other women messaging you at the same time. You're just there to offer value and if she does not want to take it, then you're just going to move on to the next one.

"Show your willingness to leave at any moment if she's not putting in much effort as you are towards the meetup. In reality you will never close the door entirely, but the idea however is to make it look like you might."

Text game can go back and forth more times than you can imagine. The trick is to sit through it, take it like a man and keep moving forward. At the end of the day, if she's responsive no matter in what way, then it's going great. Patience.

Urgency can instantly spark the attraction. If she feels like she's about to lose you for an example due to you moving to another city, she'll be more inclined to meet up.

"Never accept an answer from the girl if it's very high up in the air. Always be sure to get a firm answer."

Leverage

The main focus when playing the text game is to build leverage. When enough leverage is built, she'll feel comfortable meeting you in real life. Some girls are easier, some harder, but the rule of building your interaction up to the point of where she's ready to meet you, will still be the same. The more she's invested in you, the more she will be inclined to go out with you. The more time she spends on talking to you, there more she'll be invested in you. The more cool shit you'll write and that she is able to respond to without hesitation, the more she'll talk to you.

Handle the logical waypoints towards meeting up, but at the same time with each text convey a little bit of your personality. Flirtation, humor, cool facts about you etc. Increase the leverage that she'll have on you by moving it forward with each step. If you're moving forward without part two, then she'll feel the uncomfortability and cannot separate you from tons of other guys who are messaging her at the same time. If you give too much, she'll sense neediness and will lose attraction. If you're not moving it forward, then the conversation will go nowhere. Every text should have a purpose, but also this sense of flirtation, coolness and humor to it. Balance. Purpose without agenda.

The best way to go about text game is to hit her up with a message while imagining that you've just had an orgy with super-hot models half an hour ago. This will eliminate creepiness, neediness and projects normal and confident traits right off the bat without you even applying any weird techniques that some other guy in his rip-off expensive online program wrote about. By adopting this mindset you'll be you with a small exception – you'll be a high value guy. Also, as you see, I emphasized simply sending the message since if you do not take the first step, nothing will ever happen, as it goes with real life approaches.

I've had tons of women who I asked out just once and after them saying no, I just put them in a friend zone, texting as a friend and not in a man to woman kind of way, sending funny pictures of me goofing around with other girls or being in the gym or reading books. The girl will start to feel like she made a bad call not coming out with you in the first place and the chances of she being attracted to you get higher and higher. She will most likely implement the meetup at some point on her own and that's when you're in control, you have the power to either date her or not. Funny how fast the tides have turned, eh?

When to arrange the meetup?

Today or tomorrow. Don't even text her if you can't fit her into this time schedule. Unless she offers you a date on which she's free, don't think ahead that much since there is just no need what so ever. Men are logical thinkers and find it completely normal to arrange a date that's not that close in the calendar. Women however operate on emotions, which can change extremely quickly. So the girl who's really into you today, may lose interest completely the next day. Also, she might get discouraged, get scared, have some other gentleman caller snap her off and all that, there are many other reasons why it's essential to make the meetup happen as quickly as you possibly can, pick her up after work and spend a quick 30 minutes with her to create leverage, pretty much whatever you can think of that would get you to see her sooner – do it.

Same principle applies to kissing, implementing sex and so forth, depending on which level you've reached with the relationship between you two. In the world of dating it's always better to rush things and then apologize for mistakes later rather than playing it safe and end up not getting rejected, but at the same time not having the chance to win anything as well. It's better to try and fail than not even play the game. If you don't play the game, then the outcome is simple – you don't show up, therefore nobody even knows you exist. How can someone who does not exist, earn a reward? The answer is simple. He can't. Another reason why you should invite her out as soon as possible is because interest can be lost really easily when the conversation gets too long online. The sooner you ask her to meet up with you, the better. The opposite side is to talk to her for a very long time, create solid comfort and then invite her to where ever it is that you have in mind. She'll be inclined to not flake and say yes, because she literally has no counter arguments since you've been doing a great job at befriending her. Then, when you've reached the point of meetup, handle the conversation as man to woman instead of staying just friends. Man has to take charge, there is really no other way around it, and if you've built enough comfort in her and shown your value as a man, confidence, fun and direction in life, she'll happily accept your implementations. Not all of these traits are mandatory for sex, but they will improve your options by a lot, especially amongst high quality women.

In the pool of over 3 billion women on our planet there is nothing that's worth losing since you can find another one fairly quickly, so don't be afraid to fuck up and push to the next stage. It's better to be labled as the fuckboy than a friend. It's simpler, more direct, conveys more value, the chances of sleeping with her will be higher and there is less emotional drama. Also, it's important to keep in mind that women will respect you for going after things you want.

Text game can be really plain and simple without any fancy artillery. Attraction is built in real life and very little by texts. The best you can do is to be direct, funny and calibrated. Do not mess around too much, you are not here to be her next text buddy.

When to stop texting her?

You're done only when she blocks you. This will maximize your learning curve and also your results by showing massive persistence. This is called burning sets to the ground. It will provide you with massive knowledge on when to back off, when to go in, what to say overall and what can be considered to be "too much", so you would be more experienced the next time.

Do not be mad or confused if she does not respond to your texts. Do not think she did not receive your text either, because she did. She also read it and is simply thinking of the response, or is just too polite to say not now, which is usually not a bad sign since she is not ready to cut you completely off, so consider yourself to have some value in the eyes of her.

Text game is the most effective when you're determined to meet her, otherwise you will not push as hard for the meetup, which is crucial for text game since it's harder for her to say yes through the phone being in her comfort zone.

Online Game and Tinder

Since Tinder is a big part of our dating culture these days, here's a summary of having success in it.

I've tried online game with all kinds of pictures and trust me – it's better to just have a great profile so that the girls would actually respond to you on dating sites.

The pictures most guys post on Tinder and other dating profiles are terrible. The stuff that you have to explain, delete it. All of following are freaking awful.

Group pictures. Which one of them are you? Delete it.

Drinking? Are you an alcoholic? Delete it.

Guns, swords and other weapons – Are you a psychopath? Delete.

Smoking - Delete.

Sunglasses – too much. Delete.

Angry facial expressions – Delete.

Ugly clothes – Delete.

Other girls on the picture – Delete.

Creepy shot done closely, idiotic pictures taken at long distance – why would you even? - Delete.

I could go on for almost an hour, but to save you from this boredom I'll give you the tips you've been waiting for. I'm not saying these pictures won't get you matches, because they will, but not much. Of course there are girls who like such shitty pictures that portray even a shittier mindset and the lack of knowledge on female psychology and there are some girls who will still like you thanks to some fucked up reason. Usually those girls don't have much quality or are too optimistic. When these optimists get enough creeps messaging them dick pictures, lame pickup lines and other stupid shit like this, that optimism will be gone relatively quickly.

The main picture has to be something of high quality that will portray your face and your cool body language. It can even be a selfie, if everything else is out of the question. Other pictures should have a vibe that you did not plan them to happen, meaning they were random and done in heat of the moment. This way the girl can see that you have a cool life and don't need to set up any background to make yourself look like someone you're not.

Another point I just have to point out with online game is that all the women you're messaging, you must take them as equals, otherwise you'll simply fuck up the conversation by putting her on a pedestal, thinking she's the one. You're the fucking one, not her. Learn the ways on how to interact with women online first and then worry about the one, if you even want to at that point. Every guy who's learning game has this one girl that's on top of their list, who they care the most about. Probably all of your friends have already seen her tinder pictures as well because you can't stop bragging about her. This is sadly not how the dating world works and is certainly everything but optimal.

Get the rotations in place, approach a lot to get their contacts and have a great profile online to get tons of matches and then start messaging them one by one without putting anyone higher than the other. This allows you to be free with expressing yourself and bring out the coolness in you. Like really, you don't even fucking know most of these girls, you can't just put her on a pedestal for responding to you or having great pictures of herself. Don't make them be that big of a deal for you. It will just make you come off as needy, therefor unworthy.

All of us have been fantasizing about this one girl, all those late nights and countless dreams of your life together, the names you'd give your children...

Understand that you do not know her. She is most likely not the girl you'll spend your life together. Have fun with her, that's the way she's going about it regardless of your actions.

As it was already stated before, the best way to text is to imagine yourself having an orgy at the same time while girls texting you left and right at all times. How would you treat this one phone number you got at the club last night? This is exactly how you should act. Zero neediness, full on value offering and asking if she's up for spending fun quality time with you. Best way to approach text game that I have been able to think of.

By implementing this way of thinking in your head you won't be texting her like she's the one, you'll be asking cool shit, expressing your personality and coming off as a guy who has his shit together. That's pure attraction right there.

This is an action based book, therefore the rest of upcoming chapters will be focused on the real deal, the real pickup that's done by putting yourself into the storm and coming out of it alive, as shockingly better and much more powerful.

Pickup can be really fucking hard

"Thoughts, if gone though over and over again, soon become your reality."

If you've been going out at least few times in your life with the intention of finding a girlfriend or something remotely close to that experience, you've probably experienced the kind of night that just feels like it's too damn hard to keep going with this. Frustration, tiredness are eager to bring your down and make you stay home on the next Friday night. This feeling can be summed up by a concept that the book called The War of Art is all about. Resistance.

Resistance is a block that will prevent you from doing the thing you really need to do. Funny thing is that deep down inside you're actually wishing you could have the strenght to do whatever you feel resistance towards. Even funnier is the realisation how we all have that strenght for us to use any point what so ever, we simply don't know how to find it since we haven't been supplied with the right tools. Schools don't teach this. Most parents don't teach this. But I do.

I've had so many nights, could not even count them all if I wanted to, where pickup seems like the hardest thing in the world. These nights have happened merely because of the weak, negative, bitter looking, excuse searching side of my brain coming out to the surface. This is something I want you to be really aware of. There are times when you feel like you've fucked a million girls, life is easy and fun as hell, and there are no problems in the world what so ever. But then, you'll get those other times when you feel like a virgin whose manhood had been viciously taken. These moments happen only because of your current mood that's dominating at the time and act as a self-fulfilling prophecy. What you believe and think about is what will happen.

A lot of these negative emotions that you feel on nights when pickup seems extremely hard, are actually good. It's not a bad thing that you feel this way, they are indicators of your humanity. I know people who don't have that, who do not feel emotions and feelings, who are full plain psychopaths, and can do whatever the fuck the want without feeling sorry for anyone. So don't be angry or feel bad about yourself for feeling such things as fear or approach anxiety. These are healthy mechanisms in your mind that are looking out for you. Now the problem is this: Let's say you're a chariot rider. An experienced rider is able to whip the horse just about enough for it to go in right direction and not just throw you off the saddle. If you're an inexperienced chariot rider, then the horse might just start to run all over the place. It's not the indicator of the horse being stupid or weak, it's just the opposite. The trick is all about whipping the horse properly for it to speed up while not freaking out.

This is exactly how we, humans operate. We feel emotions that are there to keep us from getting harmed. In order to be successful in game or anything for that matter, we need to whip the horse in our mind properly for it to go in the right direction.

We fail only because of fear, nothing else. Every problem that you have right now, its origins can be tracked back to fear, which is always the fear of death, fear of losing something really important to us. Fear can only exist in our own mind meaning it's not real in any shape or form. Fear can only exist about future, but since future has not happened yet, therefore it's not real, which makes fear not real either. Danger however is very real, and the difference between these two can be, at times, really hard to find. It's up to us to be able to see the difference between these two. Approaching a woman for an example will not put you in danger whereas running into a fight against three tough dudes most likely will. We must recognize the difference and act accordingly in order to live our lives to the fullest.

Pickup can be really fucking easy

"The difference between an introvert and an extrovert is that one spends energy on interactions while the other one gains energy energy from interactions."

As I'm sitting here right now it's really hard for me to remember that I've ever had a girl blow me off, ever had hard time with learning pickup and approaching a woman felt like committing suicide. How did I ever have so much trouble learning something that in reality is so freaking simple? Why do I even have to teach this to you, if it's so damn simple?

Don't worry, I've not gone off track nor changed my value system and the way how I see the world. I'm simply experiencing my winner's state of mind right now at this very moment, which is exactly the opposite to the one I talked about in the previous chapter, and which is also in the pickup community known as being in state. This mindset is accumulated doing the thing you're afraid to get yourself into and doing it so many times that your brain totally forgets how hard it was for you to get here and adapts it as a part of your new comfort zone. It's the state of happiness, joy and total fearlessness, it's the path of success. The person who's experiencing this mood for themselves, has lost all fear towards the endeavour he's in and does it out of joy, not using force also known as willpower and has tapped into the state of power, which represents understanding and being free of any kind of pressure.

There is no right answer whether pickup is hard or not. Pickup just is. Whether it's hard or easy, stupid or fun, useful or not, all depends on your state of mind, how you're feeling about yourself and about approaching women in general, do you feel blockages and limitations or are you free to do anything? Your emotions, your mindset will determine whether you feel fond of pickup or is it something sinister and will require tons of willpower to get through.

How to achieve this state of enjoying pickup to the fullest and feeling like you're the shit? Repetitions. Tons of repetitions, proving your subconscious that it's better to be this way, since our subconscious mind responds do experiences rather than logical arguements. The more you do the thing you're afraid to do, the more you'll begin to love it since fear is replaced by a new thrive of making up for lost time. In my case and also with most people I know that are not born as natural womanizers, will all feel stifled, too much in their head thinking about all the possibilities that might go wrong, over-analysing and all that sort of stuff in the beginning of the night, but after getting the first few approaches out of the way, they'll in the bone zone, feeling like on the top of the world, free to take on anything, figuratively, of course. It's a dellusional state, but it's a necessity to get through the barriers that eventually will lead to a successful life. Every great person is a big crazy, just like Steve Jobs has said once. Any normal person would quit since it's not normal to beat yourself up like this. Here's the thing though, any normal person ain't a success story either.

If you're the guy who's naturally not that great with women and are not a natural born socializer, and more like kind of an introvert, then this chapter will fit you quite nicely, same with the solution to your problem. First few approaches usually require the force method of pushing through and using willpower to destroy your weakness that, in this case, represents failure to take action. After you've approached a couple of women, you'll be in state in where you feel awesome about yourself, and feel like you're that natural guy who's the master of seduction, and who most of us have always wanted to be. In this state, anything is possible and is also tremendously attractive to the opposite sex for more than just one reason. You'll be the guy who fits the type of which most girls wish approached them. All thanks to the warm up that can only take few minutes. Talk about magic pill.

For the new guy

"The most masterful pickup artist does not care about the outcome, and yet is able to be the most engaging guy out there. Girls will want the best guy they can get, not necessarily the best guy out there. Show intent, but at the same time have no outcome dependence. Master this paradox."

If you're new in game:

- Don't be afraid to look weird or stupid

- Don't be afraid to get out of your comfort zone, do things that excite you without much hesitation.

- Don't be afraid to be over the top crazy, this is what makes your skillset grow.

- Always approach without hesitation, it's about getting the reference experience, that's all what matters.

- Forced to go out alone? Excellent. The harder the task, the bigger the reward.

It's almost a necessity for the new guy to make himself feel like home whenever he's in the club, bar or any kind of venue that's designed for pickup. Jump up and down, do push ups in the club, dance like your life depended on it. We all understand it might be a little whacky, but it's essential to get the feel of this kind of life, what people respond to, what is considered to be too much and how to calibrate yourself to be charismatic and attractive right off the bat. If you're thinking this is too unorthodox and a stupid thing to do, then you have to realize that this already IS the much anticipated shortcut that will get you ahead. It's really damn impossible to make it any shorter than this. The basic idea of this is if you don't test the limits of social interactions, if you do not go all out, don't try out different things, then you won't have any reference experiences to build on. There are no victories without failures. You will probably not be able to have sex on the first night you go out after being done with this book, but what you will have is a shortened learning curve that will make you better than anyone else on your level and it will also do it much more faster than anybody else is able to keep up with. It means exactly what you're thinking right now. Without going through this beginner's phase, you will NOT reach anywhere in terms of having success with women and becoming the guy that all girls want and all guys want to be. Work needs to be put in, and smart work for that being. I've taken care of the smart part and a big portion of work, now all you, the reader, have to do is to put these principles into real action.

The most successful beginner is the guy who's trying to do new shit, not the one who's trying to figure out the way of doing less and shortening the learning curve without having any authority to do so, meaning he will fail miserably. Forget the ego, don't worry about not being cool enough and simply take on whatever's appealing to you and feels good in the heat of the moment. As for a guy who's fresh meat in this industry, this learning curve cannot be skipped in any way.

For the second part, to make you more calibrated:

- Open(talk to) as many people as you can

- Do not be afraid to groups, boyfriends, friends, security and any of that stuff since your interpretation of what's her relationship level like, will most definitely be false. Open all.

- Use common sense. If you feel like you're not talking enough, calibrate yourself to the situation. If you feel like you're doing too much, do less. Be aware of your situation by doing a recap of your nights and also paying attention during the interactions.

- Play around and test with different ideas that come in your head. Use your own creativity in an interaction.

- After you're done for the night, do a recap and rethink your actions. This is how you'll learn and prepare to reach higher level the next time you'll be out.

- Memorize a story if you have to, but don't rely on its quality being the game changing factor. A story is just something for you to pass the girl's time with while she's getting to know you. Quality of it is secondary, primary is your energy and how you're feeling about yourself, her place in your mind, for an example whether you're putting her on a pedestal or not, and who you truly believe you are in general.

The more I repeat myself, the more likely you are able to actually do it.

Progress vs Fun

"Prioritize fun, but make progress during your journey."

There are two types of techniques you can use when going out and having the intention of meeting girls. The first one is to hit it hard, force yourself to approach from the first moment you get to the venue, push your emotions and feelings to aside and have a clear sense of focus on picking up women. This works great, since you're proving to your own brain that nothing bad is going to happen when you live this sort of lifestyle, no angry boyfriend or a father is going to kill you for talking to their beloved girl, you're shaking off the haze of being stuck in your head and eliminate mental debates on whether you should or should not approach the girl in the first place. When you walk around the club and don't have a clear sense of why you're there, then you'll end up getting in the spectator mode, whereas when you're pushing yourself hard to getting the results you desire, you're taking action, which gets you out of your head, puts you in the zone and make the night feel overall epic.

The other method is completely on the opposite end of the spectrum. It's all about acting as you feel like, going out to relax and completely enjoy your time, hitting up women whenever you feel like it since having fun is your main focus. The main idea of this is relaxing when you get to the venue. It's about not putting any sort of pressure on yourself and leaving the force method completely out of the picture. The club is here for my enjoyment and I'm here to chill. Maybe grab a drink, relax with your buddies and calm your way into the venue to relax.

Sometimes you might wonder depending on your personality type, that the pressure to furiously hit it up and forcing yourself into the zone is actually making you feel very reactive to bullshit, it's making you feel like you have to prove to yourself that you're going to pimp it up. Rather being this natural guy who is enjoying his time, you'll feel like this chicken with his head cut of running around chasing something that isn't even there in the first place.

The whole situation of this is like a double sided coin. In one way you want to relax and feel the vibes of the club, enjoy the moment and doing exactly what you feel like doing. In other hand you want to approach hard, make the time you're spending at the venue worth something and make solid progress as fast as possible to reach new heights and explore new levels of the art of pickup.

The most optimal way to approach this matter of conflict is to adopt the side of the coin, which feels most appealing to you at the given moment. It all comes down to your personal preferences and where you want to ultimately be in life. For the guy who's going out, having loads of fun, but has no solid results with girls, maybe a few lays here and there, but is overall lacking of pickup knowledge and would also want to become better at this, should focus on more results and less on relaxation and just hanging with the bros. But for someone, who is completely burned out from approaching women all night, who feels like this shit is getting tedious and is a negative influence on his state of happiness, should definitely change his style up. It all comes down to your own personal preference and doing the things that you believe are necessary for you at the given time, which requires complete honesty with yourself and your emotions to know what the right approach is.

If you keep pushing yourself hard against your own will and not being aligned with your emotions, you're going to be stressed, you're going to make others offensive towards you, you're going to feel shit within yourself, your happiness feels rushed and forced and it's completely unnatural. Picking up girls should not be something you're going out to do, it should be something that happens naturally thanks to your intention of moving in that direction, but also having fun in the process. The whole purpose of picking up girls is having a fun time and enjoying life to the fullest by exposing the side of life that's in the dark, yet really important to master for anyone, and by removing fun and merely focusing on results will make you the kind of guy who will not be able to attract almost anybody. People don't like an uptight, overly nervous and needy guy, who is extremely dependant on the outcome. The kind of guy who is liked, loved and also fucked by beautiful women, is the guy who's having a great time with other people and moves things forward when it comes down to do so.

Sex is a goal, but it's not the destination

For a beginner this concept can appear to be shocking.

A critical part of life in general is that some guys get in pickup believing the evolutionary side of this which means the entire point of living is to survive and reproduce. You have to realize that this is your DNA's agenda, not yours. While your DNA is a part of you, it does not mean you have to run around and have sex all the time, to get ahead all the time and be on top of your things at all times. This is a big thinking pattern amongst most guys, who are thinking they have to get laid in order to feel happy. Coming from that mind frame is really unhealthy. If you cannot enjoy being here at any time in any situation doing whatever the task might be, then you'll probably won't enjoy sex as much either. Sex itself is the act of having fun. A guy who is not enjoying his life simply does not know how to have much fun, so sex will not be as pleasurable to him as it could be.

For many guys, sex is all about fucking as fast as possible without enjoying the little things before the ejaculation. It's like the only parts of sex they really enjoy are the orgasm and the feeling of accomplishment, since the successfully picked up a woman. These are just some sides of sex and alone will not produce the whole package of fun. It's really recommended to enjoy the little things, to feel present and find joy in every moment you live through. Desperately waiting for something like a better day, a better job, a better business oppurtunity and not being satisfied with the current life that you're living, go hand in hand.

Sex should be your end goal and you should do everything in your power to work towards getting to that specific experience and play this game to score, but do not forget the true meaning of pickup. Sex is just a bonus, but the person you become through learning this skillset of seduction will be the ultimate price. In my experience, a high value guy is not built through making money, becoming physically really fit nor reading thousands of books. The true value is accumulated through learning social interactions, especially pickup. Everything from what I just mentioned is positive of course, but can mean absolutely nothing without having the skills of seduction available for you to use at any given time. It's not just sex or being able to seduce women. It's about being a social beast who is able to reach the top in any environment.

Good game

Good game is like plastic surgery. Everyone says plastic surgery is salacious looking and just not worth it. But if it's good plastic surgery, then nobody can tell the difference and many even think you look freaking great. Exactly the same concept applies to game. You cannot tell if the guy is gaming, if he is really good, since it simply looks natural.

You must first put yourself into the state you want others to be in. If you're going up anxious, weird, scared, needy (I need to do something!), with the mindset of "I need this to work", then you're already shooting yourself in the foot. As you go up and approach, whatever you feel, they'll feel. That's one of the ground rules in game, the law of state transfer. If you want them to be fun, then first be fun yourself.

The larger problem behind this is described with a simple question: Are you enjoying life? Work on your game, but also work on your life. In doing so your life will emerge into your game. Fitness, knowledge and making money are all great things that should be focused on, after all, they offer us the life quality of a true king.

Always approach no matter what state you're in, how you're feeling and what your anxiety level might be. There's no need to make this chapther, the mastery of self-development, into a criteria that you need to apply right away in order to socialize with women, however it's necessary to be aware of this concept. Improve your life and become better every single day. If some days you fail and feel like shitty, don't worry about it and still go out to practise pickup. Tomorrow you'll be back at it doing amazing things with your life once again. Remember – women don't care about your external value, they value what's inside no matter how cringy it sounds, it's true.

The end goal is to enjoy life and pickup definitely has one of the highest chances of getting you there.

How to make your brain work with you

Game is a process of finding the truth, whether it's about social interactions or your own mental state and value system. It's a process of going out, getting the experience, learning the social principles. No matter how bad you are at start, but keep going out, getting the new reference experiences, exposing yourself to new and inconvenient situations and facing grand social difficulties, you will get better no matter the circumstances that have been laid out for you. Whatever effort you put in, you'll get back exactly as much. The guy who goes out for seven nights a week, will eventually end up getting good at game and learn how to get sex easily whereas the guy who only devotes one night per week on learning pickup, will be at the level of the first guy seven times later. You can't cheat your way to victory here, it's all skill. The way we develop skill is exposing ourselves to new information and experiences, since our brains are tremendously adaptable and will learn the new skills fairly quickly, if we just dare to put in the effort.

However, if you don't go through the process, if you start off with negative, bitter and dysfunctional assumptions, believe the unhealthy and false ideas that hold you back, then the learning curve will be extremely long and there's a grand chance that a guy with these traits will not get to the finish line at all. One of the biggest problems guys have in game and in life overall, is they treat their assumptions as facts.

Do not treat your assumptions as facts.

What is a fact? You went out, talked to five women, out of which two were hooked. That's a fact.

What is an assumption? Girls don't like me because I'm not rich, I'm too short or the girls don't like sex. That's an assumption. Those are theories and certainly not facts.

This is exactly what happends to the ones that have not received proper educational information on life's basic principles, which are the foundation of successful dating, becoming rich and being successful in any endeavour. People have an assumption from the beginning, then will learn the ways of having good game based on that assumption and end up being stuck at some level for not being able to understand the truth due to the lack of right knowledge. If the underlined date is false, then everything you'll build on it will not be used correctly and will not produce much results since the foundation is some total bullshit that is bound to collapse. As long as you keep that wrong and most importantly - useless assumption, it's impossible to ever get really good at game. A wrong assumption can be extremely useful, as I explained in The Key, but in most cases, the idea of believing something that's not true, can go wrong fast and become really unhealthy.

For a long time people believed it's impossible for a woman to run a marathon untill Kathrine Switzer sneaked in while having a disguise on and finished the race in top 3. It was an assumption that women are not able to run a marathon and did not have any correct scientific facts to back it up. If every woman believed they are not able to run a marathon, none of them will.

Without getting rid of false assumptions you will never figure out the truth.

Let's say you have developed the belief of women not liking sex as much as men. That's an assumption right there. If you take that as a fundamental assumption, then what's going to come out of that? Anything positive at all? You'll start to think the only way to get women into your bed, or into any bed for that being, is to trick them into sex, that it's mandatory to manipulate them and the other way, the healthy way is that men need to prove themselves to women and offer them everything such as gifts, their money, look good for them, be extremely nice and so forth. This type of mindset is the worst one a man could ever adopt to himself. Period.

If you assume that all women love sex, then you're going to get mostly positive reactions, you'll have a positive look on the world and will have much more fun than the other guy. It's an assumption, and also not entirely truthful, but the fact that it's tremendously helpful, will overrule this argument. If the story you believe in is helpful, then there is no point in questioning the truthfulness of it.

However, both of these, whether it's positive or negative, are assumptions. One is healthy and the other one is not. As long as they're useful to you, by all means – keep them! But as soon as they stagnate and lose their value, get rid of them. Useful assumptions can massively boost your growth.

I want you to do one exercise. Find yourself a pen and a piece of paper and write down all assumptions that you have about pickup, what women like and everything about dating in general. Write down all the things you can come up with without any hesitation. Go! The next step is to study your own writings and think logically. Are they really true? Is this idea really that solid? Am I right about this one?

The third step is to go out and test them! Doesn't have to be some new hobby you pick up, just implement your testing's into your regular game night. Try them out, even ask around if you want to. See how people respond, see what triggers them and are they really that mad at you for asking such obvious questions or are they intrigued and are facing an inner conflict of whether they should tell you the truth about themselves or are they too anxious to even run their mind over it. All of this is feedback and will give you a massive edge as far as pickup goes. By doing so, you will begin to see the real world with all its flaws and misconceptions. You'll begin to see the quality of people, where their mind's at and who is going to make it and who is not. Really go all out and test your own assumptions, ask several girls whether they like sex or would they rather not have anything to do with it, feel free act like a rich guy and see if you can get more women, become physically really fit and see how women respond, act as a douchebag and also a nice guy to learn about people's reactions and so on. Do whatever it takes to make yourself understand the ways of attraction, since they're also the ultimate principles of any endeavour.

Once you actually get the ball rolling, step outside of your cage and do the things I just wrote about, you'll be blessed with real world facts to back up your assumptions and theories, from which I guarantee most of them will be utter bullshit. I know this from my own experience. And then you can finally choose your own belief, your core values and begin to engineer your mindset into something that's really appealing to your future endeavours.

But...

At the end of the day...

Believe in the stuff that helps you no matter its rightfulness. You're here to improve your life's quality and if you happen to find some universal truths while doing it, then they're just a bonus. Happiness and satisfaction is everything, even if it turns out to be fake. As far as you fully belive in it, you'll have the time of your life, guaranteed.

Shy guys don't get laid

First of all, this statement is not entirely true since there are women who have a fetish for shy guys. However, since most shy guys don't even go out at all, then the women who would want them, don't even have the chance to ever meet them. The whole concept of shy guys not getting relationships and laid in general goes back to the idea of she feels what you feel. Let's elaborate.

Whenever you approach a girl regardless of her current mood and thoughts, she will feel what you feel simply because the woman will always be sucked into the guy's reality and the state in which he's in at the given time. A shy guy is probably not some pickup freak and has not even tried to approach women more than once or twise in his entire life. Needless to say, he is tremendously inexperienced. Being inexperienced in dating will make you feel uncomfortable around women, since it's a new situation and our brains are wired to signal anxiety whenever those situations occur, because it's an important part of our protective system, and that will show through body language, facial expressions, tonality and through many other indicators.

Visual ques always hold much more importance than the stuff that people actually say through words. A girl might say all kinds of bullshit right to your face, but if she is giving off the attraction vibes of her being into you, and your gut feeling is telling you that behind the mask she actually likes you and is just putting up a front to either test you or hide her own insecurities, then obviously you should keep hammering the conversation untill you reach somewhere with her. It's ultimately in both of your interests, you and her, she just might not realize it right away.

Same thing with the attractiveness of all guys. A guy can talk about his bank account, his three Lamborghinis and about famous actresses and models who are now his ex-wives, but if his not giving off the cool guy vibe and don't seem sex worthy, if he does not have his mental shit together to be worthy of women, then a girl will not be attracted to him, no matter who he is, who his friends are or how much money he has. Attraction is not external, it's internal. External values are nothing more but a que to a woman to get the sense of if the guy has gotten that far with his life, than maybe he also is more inclined to have those traits that women ultimately look for.

Another reason why shy guys don't get laid is that even if they do decide to approach a woman, they're shy. The woman you approach, feels what you feel. If you're not having fun, not feeling comfortable with the situation and just pushing through the pain of hating socialising, then she will not find you attractive. It also depends on the girl of course, but the batting average for this style is relatively low at all times. However, we are inclined to start from somewhere and gaming in a bad way is better than not gaming at all. Besides, the learning curve in the beginning is fast as hell, a guy like this will lose his shyness extremely quickly and will move up in the rankings of a high value guy in the matter of weeks, if not days, hours or even minutes!

In pickup and also in life, bad action will always be million times better than no action. Without taking action, the outcome is already nothing. But by putting yourself out there, who knows what might come of it. Greatness is definitely worthy of a shot.

If you're a beginner -

Go crazy and try different styles without hesitation.

If you're advanced –

Become more calibrated and natural

Becoming advanced is about 80% of the entire skill that you're able to create in pickup, the other 20% is all about correcting your calibration and giving a finishing touch by choosing a proper direction with your style. The first 80% is easy to accumulate and comes within months, the last 20% can take years.

Outcome independent

You'll hear this advice a lot in the pickup community.

"Just be outcome independent, the outcome doesn't matter as long as you're having fun."

Being attached to the outcome will make you more vulnerable to the women's comments and remarks about you, you'll not be able to handle failure as well and you'll end up being in a shitty mood all together since learning pickup is messy and emotionally painful. It's not possible to attract every single girl, not even if you master the skill of picking up women. It's important to realize that not everyone are going to like you. So if you're outcome dependent, then you'll be influenced by the comments you're going to receive more than you actually should be. The quality of your entire day will be reliant on the feedback you'll receive. If it's negative, your state and mood in general will go down. At some point the feedback you're getting, will be negative no matter what you do, how fast you're progressing or how good you are, so by being really focused on the outcome is just going to be shooting yourself in the foot.

In other hand if you go out with the sole purpose to have fun and experience cool emotions, then you'll probably have a great time, but are not able to improve as much as the guy that's a bit more outcome dependant than you and probably will not close as many one night stands as you could.

A good way to think of this concept would be to imagine a store. A store exists with a mere purpose of selling their goods to the people. If the store clerk is really pushy and begs you to buy something from him, then you will most likely not be very fond of him. If he is not helpful at all and doesn't care whether you buy something or not, then you'll probably just look around a bit and then leave unless you have a clear intention of buying something. The best place for the clerk to be in is to offer assistance and guide the customer through the store showing her around, what the store is offering, what it's able to do for you and how to operate it. This would be the best mindset that every clerk could have. In conclusion, he is not being pushy, but at the same time he's pushing the direction of your conversation to the end result, which in this case is getting a sale. Pickup is the same for the most part. Same mechanics, same destination, although much rockier.

If you come from the mindset of selling youself to the girl, proving your worth, desperately trying to show how cool you are and implementing dates or even sex at all times, then she will not like it and would feel uncomfortable. At the same time, if you're too relaxed and have no intention of going out and sleeping with her, then she will also not feel as attracted to you, therefore the law of state transfer. The recipe for success in seduction is exactly the same as a professional store clerk would have. Your goal is to express yourself, share your personality, show her what kind of a person you are (cool, needy, shy, confident etc.). Everything you two do together should be moving the direction of sex, but at the same time you should prioritize having fun and enjoying your time with her. Ultimately it's another paradox of doing everything in your power to move towards sex, but at the same time not making it your main goal and prioritizing fun instead. The art of not giving a fuck while actually giving a fuck.

It's easy for the guys to get a wrong idea and go all out in the self-amusement department, do all kind of crazy shit for the sake of just doing it and having tons of amounts of fun. In other hand, there are guys who crave for sex and just having a girl around them so badly that they don't know how to relax and have fun, which is giving off unattractive vibes and pushes the opposite sex away.

What can you do?

I really think there is no better way of explaining this than sharing the mindset I've accumulated in myself throughout the years of picking up women.

When I go out, I tend to have a specific goal in mind, and the goal that I have set for myself and that I made my whole world revolve around, is having fun, fully enjoying every moment I'm able to spend in this life and not being afraid of doing the things that really benefit me, which is summed up by progress through amusement. I've combined having a great time and also being really goal oriented at the same time by making my goal having fun and breaking my fears, which ultimately are talking to women, seducing them and reaching sex. If you're new in this, you'll probably have the same fear – expressing yourself freely around the girls and feeling confident in any social interaction, which is easily broken by exposing yourself to difficult and new situations, for what we have a chance every morning, afternoon, evening and night. We have all the time in the world, the problem is us not taking full advantage of it.

Be a hard closer

Be a hard closer, and also outcome independent. A paradox, eh? How can one care and not care at the same time?

A big problem amongst guys of pretty much every skill level. You can have the best game ever, be the coolest guy in the whole club, dance with amazing and famous models, instantly attract every single girl who has the guts to walk into the bar in and basically be the coolest shit in two mile radius, yet on most nights you won't score with anyone because the concept of being a hard closer is completely unknown to you. The idea of having a certain goal in mind at all times has been implemented into my brain so deeply, because when it comes to competing for a girl with another dude, being a leader and getting the girl to the location where sex could happen is all about being a hard closer unless you're willing to lose her to some drunk guy who just grabs her and takes her away, who knows nothing about the science of attraction we talk about here today, yet enjoys the spoils thanks to simple luck.

Back when I used to have much weaker game and did not really attract girls as much as I'm able to now, I still got laid like crazy, which will totally seem like playing against all odds, and winning every single time. Sounds crazy, right. How was I able to do that? By being persistent in a smart way. I was not able to attract many girls and I was completely aware of it, since I knew my game well, I knew what kind of people buy it and who are entirely disgusted by it. Let me tell you right now, there weren't many buyers, who would see me and pick me right away. Then again, there rarely is. The only thing that I excelled in was knowing the girl's buying temperature, which is used to gauge the attraction level that a woman feels for the guy and her current emotional energy level, and knowing exactly when she was ready to have sex with the guy she just met and who she picked over me to spend her time with in the club. Since those guys these girls are with are mostly nothing special, just some ordinary construction workers and store clerks, sometimes even drunk degenerates, who have absolutely no ideas on how to successfully handle her. Girls are just attracted to them because they're easer to relate to since I'm some hardcore pickup guy, who is out for blood, meaning pickup is like work to me and I take it extremely seriously, whereas the other normal guy who just came to the bar to drown his sorrows into a glass of strong beverage, has regular ambitions and is more of a sheep opposed to the wolf that works hard every single day for the life of his dreams. Sheep are easier to relate to, since the girl will in almost all cases, be also a sheep who is having a tough time handling life due to the lack of right knowledge. The most perfect thing to do, if you're able to call yourself a wolf, is to be calibrated and recognize girl's feelings, emotions and not be some kind of a overstimulation. The importance of being chill while also projecting values of a wolf on yourself is the best place to be at.

If I roll in at the right moment, for an example at 4am, whereas the girl has been partying since twelve, and am able to draw her attention, she'll be hooked right away and will come with me to an afterparty at my place in the matter of few minutes, so pretty much instantly. Why? Because the guys before me, who have bought her drinks, danced with her, spend hours of keeping her company like a good sheep would do, have already done all the work for me, building her buying temperature and getting the girl into the state of being free to express herself and okay with enjoying time in the company of strange men. Therefore, I think of it as it's my duty to take it from there to offer girls real experience instead of some drunk dude who would probably fall asleep in the taxi without even knowing where to go.

Being a hard closer means not being afraid to kiss the girl, guide her to taxi and drive to your place, basically just guiding the interaction in the direction of where you want it to go and not giving in before you get some clear signs of her being totally against it. All of this may look a lot like manipulating, which it kind of is, but you cannot deny the solid fact of girls wanting to have sex, in fact they love sex, maybe even more than guys do, but they need to experience all of these stimulating emotions before actually getting to the end game! Think of it as a movie. If you were to skip the entire movie and just go to the end scene, then the movie would not have much value. Guys can do that perfectly since they're all about the end goal, that's just how we're designed. Girls, instead, need to experience the whole movie before seeing that end scene, which in this case represents sex. To meet a guy who's cool and also knows when to go for sex is an absolute bliss for them. In the end, girls don't really care who they're going home with, and if the other guys have provided the whole movie excluding the end part, then it's really damn easy to take over, if you're able to project at least some value right off the bat when meeting her. Girls are also tired of being in the same club for hours, so they're pretty much inclined to leave anyway, either with or without a guy. If it feels like I'm taking advantage of these girls as many of my old friends used to think, it is certainly not the right interpretion. A good pickup artist simply makes sex available for the both parties and takes all the responsibility off the girl's shoulders, so she could be free, bring emotions of desires out with ease and without being slut shamed and made fun over for sleeping with a guy she just met. Keep in mind that sex should never be forced, in fact, there is no need for it anyway since everybody love sex, however, getting to the sex location often needs to be, but it has to happen by taking charge while offering fun. It's the principle of making her do something that she will thank you for later. It's like with a good salesman, who for whatever reason makes you buy his product that happens to offer you lots of value and usefulness and you'll be glad you bought it. Same idea applies in pickup. Nobody is leaving from your place with a bad experience unless you're absolutely terrible at sex.

You want to be a hard closer, but if you're too much of a hard closer, then the girl won't sense that free flowingness, that cool guy vibe and you'll come off as desperately needy. Thatswhy it's mandatory to enjoy your experiences and not be too goal orientated, but still be moving in desired direction with everything you do. Take charge of the interaction by deciding where and when to leave, but at the same time be sure to take her needs into account. If the girl is not ready to leave with you, then it's only because you haven't built enough comfort with her, meaning she does not feel completely at ease with you. Comfort can be built through being chill and calibrated, the very same traits a hard closer lacks of. It's a double edged sword, one must balance the enjoyability of any moment and goal orientation in order to be successful at pickup.

Once again, enjoy your experiences, but also be aware of the direction your interaction is going and therefore guide it towards sex by using the most fun way you can think of.

Fun melts away resistance.

The right way to think

If you'd be given a chance to choose your social circle out of all the people in the world, who can you name right now? Who come into your mind right away? Would you pick Oscar winning mastermind actors or settle for insignificant people from the sports bar even though in this current example all doors are open to you? Let's face it, you'd most likely pick famous soccer legends, movie stars, millionaires and overall cool people to hang out with, who are good at what they do and would be really fun to spend time with. This is a common choise for all humans since it just makes the most sense. We like to be around cool, fun and influencial people.

If you follow this concept, then most men would love to hang out with people who are valueable and who offer stimulation whether it's low or high. This allows them to feel like they have been accepted by a cool dude so they can be happy about not being a fuckup and actually having some value in their life that ultimately is nothing more but a distraction from their reality. In conclusion, we are drawn towards people who are able to make us feel good about our life whether it's spending time with people of lower class to feel superior or just the opposite to feel higher than we actually are. This is low vibration thinking for the most part, thinking we need to distract us from our problems instead of stepping up and solving them. It's not healthy and represents insecurity and it's just what our society is designed to do for the most part. There are small hacks that actually make us evolve and produce value, but those factors mostly affect us very little, only a very few of us actually use it as leverage to create something grand, for an example Steve Jobs and Albert Einstein. These two great men used their circumstances as leverage to make something of themselves, whereas some other dude would read these signs differently and not even embark on that journey. The biggest difference is the mindset, whether we use the occurences in our life to move forward, backwards or stay the same, which ultimately either makes or breaks us. Occurences that happen to us will mostly be the same, our attitude towards them, however, differs.

It's important to take everything as feedback for yourself. Don't care so much of what other guys or girls are using you for. Be aware of it, but don't think of it as something very important. The real thing that you should be focusing on is breaking down your days or nights, basically the entire time you're awake, see what kind of people want to be around you, who you attract and what you could be doing to get even more high value people to like you. Maybe you need to be more fun, maybe you need to be more confident, maybe you just need to care less or maybe you need to care more. Whatever it is, there is always room to improve and move in the direction of which you want to go towards. Life is just like a road that does not reach its destination before death. Untill that point, the road never stops, meaning the experiences and the improvement or disimprovement does not end. Since now we've established that the journey does not end without death, wouldn't you agree it's rather better to keep improving instead of stagnation? If you are already getting women that are hot, then think about what you could do to get women that are smokin hot! The key word here is to improve. Make every year, heck, every month even, better than the one before.

It's important to always keep in mind that in order to gain something from a girl, for an example sex, loving relationship and so on, it's essential to offer value to her. She is not going to associate herself with you if the value exchange is not mutual. Making her have fun, letting her feel loved and valueable, giving her attention, offering support in difficult times – doesn't even matter much as long as you just need to go in and offer something. It's not like you go in and ask for sex. The right way to do this is offer her sex while also being a sex worthy guy, not just ask or even worse, beg for it. See the difference here?

The right attitude to have towards the girl will always be this:

"I can easily live without you, but it would be extremely dope if you joined me on this amazing ride."

The goal is to give her the idea that you don't need her to live an amazing life and have fun at all, but you're talking to her just to offer her to be a part of it. No signs of unattractive neediness while projecting lots of self-confidence, fun and every other great value type conveyed in one sentence, that should not be said, but written on you as the way you hold yourself, walk and talk, the way your eyes move and most importantly - your attitude towards her and life in general.

Instantly become worthy of sex with anyone

We are going to sort this out in your head.

Pickup is hard only because you make it hard. Pickup itself is relatively easy. The only reason you feel like it's hard is because you have not sorted it out in your own head that you're the shit and you're worthy of hot women. This belief will make you uncomfortable around all women and in order to be a master of game, this needs to be terminated.

If you're somewhat decent guy who is not too bad, but not too experienced either, then you'll probably feel comfortable around women that look bad or just alright, but in front of the hottest ones you'll typically lose your shit and suddenly become extremely uncool.

If you look at the techniques of pickup, what to say, how to act and everything like that, then a lot of it is not about what you do or say rather than how you feel when you're in there, talking and interaction, spending time with people. Learning the ways of a superior man will automatically fix all your behavioural mistakes, rather than fixing your behaviour, but mind staying the same. Knowledge rules the world, which ultimately on a macro level cannot be successfully faked. The same compliment that you gave to a girl once when feeling completely confident will be completely out of order with a second girl if you're feeling a bit down and insecure. The first girl will think you're so different, funny and cool. You say the same, but use a different attitude, to the same or even another girl, and she will intimidate, push you away and just make you look like a dickhead or a psycho.

"I can see you picking up a girl whose average, but do you have the level of game needed to pick up a hot one?"

In order to pick up the dime piece, it's both harder and easier at the same time. In one hand you'll feel like she's playing in higher league compared to yours and this will make you feel less confident. In other hand she is easier to seduce, because she is not used to really cool and confident guys hitting on her, since most guys don't feel entitled enough for her. Ultimately it's all just a mind game. Harder for the inner game, easier for the outer game. If we look at it as a third person and the guy has his shit together, then picking up the hot girl will be tremendously easier.

A girl who's typical, not the hottest, but also quite decent and okay, has met a lot of guys who have sorted out their worth in terms of her and she is used to it. A girl who is really fucking attractive, has not met so many guys who have sorted out that they're good enough for her.

You have to sort it out in your own head that the things you say and how you act are worthy of her time. Once again – it's not about what you do or say, it's about how comfortable you are with yourself saying and doing. The whole situation can be summed up by describing it as a status anxiety. The ones who have it, lose. The ones who are perfectly fine with themselves and feel entitled, even if they're actually not considering society's standards, win. Simple.

When we approach a group of new people, we don't want to be overly weird and creep everyone one. This is just how evolution has made us to be, our survival system has designed us waiting to fit in. Back in the ancient times people got killed for getting too close to the tribesman's woman. Same principle is still stuck in our head, the shape of it although has been modified. We don't know who's the boyfriend, who's the girlfriend is and our subconscious is still afraid of what might happen if we make the wrong move. Think of it as an evolutionary glitch that time has not been able to weed out just yet. Obviously we don't get killed for stuff like approaching someone's girlfriend anymore, but by making a wrong move we might not be as likeable as we would want and the fear of same caliber still remains.

Your brain has a defence mechanism. If you don't think you have enough status in a particular environment, the brain will shut you down. Your voice will get weaker, your confidence drops and the levels of anxiety will rise just to get you out of there into a safer environment, like your mom's basement. This will prevent us to get enough attention that thousands of years ago would have gotten us killed. In this day and age we'll just get a weird look. Funny enough, we still act like it's a fear of same caliber however the danger has been completely weeded out.

Your brain will stifle you intentionally when the status anxiety is about to hit. If you want to feel unstifled, if you don't want your brain to deliberately shut you down around a girl who's sexually attractive, you got to have that completely straightened out in your own head and feel like you're still the shit, which happens by approaching more and more to get the feel of it, to make it into your reality and to prove your subconscious that nothing bad is going to happen. The worst case is literally getting a drink thrown in your face, which has the chance of one in a million. Good odds, if you ask me.

How to feel like you're the shit

Ultimately, this whole concept consists of two ideas under any circumstances:

- Finding out what your values are and living up to them

- Accepting yourself regardless of your current situation

It's a paradox.

Let's have a short exercise. Sit down, take a deep breath, and go deep in yourself and find out what your values are. For an example, to me they're reading many books, stepping out of my comfort zone, teaching people and improve their lives, be fit and healthy and live an interesting life doing cool shit many are afraid to do. This is just me though. Really think about what You care about in life, which can be literally anything.

What I want you to do here is actually live up and strive for these values. When you're living up to your own values, you're going to feel good about yourself and are comfortable to approach pretty much anyone simply because of not having any insecurities. The value of which you crave for, doesn't matter as much as mentally being able to actually go for it, to have the right mindset and work towards accomplishing goals that you set out for your own benefit, to fulfil your own given purpose. Human beings most likely don't have a purpose for their existance, however, that does not mean we shouldn't give it ourselves to have something cool to do in this life.

When this doesn't work out, when you realize you're not able to accomplish this goal of yours for a long time or maybe even never, which is usually the case since perfection by itself is not obtainable, you'll need to adapt another idea to support your cause. Now it's time for you to learn the art of self-acceptance. Accept yourself for who you are today and praise yourself for being on the right path moving towards your values.

We don't need anything, but we should want everything. Let me give you an example:

If you're overweight and your highest value in life is to be a fitness model at some point, then as long as you're on your way of getting there, you'll pat yourself on the back for every small victory and keep going. Realize that it's not the reward that you're working for, but the journey is what we all need to value the most, since it's the biggest key towards achieving true happiness.

Determine your values and work on living up to them, but don't be too harsh when it doesn't work out completely. It's important to just be on the right path, the destination will vary no matter how hard you try.

I'll leave you with an end note.

Sort your life out. You're the shit, if you truly think you are. It's not a delusion, it's the algorithm. The algorithm of being is the coolest person in the room is actually believing you're the coolest person in the room.

People want you to have fun! Nobody, who truly cares about you, who respects you and has nothing against you, would want you to hold yourself back, especially the girls who you're working on seducing. They're interested in your personality and the only way to be completely authentic and charismatic is to not hold yourself back, but still be calibrated and not go completely off the track. Girls want you to succeed, since it's also their outcome that's on a stake here. If you're a cool guy, then they will have the privilege of being with a cool guy. It's a winning situation for both parties.

Being intermediate

"A pickup artists is designed to create an opportunity when there are none."

I'm going to take a wild assumption and say you're quite alright at pickup. Don't take it personally since most guys reading this are probably not and that's totally fine, what matters is guys actually reading and applying these techniques. Skill level doesn't matter if you take action, since by doing so it will go up anyway. It's all about making progress, not about where you are at the time.

By being intermediate, you've mastered the concept of approaching, meaning you're totally okay with talking to strangers and you've gotten a few lays by just doing something, not necessarily right and progressive things but the fact you took action and did them, matters and has gotten you results more than just once. That's what we call an intermediate.

Chances are you take pickup really seriously like it's a big deal, scan the room for approaches, and look for girls who you'd like to talk to all the time and so on. If you find this description to fit your style, then recognize, that this is totally fine, but it will paralyze you if your goal is to take it to the next level. Acting like a predator, scanning the room for potential lays, knowing where the hot girls are at and thinking about how you're going to start a conversation with them is alright and whatnot, but this certain type of behaviour will not get you to the next level. In this case, if you do find this to be you, you're too much goal oriented and are not having enough fun. In order for you to reach mastery and start getting laid more, this type of thinking, this style if you will, needs to go through a calibrating makeover.

For someone who identifies himself with the description of what I just gave here, here's your new goal. Learn to have more fun, self-amuse and talk to more people without judging based on their potential for getting laid that night. Intermediates often have the habit of judging women by their looks and not even talking to the ones they don't find that hot. Intermediates also happen to prioritize sex over reference experiences and individual growth towards becoming the superior man. Sex should be the end goal, but definitely not the thing to think about every single second while gaming. One must learn to let himself loose and enjoy the moment, practise talking to everyone regardless of their race, gender, body type and when the time comes, when you end up finding a really great girl whose company you enjoy and vice versa, isolate her by taking her somewhere, where sex is a possibility.

I used to take girls to another clubs even after I had established they being in into me and probably also being ready to sleep with me. What I was doing was counterintuitive and simply a waste of a great oppurtunity, since if the girl is already down to fuck you, then just lingering around and not moving things forward will make her lose her sexual intentions towards you by each minute.

Instead, what I should have done is coming up with an excuse to show her my apartment or my car or in fact any place, that's isolated and suitable for sex. A quiet place that feels comfortable and cool like a park corner, hotel's lounge, basically where ever you feel going to and you think has potential to be a sex location, will fit perfectly. Feel free to experiment with abnormal ideas, try to implement new locations that might seem really intimidating at first, but if the one you use regularly is out of reach or you don't have your own place to take girls to, then there isn't really much other option. If you can make the situation fun, then the girl literally does not care where she is being taken. Having fun is ultimately what we're all there for.

Possibility number two – you might be having way too much fun, therefore not being enough goal oriented. I'm not saying this is a better type to be than the first one, but you're actually enjoying your nights and having a blast doing shit you love such as dancing, approaching, self amusing, therefore enjoying your time more than the guy who's just all out on expansion and growth. However, with this type the biggest problem is you not having a certain goal.

Typically, these sorts of people don't even know about game and just go out to socialize, drink and have fun. These men probably don't even know about game and rationalise women's preference with the guy having lots of money, being fit or just overly funny. What I'm saying is they do not have enough theory to know in which direction they should move towards.

Sometimes, the guy who can identify himself with this second trait, can also be a guy who has read about pickup, but is just too damn caught up in the self amusement department and finds it hard to move on and actually focus on improving, instead he just goes out to have a blast of fun emotions, yet never actually getting anywhere.

Fun should always be your way of life in the club and when going out in general, but some kind of end goal is an absolute necessity. Fun is something you should have during the entire night with every single interaction, good and bad, but it should all be leading to the grand prize – pulling a girl you like to either your place or her place, and sleeping with her.

I used to have loads of fun, talk to many people without judging their sex potential in terms of being able to sleep with them, but I did not get laid much simply because I prioritized fun and when the time for pulling was upon me, I did not close the deal, kept doing my own thing which was either dancing, going to another bar or a club, or just kept the conversation going even though there were clear signs of she not caring about the foreplay anymore, and basically just killed the attraction. Women were waiting for me to implement sex and take them somewhere private, but all I focused on was having fun and did not take it to the next level. It's important to have fun and do lots of cool shit with the women, but when you feel their buying temperature going higher just like in sales, them giving you indicators of liking you back, then don't be afraid to move things further by making out with them right away, grabbing their hand and running towards a cab, inviting them to check out your amibo collection back in your flat and so on. The options, or should I say the excuses for isolation, are pretty much limitless. Remember that you should not be too direct out in public, especially not around other people, such as asking for sex straight up without any filter, since they cannot say yes just like that because of social pressure, of uncertainty and many other totally judicious reasons. Focus on the isolation when her buying temperature is high, use pretty much any excuse to get out of the place you met her at, whether it's a club, bar, pub, restaurant, street and move her to a location where sex could possibly happen.

<u>Pro tip</u>

If you feel like the conversation is getting boring, simply just escalate, change the scenery, implement a makeout, invite her to your place, or just pretty much whatever you can think of in the current moment. Just be sure to not dwell in boredom, but also be aware of overstimulation, since it projects neediness and tense pressure. The way you open the girl is what she expects for the rest of the night from you. If you're extremely high on energy, she will expect you being in that certain state for the rest of the night. If you're calm and chill, she will stay with you for being calm and chill. If your intention is to change the energy of the interaction, do it slowly and with calibration.

Isolation has the power to either make you or break you

"There are different types of girls out there. The power of knowing what type of approach works the best for who is accumulated through trial and error and becoming aware of different personality types. Practise."

As much as I like to emphasize the idea of isolation and how much it helps you to get laid, at the same time it can be the very same reason why you're not getting laid. When you see a group of girls being out, having fun, dancing, drinking and whatnot, do you really expect you can just pick out one of them, interrupt her fun time with her girlfriends, maybe it's her only night out, and drag her to your place? This does not just happen, unless it's the night is on the verge of being over, like around 5am or so. The best bet for you would be to join in on their fun by also contributing on your own part into theirs, befriend all of the members in the group even though some of you might give you a hard time, to which you'll respond by being fun and positive, since fun melts away resistance. The most social thing you could do is talk to a group of people and have them all be proponents of you. If you go in there with an assumption of being able to build an investment with all of these different girls you're hitting on, you'll look like this massively cool dude, have social pressure of everyone liking you, therefore trusting you, the girls can feel safe with you if being left alone at some point in the night and so forth. They all will be talking back and forth, with each other and with you, everybody having a good time and enjoying the positive vibes that you're able to project on them all by being positive yourself. This type of behaviour builds a lot of attraction since you're able to lead the whole group instead of just trying to peg her off.

The world isolation sounds really creepy when you think about it. It's like you're this predator who's hunting for his potential prey, waits for the right moment to strike. The word "isolation" reeks of anti-sociality. Instead, get the whole group to be on your side based to investment, build commonality with each one of them, build serendipity with each one of them so they all want to keep talking to you, and then, at the end of the night or whenever you want to pull, just suggest that the whole group comes back with you. The chances of the whole group coming back with you is really damn slim. It's an extremely rare occasion of when it actually happens. Usually at least half of the group will fall off due to many reasons that are beyond your control. Some are tired, some have work in the morning and some are just not interested. Most of the time you will be left with one or two girls.

There is a sales technique called face the doors, which says that you should go for the biggest offer first and then work your way backwards. Let's say you're selling books door to door. When the potential customer opens the door, the salesman jumps right in and starts offering his product, the whole five year subscription.

Let me take you through one of my low energy nights

I'm sitting at home debating whether to go out or not. Luckily it does not last for too long, since I force myself to go out right at the very moment of when the negative thoughts are starting to take the hold on me. Needless to say, I do simply because the quality of my present and upcoming life depends on it. It's one of those mental debates, the war of art against resistance that's coming from inside. The best way to live in this world is to be spontaneous and use the three second rule, meaning whatever is bothering you, where ever you're in need of making a decision, make it within 3 seconds. The first thing that comes into our head, will most likely be the right one and by overthinking we are slowly killing the potential of doing the right thing. If you're not creating resistance within yourself thanks to these mental debates, then all that's left is the pressure coming from external factors, and which is by the way extremely smaller, therefore you'll have more mental energy to spend on more useful effects.

I end up going to a bar, which is filled with people who all look like they're having much more fun than me. I'm sitting here, all alone, drinking sparkling water. I can't recognize almost anyone here, people all around me are having fun, laughing, drinking, being load and enjoying the shitty music that's being produced by even shitter people. These are the thoughts that go through my mind. Just standing here, with my drink in hand and just getting into the vibe minute by minute through making myself enjoy the music. I switch from sitting to standing in every few minutes and feel intense and at unease.

After half an hour or so passes. I begin to mentally scream at myself, commanding myself to approach, otherwise I've just been wasting a heck of a lot of time. It has come to my attention that we all have the moments of where we experience mental debates with ourselves over things we should do, but just don't have the courage to step up in, and not just in pickup, but in all endeavours we'd love to thrive at. At the end of the day I could stand in that very same bar for five hours and not approach any single person, feel utterly shitty and tell myself as many lies about why I should not take action as long as I want to, but if after all that time I finally decide to step myself up and slam the goals, forcing myself to approach and give my everything seduce some woman, then this kind of attitude and action will suddenly put myself into the go-getter mindset, boosting my value by a ton and creating chances of actually making something spectacular happen. The idea of using blunt force instead of tapping into the state of power is not the best way to think, but in this certain case it's the best one you could possibly use. Anyway, after I'm done badmouthing myself, I approach and feel an incredible amount of resistance disguised as fear and anxiety. The very same moment I go over there and say the first magic words "Hi, who the fuck are you", the whole fear of pickup will slide off fairly quickly within seconds, I begin to enjoy the time I'm spending in the bar and the whole night starts to turn into something truly spectacular and I'm able to pull it together by the end of the night. I've tapped into the state of power, able to accumulate an amazing time for myself and for the people I spend my time with, and feel entirely relaxed, thinking this is who I am, this is what I'm capable of and this is what I'll keep doing for a long time.

My night has been saved. All the pressure has been taken off me. This feeling is equivalent to literally feeling like Superman, operating from the state of power, which comes through forcing yourself to take the first step and get the ball rolling. What was it that made me feel so awesome exactly? Why did my night turn around from rubbish to gold so god-damn quickly? That's the effect that a single approach and doing something so outside of your comfort zone has on us, by doing so all your fears will fade away at the same time. The act of feeling resistance and giving your all to push through it by using force to achieve freedom and power, which go hand in hand. The reward is truly epic and something no guy in the world would ever regret spending his time on.

Let me take you through a bad night gone right

"The night that tends to be the worst, has a great capacity to end up being one of the best."

One of those nights on which I'm not able to have sex with any girl despite trying really fucking hard.

Today is game night. I'm pumped hours before going out and I feel like I can't wait for it to begin. When the clock hits 10pm, I'm rushing out, get on a bus and drive to the most popular bar in the entire city. During the drive I got my earphones on, listening to Eminem's "Lose Yourself", totally ready to absolutely kill it infield.

I finally get to the bar. I'm ready for absolutely anything. There is no approach anxiety, all of it has been wiped off by hours of meditation. I choose the first girl I see and get her attention. She seems alright. We chat for about five minutes and then I let her leave with the intention to find her again later this night. Always do this with girls who are there with friends and night is still young since girls who have such logistics are not just going to follow you to your apartment before midnight. She's there to have fun and not be picked up by the first guy she meets, even if they guy is really cool. All I did with her was setting the bar really high, since amongst drunken degenerates there is no match for a pickup artist. Now the second part of my plan is to wait for few hours so she could realize there is no better option out there, then text and find her again, and proceed towards sex.

I keep at it by approaching more women, getting phone numbers left and right, establishing social connections and letting girls know I'm around. Most of them flake on me after few minutes of spending time together due to having other interests, back luck or just me not living up to their standards during those first few minutes. Keep in mind that you can be the right type for the girl, but if she has a better idea, different interest about what to do at this certain moment, then she might easily just get your number and then ditch you, forget about you due and go home with someone who she does not like as much as you, but since you not being around anymore, there is no better choise. All what girls ultimately want to have is fun, good positive emotions and to have a great night, and finding a high quality guy does not always go into that specific category.

Think of it as a bonus, which can be skipped if they're having a great time without you. If not, if they're bored or just having a mediocre time, your company will be highly expected and also appreciated.

Anyway, by that time I've spend two hours already. I've done everything on my part, approaching as much as I can and using the full power of my skills no matter the level they're on. I'm slowly getting frustrated.

I'm one of those guys who has sex with a different girl at least two times every single week either through Facebook, Tinder or just cold approach pickup. Even if I go out every single day, I still might not able to achieve my regular number of two per week. There is an element of randomness in pickup, just as in life. We cannot be hundred percent sure in anything. On this particular might I'm too much in my head, the overthinking is literally taking a strong hold on me, also ego is trying tremendously hard to take over. I have this feeling of like somewhere during today I screwed up big. In reality this situation is nothing more but just a bad night due to losing my fun vibe with the first few approaches that went well from an outsider's perspective, but since my own standards are extremely high for the performance of myself, I was blinded by my own stupidity to realize what's actually up and didn't stop to think clearly, instead saw only failure and kept forcing through it, even though "it" did not exist. Many of the girls I talk to during my time out and spend my nights with are often married or have boyfriends at home, abroad or at work, and they're simply outside to have fun. They also don't break their principles with other guys that easily. These types of girls might give you phone numbers that are not even theirs and fool around by flirting with you since everyone love a good tease every once and awhile, but at the end of the day if you're feeling a bit off, not entirely in it, then the night will probably end with you being left alone. Getting a girl to cheat on her husband or boyfriend can be done, but requires you to really own your frame, which is not possible when feeling like shit, which was the case on this specific night that I've been describing.

After the first two hours of doing nightgame my energy levels decrease to a relatively low point, I begin to focus more on relaxing and stop prioritizing the goal of reaching sex. Yet, sometimes during these periods I feel this sudden urge to not give up and still go for it despite feeling burnt out, and I force myself to approach. This kind of mindset makes me seem needy, outcome dependant and really nasty to be around. As you can already guess, I totally waste the next hour by just blowing off girls off, killing the initial attraction that's there due to being a man and her being a woman, unintentionally shifting my frame from abundance and fun to scarcity and bitterness.

At some point, after my one hour blowout rampage, I find the first girl who I saw in the beginning of this night. She's deeply hammered and barely remembers me. I obviously did not leave a strong enough mark on her, even though alcohol might have done a wild job on her, which is not really my failure, simply bad luck with the choise of this girl. At times it's really hard to know right away who's going to be totally wasted out of their fucking mind and who's going to be the designated driver. She ditches me and I ditch her, we both realize it's not going to work. At this point the clock is already around 5am.

I sit at the bar, completely exhausted, feeling like shit for not living up to my standards of one girl daily and looking back at my night, analysing everything I could remember. I see my mistakes, all of them, but at the time I just can't let go of my ego, therefore don't acknowledge them.

It's 6am'ish and I begin to walk home. Totally destroyed, mentally. Nothing special happened, few new numbers who probably won't answer my texts on the next day, or the day after that, or the day after that. I'm feeling like a complete mess in every way possible. I begin to doupt my life goals, my choise of career, the city I live in, my friends and their effect on me...

Then I remember something one of my mentors said about pickup:

"Always play it out to the bitter fucking end." - Owen Cook

When the going gets tough, the tough get going. I realize that I must hit the iron untill I deplete all my energy, untill there's nothing left. If I have enough energy to complain, then I also have enough energy to try again. Feeling dead-tired, but thanks to my ego I just could not give up, not yet. I turned around, walked back around the corner to a club. I did not go in, since it had just closed down. I looked around the venue, saw the last girls who were leaving the club, drunk, but still able to stand on their own. Thinking back now I realize how at that point I looked frustrated as fuck, ready to do or try anything, give it my all to turn the night around. I see the first girl who's coming out, force myself to be as calm as possible, do a quick ten second meditation, then walk towards her, hold out my hand, look deep into her eyes and hope that she'll play along and take it. She looks confused, yet intrigued and does exactly what I expect. I smoothly pull her closer to me like a sailor with a rope and we kiss instantly. She has the most surprised look and asks me who I am. I tell her I'm Aragorn and I'm here to take her to the mountain of doom. She laughs while I pull her to the first taxi I see. We both get in and drive back to my apartment, where we spend the entire morning, noon and afternoon. The effect of playing it out till the bitter fucking end. When I look back at it now, I realize that I was in the mindset of it's now or never, and the girl could sense that. The only thing that was in my mind was sex, I did not care for anything else, including getting beat up, laughed at nor disrespected. There was a fire in my eyes, the fire of a guy on his last life cord. As Tyler Durdan once said, it's only once we lose everything when we're free to do anything, and this type of thinking, of finding positivity in a shitty situation, taking charge with major confidence is attractive as hell. A pure trait of masculinity.

Moral of the story:

- Your mood can get destroyed very quickly, if your fun is based on getting good results. Fun needs to come from yourself, being self amused and not attached to the outcome as much.
- Ego will mostly fuck up your night, but can be useful in some situations such as not leaving without getting laid
- Don't give up untill you've got nothing left. Most guys would have gone home after such slaughter.
- Having high expectations can fuck you up, go in with zero expectations and then be amazed of the great results
- Some nights just simply suck, don't let them put you down for too long ☐ If everything fails and in your mind you've tried everything, try again
- Make having fun your main goal, everything else is secondary. Ultimately sex will be part of your goal and you'll get there not from the feeling of needing it, but from the state of creating fun, because sex should equal fun, not just accomplishment. That's also secondary

Do I have nights when I don't get laid at all? Sure, all the time. On the nights when I don't go out, don't text anybody who I met during gym session, in the store or anywhere else, on those nights when I don't have a girlfriend at home, and on those nights when I don't try much and give up too quick or be just in a shitty mood in general, there is a tremendously high chance I don't have sex. One girl daily is not possible, and not from the technical standpoint, but from your own mental state, due to your own mood swings and the occasional change of desires.

I've found that the circumstances are always the same, it's your mental state that fluctuates. It's not like you can't find women or they're not liking you, it's just your mindset. I've come to realize this after professionally gaming every single day and night, plus online dating, for over 500 days straight. So even if you fail for five hours, approach 60 different girls and can't reach any level of intimacy, you'll just have to adjust your own attitude towards pickup, maybe even towards life. There is always a girl out there every day and night who's up for sex with a complete stranger who is able to convey masculine traits. If you have decent game and still can't find her, then you're just not looking hard enough.

In all seriousness I've gone home at least 300 times if not more without any girl, from which many of those days being even without any phone numbers or names that I could look up on Facebook, without any results other than powerful reference experiences. How do I see those days? Progress, simply progress. I don't think of the day being shitty, useless, a waste of time, nothing like this at all. If the day was shitty, it's merely because I was in a shitty mindset. Life is just life. It's your own interpretation of whether it's good or not. It's important to positive, hit the field hard and you'll reach your desired result sooner or later.

For a beginner, getting to sex should not be your main goal right away. The idea is to have fun in that kind of environment such as the club, bar, talking to women during daytime on streets. Have smaller goals like being able to approach, to hold a conversation for three minutes, getting her contact information to meet up later and so on. Sex should be high in your list of goals, but look at it as a step by step process and while you're at it, do not hold back from celebrating every small success.

The Dance Floor

"He who would learn to fly one day must first learn to stand and walk and run and climb and dance; one cannot fly into flying." - Friedrich Nietzsche

One day, after being part of the pickup community for just a few months, I was sitting at the bar, chatting up some girls. Suddenly, they left and I was left without an explaination. Looking back I know exactly why it was so. I was simply not experienced enough and they could easily feel it form the way I was physically behaving, so it's the lack of both – confidence and fun, failure of creating strong lasting attraction. I was good enough swipe them off their feet and have them join my table right away and keep them there for fifteen minutes, but that was basically about it, that was everything I was able to play out. After they got up and left me, I was left with large confusion. I did not know what went wrong, in fact, I had no fucking idea. I was looking around the bar and noticed the dance floor that was packed with drunk guys and a few girls. I felt like letting off some steam, since if we don't understand what we're doing wrong it's our usual reaction to get frustrated and mad, went up on the dance stage and just threw my whole heart on it. For the record, I had, and I still don't, no idea how to dance and have trouble even figuring out the rhythm, which scientists believe to be a genetic disorder. Despite this obstacle, I danced like crazy, moved my limbs in any way I wanted to, did not care about my appearance, my reputation at all and surprisingly had tons of fun, way more than with those lovely girls at the table before. Whole act of this lunacy felt ten times better than chatting up women simply because I was burnt out from all these nights of pretending to be a quote in quote pimp. Hitting up the dance floor, using it to do stuff what the ordinary person would call stupid and during this act enjoying myself entirely was an act of letting go, losing all stress, throwing every bit of expectation I had for myself into the trashcan and fully experiencing the "now". Needless to say I got hooked right from the first minute and decided to try approaching girls by simply going up to them while dancing and without saying a word. As a guy who's just few months into game, who has no solid experiences, little to no self-worth and is unable to unstifle himself from the horrors of modern world, first few days were completely shit. I was able to dance with women alright, I even had a few girls being really attracted to me, yet I did not know how to pull, whether I should move things forwards with a kiss or pull back, so the dance was all I experienced. It was like your first day in preschool, no idea where to go, whether you should chat up and create a conversation with someone, literally a complete mystery especially if you're unable to read social ques just like I was.

Most guys will avoid the dancefloor like a plague by making excuses such as they don't know how to dance. The thing they don't realize is you do not need to know any dance moves. You don't need to take salsa classes. You don't have to participate in samba lessons. You don't have to look good or be "politically correct" when dancing. Dancing is the act of letting go, of enjoying the moment. It does not have to be logical and there is no correct way of doing it. The trick to be a successful dancer is to do whatever you feel like doing, move your limbs however you want to and dance however the fuck you feel like dancing. If you're getting a high from it, then obviously you're doing something right. Only requirement for a successful dance night is to actually do it and not care for the dellusional judgements we think others might make. In reality, the more weird and mad your dance moves look like, the more they envy you for your ability to enjoy yourself. The ones who judge, are jealous. For real.

"Dancing is about forgetting everything about your past and future, and feeling happy while being in the moment. If you're not feeling it, then you're not a successful dancer."

If you're having fun, feeling relatively confident and comfortable with yourself, then she will get sucked into this world of yours, she will buy in, it will make her laugh and make the fun bubble expand. Spin her around a few times, spin yourself a few times, that's it. The entire technique in a nutshell. There's no point in trying to impress women with complicated dance moves and shit like that. Thinking like this, especially if you're not able to live up to this expectation, will make you stressed, stifled and extremely anti-fun, besides, if you do know some cool moves, then it has a high chance of looking like you're trying too hard to impress some random chick who you don't even know yet. Know you're the shit, you don't need to prove anything to nobody. Besides, a woman might even feel intimidated if she can't keep up with your superior skills in rumba, salsa or any of that shit. Keep it simple, keep it fun and be you without hesitation. The payoff for this kind of behaviour, this type of thinking pattern is enormous.

By being very physical on the dance floor from the very moment you take her there or even meet her there for the first time will project massive value from you. She will see that you're a leader, confident, smart since you know what women like, not being afraid of what might happen and also projecting your value onto her as a men, and since she's a woman, probably, she'll feel instant attraction and very rarely won't accept the invitation. When I see the woman I've approached hesitating over my invitation, have second thoughts and all that, I'll just grab her while being in a fun vibe and dragging her to the dance floor. It's important to yourself be in the state you want the girl to be in before doing this though, because if you go up with a really shitty attitude and a nasty mood, then you will most likely get rejected right off the bat. Self amusement is the key for success on the dance floor, already having fun with yourself or your friends and then bringing the girl into your fun world.

One of my favourite openers of all time in pretty much any place that has at least some sort of music, is to just walk up to a random woman, pointing out my hand with major confidence and belief that she will take it no matter what, while at the same time having a big smile on my face and start doing some dances with her, spin her around if the buy in temperature is high, despite the occasional shitty music that I might not like and the socially inappropriate place that might not look appropriate the first time. My goal is to make her day better, to offer value on my part so she could experience and see what a great guy actually looks and acts like, and in turn have an amazing time with her whether it's having sex, making out or just having a really cool chat that will lead on to a date the next day. Whatever happens, happens. I don't approach the set with the idea of "get" a make out, "get" sex from her since that's coming from the mental frame of taking, which is mentally unhealthy and will fuck with your brain by making one see pickup in a negative way. Instead, I go into the set to give, to share my personality which is really important when it comes to actually getting somewhere with the girl. If you're approaching her with the feeling of she's going to be stuck up and bitchy, then she will most likely be stuck up and bitchy simply because you were expecting her to be this way and on some deep energetic level she can actually sense that right off the bat. It's a self-fulfilling prophecy and also a paradox. Energy transfer and subconsciously reading body language is a real deal, therefore the way you carry yourself and what you expect the girl to do will most likely become a reality, so I advise you to always be positive and don't worry about rejections or anything like that. If you approach this matter with a positive mindset, then the chances of a girl being positive back will be the highest. You've done your part and the rest is up to her, which depends on the kind of day she's having, the experiences she's had and the way she sees the world. For a guy who has a real understanding of how to attract women, won't get rejected, because the girl rejects herself.

The things that seem uncomfortable and weird, they feel inappropriate to take on because nobody else around us is doing them, therefore no social proof, so if you decide to be the first one, all eyes are on you. If you see three people dancing on a street having fun, it becomes much easier for you to do the same whereas if everyone were shy and would not do anything uncommon, then you would also feel much bigger resistance towards dancing in public. Social proof. Every party, big or small, needs a kick to get it started and from the game's perspective, this force of will usually has to be you. This is not only about dancing, it's everything. If nobody around you is kissing, then it's also something new that you most likely have to implement. If there were three couples around you and the girl you just approached and they all were making out, then your woman is going to be there times more positively receptive to your sexual implementations. The more you put yourself in the position of being the kickstarter, the more you free yourself from the social comfort zone, the more comfortable you'll start finding acting in such manner, the more girls will be attracted to you thanks to your rock solid confidence and manly traits to act freely and as you want to, the more free you'll be in terms of your mental state and the more you'll start to enjoy living without social norms putting limitations on you. This is the freedom that the game offers to the ones that are bold enough to take that leap of faith.

"Work like you don't need the money. Love like you've never been hurt. Dance like nobody's watching." -Satchel Paige

Having mastered the technique of sexual dance has some extreme benefits. I've found that the girls that are not really into me, yet still decide to answer my request and come and dance with me, end up being tremendously turned on by me in just a couple of minutes. The definition of going from zero to hero. Girls are extremely sexual beings. Most of them have the capability of being turned on from small and simple things such as the physical contact, the guy slowly rubbing himself against her and everything assosiated with such. The act of sexual dance is like a button for any woman to be turned on in an instant and be prepared to have sex with the guy, if her personal boundaries let her. The step of removing those boundaries are destroyed through building more comfort.

How does one apply sexuality in his dance moves? Simple. The stuff that actors do in movies, the way they smoothly squeeze into the girls personal space and end the interaction by kissing her is exactly how it works also in real life. If the girl's buy in temperature is high, then you'll be able to pick her up, spin her around and even kiss her in the matter of seconds, minutes in worst cases. If her buy in temperature is low, then start with simple moves and work your way up to the grand finale through skilful and smooth progression.

Leading is super important

"A leader is one who knows the way, goes the way, and shows the way."
- John C. Maxwell

If there's one thing that implements you being confident and fun at the same time, it's being the leader in your group. Leading projects confidence and knowing what to do will keep the girls stimulated at all times, the perfect combination. Leaders are well respected and in game they rarely feel the pressure of doupt coming from the group. It's like the cane which controls the fun all of you are having just being trusted to you without anyone questioning your decisions. All you have to do is to take charge and be the one that decides where you and your gang goes.

Men have to lead. This is not because it's some myth that some masculine famous historical figure once said, it's because it's male energy, plain and simple. Male energy is designed to lead and female energy is designed to follow. If female energy is not following and the male energy is not leading, then it's not balanced and therefore dysfunctional. There is a reason why women like guys who can take charge and men like women who are able to satisfy and support them in every way during their journey. Men are born to be the tribe kings, no matter how big the tribe is. In the case of relationships it'll be just you and your woman. Women however are born to be natural supporters, to be really good at supporting the man in his endeavours. This does not mean men cannot follow since we have to follow our teachers and mentors, this is mostly valid in relationships. If a female is overpowering a male, then she will not be attracted and he will be shown as lower value. Relationships eventually die out since man becomes more of a doormat and the woman becomes more of a leader since both parties influence each other. This is just how the social dynamics are meant to be. On a subconscious level our attraction is created by these laws alone. By being the leader, taking initiative and always being the main decider on what to do, then girls will automatically be attracted no matter the quality of the direction you're taking. Law of the jungle, my friends.

In my experience you must be the guy who's making the decisions. Doesn't really matter what you do or where you take the girls, just be sure that your locations are finally leading to the destination where sex could take place.

I've had tons of experience with groups of girls, in which there's always the leader, the girl who everyone look up to. To approach groups there will always be power wars since the girl does not want to give you the influence over her group. I usually befriend the whole group and make the leader feel like she is outnumbered, after which she will always join your side and let you take over. Sometimes they are even bitchier and push you aside very strongly. Rememeber that it's not because she doesn't like you as a guy, she is just threatened to lose her power.

Pro tip: Never take a girl to play pool nor play any other game of that type. Being forced into extreme accuracy will destroy fun and kills the whole vibe in general. Keep the activities fun and simple like dancing, talking, chilling and so on, do not try to bring the logical side of thinking into your party since fun and logic do not work together, therefore slowly destroying the chances of sex.

If you have a blockade with language

There is no need for you to talk to the girls in English like you see most pickup artists operating, just talk in any language that's appropriate for the situation. However, there are guys who have just moved to another country and are purely reliant on using their 2nd or even 3rd language in order to create a conversation.

If girls are having a hard time understanding you, then my first solution is to just brush up on your English.

The second thing I would say is it does not matter if English is not your first language. What matters is how you're saying it to the girl. Voice tonality, eye contact, your body language and style in general – everything here is more important than the words that are actually coming out of your mouth. You can go up to a girl and just start speaking in a random language like Spanish and she won't understand a word you're saying, you're literally speaking gibberish and complete nonsense in terms of her understand you, but if your voice tonality, eye contact, body language that conveys confidence and your whole vibe projects a guy who's sex-worthy, confident and cool, then your words are just something you say to create an illusion that you two are actually talking while you're actually just experiencing each other. She will like that because a guy like that is bringing out masculinity and just differs so much from the regular loser's crowd.

Girls don't care if you're fluent in English or not. The fact you're going up to her feeling scared and embarrassed over your lack of skill in a language will project insecurity and just makes her not be attracted to you. The words don't matter, but your vibe, your energy, the way you feel about yourself does matter and is also the deciding factor of your success with women.

Still having no success with women

"Be in it to win it."

If you keep getting rejected constantly through cold approach, girls in your social circles not being into you, then your approach is to be blamed. I'm not talking about what you're doing to approach women, I'm talking about your approach towards pickup as a whole. There is no other reason why you would get rejected so fucking much. So why does your approach suck? What are you exactly doing wrong?

Having no success with women can be blamed on your techniques in cold approach, but the thing that it ultimately says is that your approach towards pickup is most likely flawed as well. Once one gets his mindset right, realizes what game is all about and how one should approach women, the idea and intentions behind the scenes, then every little technical mistake will be fixed almost simultaneously.

First of all, look within yourself, be completely honest and ask yourself: Am I really the cause? Is my approach towards pickup triggering this?

The girl who just rejected you so harshly might just have a bad day. Maybe she just experienced a divorce. Maybe she got fired. Maybe she had a rough day at work. Maybe she's just in a shitty mood. Maybe she had seven idiotic guys approach her today etc. Most girls who seem to have no interest in you at all are the ones with certain principles and ideas that make them pretty much a menace to be around. These kinds of people are not having as much fun as someone who's positive about life and enjoys every moment.

Most of the girls who reject a guy right away are either on an autopilot and act this way to make a guy show his value right away by doing more than a regular day to day approach and in addition run after her for a while, the game of cat 'n mouse, or they're just having a bad day, plain and simple. With those girls your game has to be on point, only the most advanced students are able to pull this off. Can't show any weakness, hold your frame even more tightly than you've learned so far, not flinch nor get baffled and keep plowing through it while enjoying your time you're spending with them despite girls constantly throwing qualification tests into your face. It's not necessarily a harder set, it's just more challenging and requires a more advanced knowledge on the game, yet often times much more direct, skips through bullshit and the end of the night pull can happen much sooner.

If she's just having a bad day, change her mood by being in a state of which you want her to be in, which should be positive and fun. If she's a "bitch", acting all superior and everything, then just plow through it without losing the frame. It will test your character a lot, puts your skills under the pressure, but is extremely rewarding in the long run since you'll look like a high value guy who's in these days is really fucking hard to come by. Less bullshit that's triggered by both parties preferring directness and getting straight to the point relatively quickly always equals a faster pull. This is done by knowing what you want and acting towards getting it and not just implementing sex right away. The idea is to spark attraction in her by being a man of purpose and giving her the thought that she might lose you at any point if she decides to refuse, therefore skipping the boring parts and reaching your preferred results a lot faster. However, this type of angle does not work with any girl, which is why reference experiences are so god damn valuable since the more one goes out, the more he is able to recognize different girl types and know what they like and how to get it just like pulling a tutorial from the archives.

"An important key to a successful interaction is matching your energy with the energy of another person."

The reason why guys get rejected constantly ultimately depends on the guy and his mindset, his ability to adapt to the situation while not losing his frame and personality traits. The knowledge about the different types of females comes naturally within time. However, there are two ways of approaching pickup that can really diminish your results. One is that the guy is too extraverted and scaring the girls away by being so over the top that nobody is insane enough to stay around him, which is by the way a natural way to act like when a guy is just in his beginner's phase. We all know when we're being this type of guy, it's all about being honest with yourself, looking at it from a third perspective and putting yourself into other person's shoes. It's important to match your energy levels with the other person, this is what creates charisma and makes them feel like you're really easy and fun to talk to. The name of this game is to eliminate differences by increasing similarities and in this case it's also to be more normal looking and relatable to the girls you're trying to pick up.

A girl is not going to sleep with a guy who acts crazy which is totally out of the norm or seems like his trying to hide something by putting on a mask. A girl is going to sleep with a guy who's being himself, and that himself is also a high value man.

Another reason why guys get rejected constantly is their half-step approach meaning they do not actually mean it. They do their approach just for the feeling of doing it, to be able to go home and having the sense such as at least they tried. The heart, the desire needs to be in it, the will needs to be there. I talk about this constantly with my students who are so baffled from doing the approach that they don't even think about the possible result and focus everything on just going up to her. This type of thinking is alright for a beginner who just needs to overcome the fear of approaching random strangers, but if this is where you stay for a long time, then something has got to change. One has just expanded his comfort zone by an ounce and then stayed there without realizing the rabbit hole goes much deeper than this.

Many guys are causing the rejection themselves by not beliving in themselves enough and from the lack of self-esteem. Many guys think their approach is not going to work, because they don't want it to work since it would open up a new door for them after which the fear of uncertainty kicks in, which brings the result of getting rejected almost every single time they go up, which in turn reinforces their negative beliefs they have about game, like pickup not being the right path for them, pickup not working and being all just a scam, or thinking they're just not cut out for this and so on. And of course they could not be any more wrong.

Why are we intentionally engaging in certain behaviours that will not work? The answer is simple. It's not the darkness that scares us, it's the light. What we actually get a nice responds and the girl starts to listen to us? Most of us don't know what the fuck to do in this situation, it's a completely new level of interaction and they're afraid of new experiences. They're afraid of upcoming challenges and new confrontations between the reality and their ego.

"Even if my approach is successful, the rest of the conversation won't be." How do you expect to get on level two without completing the first one?

If the girl actually stopped and engaged in a conversation with them, they would not know what to do with her. It's scary, I get it.

This occurrence is exactly like the infamous validating whistle many guys occasionally do in the presence of a hot girl, the random sexual comments they give out to the girl and which look totally inappropriate. It's all on the same plate with the idea of being scared of the outcome. Like Joker once said, he's a dog chasing cars without having any idea of what to do if he actually caught one. We deliberately sabotage ourselves by totally destroying the chances of being with a certain girl to feel like we tried something, but failed and get that peace of mind for a while untill the next one arrives, but in reality not actually doing enough to get any progressive results. Everything about this idea is equivalent to a bad workout. Not progressing in the gym and just half-repping every exercise, not challenging yourself with heavier lifts and longer distances, but still paying your dues and going there every week just to get it off your checklist.

The trick to fix this dysfunctional behaviour is to just become more ambitious, set higher goals for yourself and realize how easy your desired results really can be if one just expands his comfort zone by stepping up. Build your self-esteem through various projects, mentally training by engaging in activities and habits that are challenging, and just being more understanding of the whole world through acquiring more knowledge through theory and its practise. Recognize that you will never get a girlfriend who could satisfy you if you do not change your ways. You will also never be able to feel at ease with yourself if not done so. It's just a choise you have to make at some point, either go in it to win or don't go in at all.

The friend zone

"Loneliness does not come from having no people about one, but from being unable to communicate the things that seem important to oneself, or from holding certain views which others find inadmissible."

– C.G. Jung

If you can get to friend zone, then you could have also fucked her. That's just because if you can get that far, that you have enough connection with the girl to have sex, you just didn't have the balls to go for it when the time was right. It's actually quite understandable. You go out, and as a beginner you'll have a hard time connecting with girls, and then, like finding a needle from a haystack, you meet a girl who is cool and you enjoy her company. You feel like going for sex or even proposing it to her has a chance to ruin your relations with that special girl and lose that great person who you'd like to spend time with forever.

Here's an important point to realize. Girls like sex as much as guys do. It's our society that has conditioned us to hide our urges. Whenever a girl shows interest in a guy, society tends to lable her as slut who likes to sleep around. This idea is created by butthurt guys and also girls, who have not been able to understand the laws of attraction. Those people need to justify women liking sex by those women not being respectable, which is actually the opposite of truth.

One of the most inhuman things you could do is to delay sex for whatever fucked up rationalisation. I have deep respect for girls who are willing to sleep with the guy they like on a first date.

Now, into deeper topics of the friend zone…

Once you're in the friend zone, it's quite difficult to get out. The girl has already labled you as her trusted friend and since you did not show enough sexual interest in her, then most women do not even realize that you want more from her. Women don't think by the same pattern as men do, which guys are unable to know without proper education. Not schooling, but education. The truth is – a man who's unintentionally in a friend zone has failed to establish a man-to-woman relationship and has it substituted with friendship. But it's not a big deal, since that guy actually tried something other than sitting and home while masterbaiting to various porn sites. That guy actually tried to make something happened and in the process of doing so made a female friend, from which there is the possibility of acquiring new knowledge that would help in his future endeavours in dating field. If he's able to take his failures as a learning experience, then I applaude him for it! But this is definitely not where the journey should end. Now he probably feels kind of shitty about how things with him and that girl turned out. He came out of his comfort zone and experienced pain. He probably want more than just pain, it would be nice if there was a reward for it. There is, but it will be available only for those who decide to pass the full distance. Go out once more, meet a new girl and try not to make the same mistakes again.

Chances are you're strongly attached to the first girl who you're accidently friends with. And I don't blame you, it happens to pretty much everyone. Here's what you shall do next – ask her out, for real this time, as a man, conveying manly characteristics and having a sense of purpose, a goal of where you would like to get with her. If she is not interested, move the FUCK on! She is not interested in you, therefore you should not be interested in her. There is a good chance that she was probably not much interested in the first place and wanted just some male attention. Could have been turned around if you had the skill level to do so, but since right now at this given moment you don't, then simply move on. That's literally your only option. There are TONS of girls out there for you to find. Most of them are lonely, with and without any sexual experience depending on your preference. Go out once more, talk to new women who you meet just about anywhere, arrange dates and enjoy your time with them. Since they are invested enough to meet up with you, then they must like you, or they would not meet up. And no more friend zone unless you want to be there. Have a conversation with her, but you're your intention in mind. You're either there to make friends or get laid, which is totally up to you. You are a man. Man will always have to take charge of the situation. Funny enough – women are looking for guys like that, who are able to take the responsibility off them, to make them feel at ease by relieving pressure, so it's totally a win-win situation.

Another thing you could do to move through the friend zone is to stay friends with her yet at the same time practise game and start dating many other women. She'll see you being desired and will develop much stronger feelings for you. Simple psychology. Social proof. If many women want you, then obviously there's something about you to be wanted. At one point when you feel like the time is right, when she is showing indicators of liking you more than before, ask her out and you'll be pretty much inclined to have success with her. She's already comfortable with you thanks to you two being great friends, she can spend great time with you and now you've also established yourself as a strong male which draws woman's attention. It's easy and to the woman you will seem like picking the forbidden fruit. God's garden dynamics right there.

Levels of sexuality

"Put yourself into the state of where you want girls to be at."

Don't be afraid to get sexual during nightgame, since this is pretty much the only time when this technique is really handy to use. Pulling is not always the most optimal option, but being sexual and exposing her desires will always be one of the best ways to get her ready for the pull. The more you get her to think about sex, the more you get her to occasionally touch you, the more she is inclined to let you pull her due to her high comfort and buy in level and most of all – there more she'll be horny. Look for signs in women's body language to give away her mood, see if there are indicators of interest and whether she's having an amazing time with you or is she just coping and looking for ques for her next exit. Here are some of the most common sights of her being into you:

- She is feeling rather confident around you and doesn't filter her output through words – get her number, have some more fun, then kiss and pull.
- She is already having loads of fun with you – get more sexual, kiss and pull.
- She is constantly putting her limbs on you – she's interested in you, get more sexual, go for the kiss and pull.

If you feel like pulling does not work out in this given situation due to either logistics, her buy in temperature not being high enough, she just not being receptive enough to you or due to her commitment to other friends she's hanging around with in this particular time, then just get her number and always end it on a positive note. Do not forget to implement a date (if she says yes now, it will be easier later on) and tell her of your intentions that you most definitely want to see her again. After this, simply leave and move on to the next set.

The more plans you have made with her, the more leverage you'll have, therefore she'll be more inclined to meet you next time. If possible, don't leave right after getting her number, work on building as much leverage as you possibly can, build it through the time you spend together with her, make her really invested and think about you enough so that when you call the next day and asking for a date, then she'll be less likely to ignore since thanks to your performance last night. The thought of knowing you for a while has been implemented into her brain. Building leverage, creating attraction in her and using the techniques of a pickup artist, if done right, will make it really hard for her to turn your offer down down the next day. A successful pickup artist will not tell the girl what to do or what to feel, his simply acting in a way that holds a magnetic thrust for any female. She'll think that she's gaming you, she'll go out with you out of fear of not wanting to miss the chance of a lifetime. The idea that seems like it's our own creation is the most powerful idea in the world.

Girls know what's up

"Women are always aware of what's happening, but since they are women, born with sexual desires throughout evolution, there's no reason to make it stop."

I've mentioned this before and I'll say this again. Even if the girl is utterly drunk, stupid or just not paying much attention, on some level they're aware of the gravity of the situation. Is she really coming to your place to check out your collection of miniature glass animals? Is she really that interested in your thirty year old brandy? Does she really care about your excuses that you make in order to get into her pants?

Excuses are necessary to be there, but they're not the deciding factor of why she's coming home with you.

The woman you're trying to sleep with needs to hear the excuses you have to offer in order to to take away the social pressure and the possible shame of going home with a stranger with the idea of having sex. Whole story of this process is like a process of bullshit that needs to happen in order to get to the prize. In order to reach the finish line you'll need to walk the path. But in the case of picking up women the bullshit one has to go through is actually really fun and enjoyment for the road that needs to be walked will always be there. The whole pickup experience is supposed to be fun for both parties and is also the best way how to measure success in this field.

As you can already realize, pure manipulation does not work in game. There is an element of manipulation since you're changing your behaviours for a desired outcome, control or play upon by artful, or insidious means especially to one's own advantage, but it's never unfair, unnatural or evil like the word manipulation seems to be. Social dynamics always involve some level of manipulation, it's a big part of its core. If you think about it, then every single interaction people have is at least a bit manipulative. If none of us felt the need for anything, not even for the time and love and joy of other human being, then we would not even spend time with each other.

It's not possible to make the woman sleep with you and her not be aware of what's currently happening. There is no way to trick anybody into coming to bed with you. It's not like you can slip your dick into her without her even realizing. What is true is that some women will regret the decisions that were made last night, they might feel guilt over what they've done due to having boyfriends, husbands or other commitments, religion and such, but they will never not know what's up in the given moment. A pickup artist offers the possibility of sex by creating the perfect environment for the woman to open herself up and surrender to her desires that have also been strongly increased due to the magic of a pickup artist. A pickup artist will eliminate social pressure, fears, any kind of anxieties that a girl might have and makes her able to express herself to the guy who mentally has his shit together and is worthy of sex not just with her, but with many other women. Game is all about opening up yourself and the females that you'll meet and then move on together to fully express your deepest feelings and desires to each other.

A successful pickup is really attractive, just like something out of a wet dream. A truly surrealistic experience.

One Night Stands

"The girl does not need a good reason, she just needs a reason."

Assuming you are able to approach women on your own, either thanks to my chapters that are strongly built on offering motivation or some other reason, I'll move to the technical part of a typical same night pickup as I like to call it.

The aggressive pull

"It's totally logical for a girl to sleep with a guy she just met, but the principle and the deepness of it is misunderstood by the majority, therefore ignore logical arguments and rely on emotional stimulus."

Before pulling any girl it's important to take the responsability of her, to throw them little pieces that they can latch on to, and rationalize on why they're going home with you. One of the best ways one can use for doing this is false time constraining. It's the idea of constantly stimulating and keeping her updated with somewhat false, yet very optimistic facts. Let's say a cab ride to your house takes 20 minutes and you'll insist on her coming with you by saying it's only going to take five minutes max just so she would not have to worry or be bored. As humans, we tend to love easy and quick fixes just like short cab rides opposed to taking a long one with a stranger who we don't fully trust. Make it seem like she is about to get stimulated by a new experience at any minute, like you two are just about to pass a landmark, a monument, your old workplace, the best library in town and forth, and while stimulating her with information to avoid boredom and uncomfortability it's important to also convey great optimism. It doesn't matter if you're being precise with time periods and promises since women are after emotions and not logic. By using this specific method while modifying these ideas according your own personal enjoyment, you'll be able to move pretty much any girl who's at least a little bit into you, from point A to point B without having to use logical arguments and rely purely on emotions and just pushing the interaction in the direction of where you want it to go with great and stimulating force, so that she will have no time to rethink where her boyfriend is or what to tell her friends that were left on the dance floor.

"If the man believes it, then the woman will too."

False time constraining will make her be more likely to come with you since she feels like you're in a hurry for some really important reason and this is the only time she could be with you. This technique can be used to sugar-coat the fact that you live in another town and that the cab ride will take for a long time. The idea is never to force the girl and if done correctly, then it's not even necessary in any way. Girls love to have sex and are always subconsciously looking for an excuse to sleep with a guy they like, so here you are, providing her with one – the lack of time.

Girls don't want to seem like a slut to the public eye. They don't even want to seem like a slut to you, the guy who they want to fuck, so they're waiting for an excuse which would take the responsibility off and help them feel at ease. Going back to the idea of time constraining, the reaction will always be positive if you are being positive and not forcing her to do something. Do not force, just implement with great intensity. Women are waiting men to take the lead due to the lack of courage and also because a real man is supposed to act in this way. Create an excuse to justify the peculiar idea, give her an idea that you would love to spend some more time with her, but only if she agrees to hang out with you. If she agrees to hang out with you, then make sure it's a place where sex could happen. Then, when the time feels right, get intimate, make it seem like it happened naturally which ultimately should be the case for an advanced guy, and have sex with her. The woman will thank you for your high level of skill in pickup later, even though she will not use these same terms. Women always realize what's actually up, no pun intended, and they will admire your smoothness and the ability to get rid of the distraction factors so she could have great experiences and an overall fun time. Situation of this kind will always be a win for both parties.

The only reason girls don't act like they want sex is because of social conditioning. They're simply trying to fit in, which is completely understandable in this modern world of ours. Women don't want to step on your boundaries. They'd rather not make themselves look like a slut, friends judging them, pointing fingers and everything such as this, risk their social value being destroyed or even risk you not liking them, therefore putting on a mask is tremendously impotant as a tool to successfully survive. In order to pull a girl, it's essential for the man to take responsibility and the pressure off them.

The calm pull

"Make it seem like it happened naturally through having a great time."

A successful pickup artist is constantly pushing the interaction in the direction of sex by first building comfort, then getting sexual, making her desires come on the surface, have her feel comfortable hanging out with him, and eventually make her feel like there is no judgement and no negative outcome in sleeping with him which is done through strong actions and very few words. As an aspiring pickup artist, you can propose to get a drink at your place, invite her to watch a cool horror film that you just had the luck of discovering today, sell her with the wonderful view that can be seen from your forbidden rooftop, just get her to walk with you and then suddenly end up at your doorstep by "accident"... Whatever the idea that you can come up with might be, and if can fit into the form of an excuse to go to your place, will suffice. By adding some false time constraining in here she will feel like your place is just around the corner, whereas in reality it's like a 30 minute ride.

Always make sure you'll take it step by step moving towards to the pull, unless it's the last man standing zone and you'll be able to escalate quicker. Take small baby step and focus on moving from point A to the point B, then C and then D instead of going for the F right away, which represents the location where sex could happen. You'll be able to speed up each step if her buy in temperature is high, and which is measured by your own gut feeling that's accumulated throughout experiences and simple trial and error approach. She being extremely touchy, giggling and laughing like a schoolgirl, having the anime eyes and totally looking like she's ready to fuck you is obviously a sign of high buy in temperature whereas if she's checking her phone, avoiding eye contact and not investing in the conversation as much being relatively low. Her buy in temperature is dependent on your level of game and good portion of luck. It has come to my attention that every third girl has a high potential of being totally into you, if your game is able to handle her.

Girls are different and will respond to you depending on their own mental state. In many cases her not being into you is not your fault, but her's. There is this certain group of women, rather a big group that consists of women that like you, but are not ready to sleep with you for whatever fucked up rationalization. These women are hard to have sexual actions with and might require a lot of time such as more than just a few dates, a darker daylight, or just a different and more experienced approach. If you find yourself to stumble upon one of those, which you will, then it will be extremely tedious and tremendously boring to wait for the right moment to escalate to the next step from B to C, which might take 3 hours to experience. From an economic standpoint it's not worth it and you'd be better off finding a woman who's really into you starting from the moment you approach her, but one has to admit, the act of hammering it out to the bitter end, getting the reference experience and seeing how the two of you play it out just for the sake of it is quite valuable from the standpoint of skillset improvement. Every woman is ready to sleep with a guy they really like and enjoy being with on a first date. If you're not able to sleep with her on the first date, then she's obviously not that into you and your game could use improvement. There is always that oppurtunity that you are not her type, which is rarely the case and used just as an excuse, but in all honesty – these occurences rarely happen when already on a date. If she has agreed to meet you, and she does, then she has also considered sleeping with you, came up with a yes, and you've passed the filter and will reach sex, if you can hold your ground during the date and skilfully create sexual desire in her.

This is outer game.

Inner game consists of your mental state at the time, whether you think you deserve the girl and how confident you feel, which I've already touched in earlier paragraphs and will continue to expand in the upcoming ones.

The most effective shortcut I've been able to find for you guys is to feel like you've just slept with 10 girls today and could go back to them at any given time. This will put your into the mode of abundance and you won't blow the sets out by coming from the frame of having low value and acting as a value leech opposed to a value producer. If a guy is not talking to a woman to have fun and only cares about finding someone to have sex with, then I'm sorry, but his won't have much success. Women are attracted to fun and confidence and not to some mentally small guy that only wants to fuck and can't feel the positive vibes and is unable to master the art of enjoying the moment without external substances. I'm not saying those guys don't get laid, because they do, but only in rare occasions. If there is an exception, then it's the rich or fit guy that has many flaws and is unable to feel happy, but does convey some traits that women use as a rationalization for sleeping with him. Either way not a healthy place to be at.

Women don't give you happiness, but the guy who you're becoming through picking up women, does.

Poker and Game

"Even if you're above the average with your skills, it's still not enough to be able to get laid every single night by different women. That kind of privilege comes with being one of the best. "

I'm not a good poker player. In fact, I've only played poker no more than 5 times in my entire life. I'm aware of the rules of poker, I know how one is supposed to make a living off it and what it takes to be successful at it. Unfortunately I never really saw the point of playing, bunch of guys sitting around a table, wasting time, dealing cards and playing for money. Looks like one of the most unproductive things to do as far as I'm concerned. If you're not getting paid for it, if you're not a professional poker player or not striving to be one, then all it will ever be to you is just another way to procrastinate. However, this game, the principles behind it and the way it's playstyle is in some ways exactly like picking up women.

In poker you can be the best player of all time, know every single trick and tweak that will make you the best in the whole world, but if your luck is just not running on your side today, then it does not matter. You can do everything right as far as your playstyle goes and have the biggest pool of knowledge on poker as possible, but if the cards ain't decent, you won't make it.

Let's look at a guy who's not that great at poker, but is still playing just to kill time. Even tho his friends can always call his bluffs and are overall better than him, the guy still wins thanks to a great hand. His friends can be higher level than him, but if they ain't getting the right cards, they simply will not win. However, if they keep on playing, around a hundred games or so, then those guys who whose skill level is higher, will put more money into their pocket than the guy who's not that good, but had more luck in the beginning.

It's the simple rule of life. Life can be really cruel and is able to make fools and idiots very rich while the people who actually deserve it will barely make a living. Despite all that, life is always fair.

This translates into game very fucking nicely. You could be doing everything right, be the coolest guy on the venue and still have nights when everything is just working against you whereas some other dude who got drunk and approached just one women against your 15 will get laid that night. He is not necessarily better than you, he does not have more value than you, he is just luckier than you on that particular evening. Now that seems unfair, right?

Everyone get their time to shine meaning we all have fair amounts of luck in our lives. Some get it on Tuesday, some on Friday. Luck is never the deciding factor since we all have it at some point, we all get those business deals, those opportunities that can put us on the top at some point of our life. That being said, how can we take advantage of our upcoming luck? Simple. By being prepared. A guy who's a good poker player will have bad days where he's left with a negative balance for sure, but when the good days come, he is ready to take advantage of them by being a good player and therefor he is able to always keep his win precentage over 50% to make money.

The same idea applies in pickup just about perfectly. Some nights you go out and get rejected over 20 times while on the next day you'll fuck the first girl you set eyes on. Just like in poker you might get 3 bad hands in a row and not win anything, but when you get those good hands you know how to play them and win the prize.

It's like this with poker, with pickup and with life in general. Most guys who are married get lucky and meet a girl on one of their good nights, where the odds favour them. This occurrence is misunderstood and treated as true love at first sight whereas it's simply luck, which we all have at some point. On a good night where we don't have to try so much to get laid, the guy who's absolutely terrible and has no game what so ever, can get the girls phone number, call her up for like two months straight untill she finally starts to like his persistence and goes out with him, eventually they get married thanks to the guy truly believing she's the one and the girl being sucked into his reality, and then in few years getting divorced since the connection was not the best, the guy only tried to make it into something it's not. This shit happends only because we don't have enough knowledge.

Since sometimes we have good nights and sometimes we don't regardless of our skill, we run into a conclusion. Every outcome is not entirely connected to your skill. You can go into the set, approach a girl and do everything really well and still get a bad result. At the same time you can be really shitty at game, but just be at the right place on the right time, her sex drive being high, you being her type or whatever and get a good result despite your skills being really weak in terms of picking up women.

The fact of the matter is that you can't attach outcome and result directly. You should be constantly monitoring and realizing whether you're doing better or worse since that's how we learn. In poker just like in game, there is an element of randomness. One thing is for sure tho – whether you suck in game, in poker, in business or in whatever the subject is, nothing will happen if you don't go out. My first night out in a bar was really great and I was making out with two girls at the same time without having any knowledge on how to attract a girl and make her like me. It was also my first approach. So you see, it was a good night for me and if I had more skill at that time, I would have been able to implement a threesome. Since I wasn't, I had to reconcile with just making out. I mentioned before in one of my paragraphs that I'm able to have sex on every single day I want to. How am I able to do this on a bad night? By simply just pushing forward, handling these rejections and eventually, after gaming untill 5am or so, finally finding the girl who's down for sex. You see, on a good night it would happen in the first few hours while on a bad night this shit will take ages and tons of disappointment hoops to jump through. I've spent time with just one woman for the entire night I'm out just to find out later they've got no interest what so ever in sleeping with me, has to catch a plane, is waiting for her boyfriend to come into town or whatever the reason might be due to my poor game back in the day, after which my whole night feels like I just wasted my time. Actually those have been one of my best nights overall in terms of how much I've learned. The more I learned game, the more I was able to eliminate bad nights. Nowadays my only bad night is the one where I have no luck plus no drive to push through. This is the only time when I go home alone. As you see, luck can make several nights easier, but drive and the will to succeed in game will make you beat the odds and have amazing time no matter how unlucky you are at the given day.

Last Man Standing

This chapter is specially designed for the guy who tends to find yourself alone in the end of the night and are running out of sets to approach and time.

If you're into picking up women, no matter where your skill level is at and you've been going out trying to make something happen, then shitty nights when nothing seems to go in your way are in no shape or form new to you. Even if something does come up, even if you have some great interactions and find women in who you're also able to create strong attraction within, but you still find yourself playing out to the bitter end where one ends up being the last man standing. The moment when bars and clubs are about to be closed, most people have already left and the only ones who are still partying, are mostly entirely drunk and the people who were unsuccessful with their efforts of getting laid. These are the leftovers.

In the last paragraph I talked about parallels between poker and game. From reading that you'll see how bad nights are mostly inevitable even if you're a professional. Like in poker, there is no way what so ever to eliminate rejections and flaking. No matter what you do, no matter who you are, there are always women who are not willing to sleep with you. If your game is on point, then you will not run into those girls too often, but since we're all just humans, making mistakes is in our nature despite our level of expertise. The rate of being able to get laid fluctuates a lot due to our emotional states and mood swings which happen more than you might think. Our energy changes relatively quickly so that even just one negative thought might put us on a rollercoaster of terrible results. Being the last man standing and being part of these so-called leftovers is something any aspiring pickup artist will experience every once in a while. Nobody wins every single time unless he looks at the losses also known as learning experiences as victories. From a psychical standpoint, winning every single time is not an option. But from a comparative standpoint, it is. You can win every night in terms of your life moving in the right direction, full of learning, experiences, and eventually getting closer by each day, but you can't have a good night in which the girls just fall into your lap every single time. Being the last man standing is one of those types of pain, which is inevitable.

There are several directions in which you can go if you are the last man standing. You can't eliminate yourself being one of these so-called leftovers, but there are several ways of which you can take in order to make the best out of a shitty situation, which in this case is eliminating the pain of defeat entirely. If the end goal is sex and you'll end up getting sex even though it has taken you five times longer than you originally expected, then it's not really a defeat, it's simply a longer day than usual. All of these paths are really easy since in this time period, where the curtains are about to be closed, most women who are down for sex, have lowered their standards quite bit and are just looking for a guy that's able to fulfil just a few criterias, which mostly consist of just going up to a woman and showing your intent through your words and actions while being totally okay with it yourself without any judgement. It doesn't really matter how you approach her, what your value level is like and how your night has been so far, the goal is to show intent and lead very quickly. Show her that you're up for sex and implement a game plan of which she could swallow and act upon. The leftover girl has been most likely approached by many guys during the night and she is very much aware of the whole drill, so you just cutting through that whole small talk bullshit will make it much easier, much more attractive and effective in many ways.

What you might have not been able to realize is that the more time goes by, the more receptive the girl is going to be towards your implementations, the more she'll be tired and just skip to the good part and the more she'll be anxious to leave, preferably with a guy. Being the last man standing has some extreme benefits. Think of this as a video game where every new level you embark upon is easier from the last one. The more the time goes by, the more girls likely it is for the girl to be in a state in which sex is easier and faster to implement. What should one do if identified as a last man standing?

"The later the time is during night, the more direct a guy should be."

Approach, talk for like a minute or less while conveying sexuality, and pull, simple as that. Just about anything will suffice as long as the plan of where you two are going seems acceptable and offers fun. Put yourself into the position of the girl and think what you in her situation would do. The biggest thing that guys always realize when doing so is that girls just

269

want a normal guy, who's not insecure, not weird and who is able to keep her entertained. The question of sex depends all on the guy and whether he's capable of implementing it due to his own inner battles of unworthiness, habitual principles and so forth. One can tell them about something cool in his house that the girl and her friends should check out, the booze collection he has or just offer them a place to chill 'n relax. Sometimes I even use the "I'm having a party" excuse. Whether you actually have a party or not is totally irrelevant, since girls are not dumb and deep inside they know what's up. It can be called manipulation, but it's more about creating the possibility of sex in a fun way which will make it easier for the girl to fight her own inner battles on whether she should come or not. Most guys are not able to do this smoothly and tend to give away their power as a man. Most guys don't even sleep with a girl after a long night out at the club, this privilege is only for a very small percentage of guys. It's a large playground, on which only a few know how to play.

In conclusion, a great way to get a girl to your house is to simply offer her something fun to do over there and show initiative by being really persistent with your invite and truly believing in the quality of it yourself despite what it actually might be from an outsiders perspective. Remember to not beg, but to offer. Big fucking difference. The last man standing game method is really straight forward and very fucking simple, which revolves around you doing the same approaches as you'd normally do, but by using more sexuality and skipping most of the small talk bullshit that can usually go on for hours. Now of course you can't just successfully invite her out of the blue without having any leverage, so at first you start finding out what she's up to and then regardless of her answer hitting her up with an invite to the location which is yours to choose. Last man standing is one of the shortest and most successful pulling techniques in playbook thanks to the perfect timing and the most optimal approach method for that perfect time.

Alcohol and Game

"First you take a drink, then the drink takes a drink, then the drink takes you." - F. Scott Fitzgerald

In all honesty...

Throwing yourself into pickup by using alcohol to calm your nerves can be really good for you from the aspect of getting good results. It will make your game look better, especially if you're a beginner or even an intermediate. By drinking alcohol you won't have much trouble approaching women, feel more confident, appear to be funnier and have more of a cool guy vibe all together. Long story short – your game will be boosted to a certain level for that one night. And this is the whole point of this topic.

If you find yourself to be that guy who drinks every time you go out, then that's what we call an alcoholic and not a pickup artist. Also, it will not help you improve your life, have an abundance and a high quality of women and be a strong and valuable person who's happy at the same time. All these fantastic traits will be out of reach. Funny enough, we drink to feel happy, yet it makes us even more unhappy. As a beginner or an intermediate, you'll just be slightly better than usual and have a higher chance of getting laid on that specific night, but that's all what you'll ever be under the influence of alcohol. You can boost your level from three to four, but you'll never reach five without giving up on drinking, plus, once you do decide to quit, then you'll be back at three or even lower.

The second thing I want to tone out in here is that you will not make any progress in terms of your game while heavily drinking in order to find courage. Few zips are not going to destroy you, but a few cups or bottles that hold the purpose of creating courage within you will most definitely go under the description of a waste of effort. Think of success in game as a main road and those nights when you drink alcohol as a side road that's inevitable since all roads have some small paths that lead elsewhere, but they will not take you to any place worthy since the destination is at the end of main road. The highway, if you choose to embark on it and stay on it without getting distracted by the small little roads, will take you to grand cities such as Las Vegas, New York, San

Francisco and other big and fantastic places while as the side road will take you to most likely to a waste ground, literally.

We all have those days when we just feel like going out, drinking till we can't take any more of it, puke and just experience this path of degeneration for just one night with the purpose of rewinding, of letting go. This sort of action is perfectly fine, I even encourage people do have such nights all the time. Unless you're making a habit of it, they're completely safe in terms of your progress and mental health, and will even improve your game by showing you a glimpse of how terrible it really is do go down on such path of self-destruction. We are not able to understand what we have untill we lose it for good, which is exactly the point that alcohol is here to help us with to entirely understand. For an example I myself consume alcohol around three times a year just to switch it up a bit. I will not improve in terms of game on that specific night, but my mind does by seeing how bad that side road, that kind of lifestyle really is for us, which overall is making me see the world more clearly and reinforce the idea of me being on the right track with my life. A powerful reality check.

Why is alcohol so bad for game?

Alcohol makes us unable to analyze our nights, we cannot truly feel our current mood in interactions, don't understand how we would really act and might even develop a false idea of ourselves. On top of all this alcohol makes us unable to realize what our level in game is like. If we were to talk about health, then alcohol is killing our brain cells, which means our emotions, our fears and anxieties will not come out as easily due to the lack of neurons being destroyed. It's like we're degenerating ourselves to lose fear without actually working for it. It's just like nuking the entire web of knowledge just to remove a few cells that bother us. Due to all these factors we're unable to imrpove, feel shitty most of the time even when being off the influence, lose our health, get addicted to external stimulus, which is extremely counterintuitive, and push positive vibrations to the side.

People say it's easier to get women if you drink alcohol, which they rationalize with being able to let go, have more fun and confidence. But imagine doing the exact same, being able to get into the same mindstate, have the same flow as someone does while drinking like a maniac, but without a single drop of alcohol. Drinking will destroy your fears for that short period of time and once the effects wear off, you'll be back where you started, but only with a slightly worse mental and health condition, therefore making it harder to crawl out of this black hole.

If you work for your skills, they'll stay. If you take a shortcut, you'll get even worse due to your paradigm changing to something that's dependant on factors that are not coming from within, but are external. If one find this happening to him, his whole life will be on a path of degeneration or as I like to call it – totally fucked. If one is reliant on things that are external, then he will always find himself to be miserable. External factors are of low quality in terms of happiness stimulus while also being extremely unreliable and out of our control. Cars, houses and even other people can much more easily dissapear from our lives than our mindset and the way of how we see the world.

Alcohol will get you to a certain level of expertise no matter your actual skill level in being able to pick up girls. If you happen to be above the level that's achievable by using alcohol, then spending the entire night getting drunk and then hitting up ladies will make your performance be weaker. If you're not that good, then drinking will be an improvement that might help you get laid, but even if that happens, you will not remember much nor realize what you did right or wrong, have no clue on where your sticking points could be and what to focus on for the next time. Drinking is short term pleasure and mediocre results while also avoiding the inevitable and moving through life without much progress. It's either the long term fix filled with true happiness on the way, or a quick stimulation that will act as a painkiller, yet has no ability to be the cure, and is doing nothing more but pushing one's date of transformation further. You'll either face your demons right now, or you'll face them later. You'll be unequipped either way and the sense of fear will destroy your happiness along the way, so the only sensible thing left for us to do is to face our demons as soon as they come up.

How to build deep connection

"Creating deep connection is about reducing differences and increasing similarities."

The first client in my whole career of teaching pickup was extremely terrible in interactions with women. I'm not talking about someone who has never gotten laid before, no, not just that. This guy had barely even said a word throughout his entire time in school. I'm talking about no friends what so ever, well, ever. I don't think I've ever seen anybody worse than him in my entire career as an instructor. This guy was an extremely tough challenge for me as I was just starting out to be a dating coach, had little to no experience with coaching and did not exactly know how to properly point out sticking points of my clients depending on their specific needs. This guy being a total social failure throughout the entire school had such a heartbreaking background that even though he turned out this way, nobody would ever hold it against him and be rather happy that he was not pushed to the point of committing suicide. The more antisocial one is, the harder it becomes to actually break out of this zone of fearfulness later on. On top of all this the guy had a severe stutter that was clear to see amongst every single word that came out of his mouth, and that he still has to this day. Experiencing this kind of dreadful condition from such an early age would make anyone give up socialising and completely drop the idea of making friends or finding girlfriends. When we are kids, we don't know much about living the good life, and as adults we know even less. As a teenager, a person with this caliber of problems would just try to skip school, avoid social confrontations and keep to himself whereas an adult with the same level of problems would become even more bitter and experience a much worse quality of life which is purely dependant on our quality of thoughts. The mould of inferiority had been ingrained into this guy's thinking pattern so deeply over these years, it was like trying to change a fifty five year old Christian who's been with his beliefs for his entire life to suddenly within days adopt the ways of a Muslim. Seems impossible, right.

Let me give you a glimpse of the gravity of this situation talking from personal experience. If you grow up with a severe stutter, depression is really quick to come. Depression makes us tremendously demotivated and therefore unable to learn any new idea that would better our lives.

On top of that, having a stutter destroys your desire to talk to people, every single social interaction, whether it's between you and a stranger, friends or even your parents, feels like hell on earth. Unable to construct life goals, unable to have fun and life seems like a chore that hopefully will end rather soon. When this guy finally decided to learn game, he had literally nothing to talk about because he did not focus on anything as a child other than just barely passing exams. He did not have any hobbies, he did not read books and he did not even watch any movies. Without information output there is literally nothing to talk about. All the celebrities, political debates, anecdotes and everything that a normal guy would talk about where out of the question simply because he did not know much about anything. Having nothing to talk about due to having no passion for literally no subject what so ever is definitely a tremendously big obstacle not just for an aspiring pickup artist, but for all of us.

In reality, it's very possible to pick up women without any kind of verbal communication at all and also to be really successful at it, since in a man to woman interaction the secret of success lies in the sub-communication, words are just a cover to not have two people stare at each other and create the awkward silence that most of us try so hard to avoid. Most of us are not comfortable when left alone with own thoughts, so we listen to music at all times, find some stimulation for the brain to focus on, therefore never actually learning to know ourselves and ignoring the most important part about being a human. Without one knowing himself how can one even become something? In order to be something one must to know what he is. In the case of my client however, since his self-confidence and self-esteem were so god damn low at all times regardless of his mood or the people he spend time around. In the book Power Vs Force by David R. Hawkins, there are levels of awareness that we all operate on. The scale goes up to one thousand, which ends with enlightenment. On the opposite end, it starts with shame. The person whose entire thinking pattern is operating on the level of shame is experiencing thoughts which want him to be eliminated from this world of ours, he feels humiliated at all times and life is just pure misery. Needless to say anymore, but this guy was in the bottom of the pit, lowest of the lowest, operating right on the level of 0 to 20, feeling shame, humiliated and wishing to be eliminated. This guy did not have what it takes to even try and improve his life, yet, he had the guts to come up to me and throw himself into the world of pickup. An act from a man who has nothing to lose and he knows it, therefore realizing there's only to gain.

If you'd collect all my motivational speeches that I've done for this guy all together, they would take away well over a hundred hours of my time. The quality of these speeches were surprisingly high. They also made me discover a new talent within me, public speaking and coaching. Before this first client of mine, coaching was just something I wanted to get into. During the process of coaching him I realized how gifted I exactly am, how well I'm able to pass on my own knowledge in the most understandable way and the kick I got out of helping a fellow human being. I was picking the fruits of my 20 years of experience that all played out in a way that was helpful towards developing a great mindset for a public figure that could be heard by many. Anyway, despite me trying hard to transform this guy, always coming up with new material that would transform any other guy to the next level, these talks did not have much effect on him, since the level of deepness he was in with all this negativity was absolutely insane. This was the first time when I fully realized that transformation has to come from within, outside factors are nothing more but influence that shape us throughout our lives. In order to change right now opposed to in a few years, one must want the change badly. My motivational speeches would have worked only if I met him every day for at least a year, constantly bombarding him with the knowledge that he needs to hear. However, I did not embark on that long, slow and tedious journey. I found a better way.

Einstein had said that if the problem is the mind, then the problem cannot be solved with the mind. Realizing this as a coach was the absolute breaking point in my work with this deeply ill twenty four year old ill boy. I got some power stance exercises from a Paul McKenna's book "Instant Influence&Charisma" for him to do every time before we went out and the results started to show. It's the type of brainwash that we choose. Listen to a tape that contains the knowledge of what you want to know, listen to it over and over again in the beginning of each day, and soon enough, despite you paying attention to it or not, you'll be thinking just as the tape encourages you to. After some time after dealing with his fears and mental blocks that stopped him from taking action, we moved on to the topic of what makes someone a good conversationalist and portrays him as an extremely charismatic person. Since this stuff focuses more on what you do rather than you feel, it's perfect for such a hard case beginner. All about the technique to get results and also feel better without solving this shit out in your head alone. Tony Robbins had once said that if you force yourself to smile, you'll instantly feel much happier. I find this to be true, especially from my own experience. Same goes for other things such as dancing and talking. By forcing yourself to jump into the pool of unknowingness, our brains are put into the state of survivor mode, meaning we begin to operate on full power to accumulate cool things to say, to do and to be accepted purely because of the pressure a new situation has on us. For instance, if you don't know what to say to a girl you're about to approach, and still go up to her and say hi, you'll begin to see that in the matter of seconds your brains starts to find topics to talk about. I rarely find anyone just standing there saying nothing without actually wanting to do so. If you want to talk, you'll find a way to talk, and you'll find topics to talk about. That's just how things go. The trick is to say hi and let your brain work everything else out for you, just like being on an autopilot.

As much as I've talked about the mindset that one should have to attract the hottest of women, there are small tweaks and tricks that any aspiring pickup artist should learn in order to optimize his results.

The books I've read on body language, posture and creating rapport seem all too complicated and most of it is in my eyes simply unneccessary. There are however many cool tweaks and trick on how to become extremely charismatic and make people just want to stay around you, ask you out, invite you to the right parties to meet the right people. In my eyes, creating the perfect social life that's differently accustomed to everyone, is really something we should all work towards. One of our deepest needs in life is to be able to experience other people, therefore making it really high on the list of our subconscious priorities. These techniques that I'm about to share are definitely a wonderful start and make you see results pretty much on the same day you implement them in your behavioural system. In order to have this work for him, one must be at least somewhat outcome dependant.

First of all, deep eye contact is really important to have. But, if you looked someone in the eyes at all times, it's going to feel a bit weird not just for you, but for the other person as well. Let's be honest – you'll look creepy as fuck. What I advise you to do is to hold eye contact only for about 50% of the entire conversation, switching back and forth whenever you feel like it. If you got something big to explain, then be sure to switch out from time to time and then get back in a few sentences later, but if you're just there to comment on something, to leave a remark, then keep eye contact. It's really difficult to explain this without getting too technical and we already know what's going to happen in result of such action. Humanity will start to diminish and your conversations look robotic, unrealistic and simply unreal. Now you'll know the basic idea and are able to implement it to your style however you feel like it.

Deep down inside I believe we all have built in a so-called "creepometer". We all know when to look someone in the eye, when it's too much to do so, when to look away and not make her uncomfortable and so forth. Some people just put it into use at all times while most of us don't even acknowledge its existance. What this creepometer, a word that I just made up to have a deeper impact on you regarding this topic, does is telling you exactly what's creepy and what would be too much to do. It's like a guide that can make you charismatic, if you let it work for you. First task is to simply find it and this is what my techniques that I explain here, are here to help you with. These tips such as the eye contact thingy that I explained just now are not just something you learn and apply in your behavioural pattern, these are for activating your very own creepometer that naturally goes with your style. We all have it, but only a few of us actually have awaken up to using it effectively. First we need to adopt the behaviour, then move on to calibrating the skill to fit our personality and our own person style. Creating charisma and having good game takes time, it's by no means something you develop overnight, but by making a start towards this goal you'll become a lot better overnight.

Giving a firm handshake is something I've had a hard time with to learn. Funny though, something as easy as this took me years to develop. What are the benefits of a firm handshake? It portrays confidence, it makes you look like you're mentally and physically alive and most importantly – you have a purpose that you're constantly thriving towards. Now here it gets a little bit more situational. Whoever you're talking to whether it's your parents, your girlfriend, friends or just strangers you just met through pickup, notice the speed of their voice, their energy levels and according to that adjust your own to be more relatable. For an example if you're naturally a fast talker and you meet someone who talks like Jack Nicholson, feeling like you need tongs to pull words out of his mouth, then be aware of your own speed and force yourself to talk a bit slower. You'll be more relatable, he will feel more comfortable talking to you and you come across as charismatic.

Being charismatic is not so much about who you are, it's a lot more about how you make others feel around you.

Another great thing to focus on is paying attention to what the other side is fond of, what he or she is talking about, what she's passionate about, what kind of metaphors she's using. If she's a sports fanatic, talk more about sports and make yourself be interested in her subjects. If she loves movies, talk about movies. I belive you get the point. If you were to go fishing, you'd use bait that fish like instead of some strawberry icecream attached to the hook that might be really appealing to you, but not to the fish. You can argue and say you don't like to talk about those subjects and that they are really pointless and a waste of your time. Well, you don't like them? Alright. But are they useless? Most certainly not. If someone likes the subject that you're not fond of, then it's still useful because you can use this specific topic to create common ground with that person and make her like you a lot more. When it comes to topics that you're really obsessed over, then make sure you add her interests in there. Name of the game is to make the things you say relatable to the other person. The idea is not to make the entire conversation about her, an ideal situation is to make it fifty-fifty or at least strive to get close to this proportion. Even coming from the relation of 80-20 and moving to rate of 70-30 will create a massive change and you'll start to experience new levels of connection with another person. A deep connection. After doing this for a while you'll genuinely become interested in other people and don't feel the need to only talk about yourself like, pardon my French, a social retard. If 70-30 will get you amazing results, then imagine what the rate of 50-50 is able to do for you. Movies describe it as true love.

Remember that I do not recommend pretending to be someone else or attempting to change you world views in order to match everyone you meet. The outcome will be confusing and unsettling for others, plus you'll start to lose the feel of being yourself. It's easy to lose your identity through this sort of extreme socially adoptive behaviour. The idea is to be interested. You don't have to agree, but you don't have to disagree either. Think of interactions as two people experiencing each other, that's the whole point of having a conversation in the first place. Every person has at least something in common with you, since we're all humans dealing with similar problems on a daily basis. Find the common piece and bring it into the conversation through topics that can interest the other person and won't be sacrificing your own personal values. The more you talk about your similarities, the warmer she will be towards you. It's not just pickup, it's the whole concept of being a good conversationalist. This shit runs a lot deeper, mate.

Our desire

"Women have value simply for being a woman. Men need to work on themselves to have value. If you switch these two concepts around in your head and fully believe in it, you'll experience a big boost in your game."

We tend to desire people who are way up higher than us. In order to get the ones that are on the next level, we also need to reach their level or higher so they would want us back. Change is always super hard for us, as humans, and admitting our own mistakes is the key component to any successful growth.

For an example, online dating services are full of women who think they deserve a man who has tremendously high value. This is a common belief amongst many women and I run into every single day. Literally. These are also the women who say there are no good men out there and that nobody is equipped well enough to handle them. Here's the thing tho. Men and women are not so different in terms of value. All levels of value exist in both sexes and they're also extremely equal meaning for every 100 guys that are on level 1 there are also 100 women who are exactly on the same level. Men of such lowness struggle to find any woman while woman of this level think they're entitled to something better. It does not matter which level you are at since there is a much more important issue that nobody seems to notice.

We attract what we are.

This is not true for every single interaction and the guy or a girl we run into, but the outcome of our life will always be what we actually deserve to be rewarded with. If you think like shit, then you will be awarded with a shitty life, simple as that. In order to reach higher distances we need to become more. Do you see the connection here? In order to get more we need to become more ourselves to be able to deserve such levels of greatness. In terms of pickup, men just need to figure out in their head that they're the shit and have the mental and character traits to deserve women while women who want to be worthy of a high value guy, must be able to answer with the same. If you get the mind right, then the body, your financial goals, your body shape and everything else will follow anyway.

"If a man's only way of attracting women is by his wealth, then he has failed as a man. If a woman can only attract men by her looks, then she has failed as a woman."

Get the mind right and everything in your life will follow.

Instead of thinking how we can get the higher value guy or a girl we should put our focus on something much more important that will help with this cause much better than any other method. In order to get more, we need to give more. In order to get higher value women we need to become the higher value man and vice versa. Really simple. Everything is a value exchange and we need to be able to respond with the same amount of value of which our desired individual is able to offer us. This is one of the grand truths of pickup and also in life.

Being a pickup artist, an impotant part of this profession is to focus on looking past these common preferences and focus on the fact that women love sex despite what they say or might think they want. Sex is something we all love, but are not always aware of. As an aspiring pickup artist, this fact is essential to understand and focus on creating sexual tension and less on making her logically fall in love with you, since logic and love have a hard time complementing each other. Logic rarely works while focusing on emotions and sexual tension works almost every time. You can talk your way into her sleeping with you, if the attraction is already there, but in order to reach that level one needs to create sexual tension first and make her be aware of you being a man. Women are naturally attracted to men and men are naturally attracted to women. This is the fruit of our evolution. Looking past all external bullshit such as money, looks and even personality, at the end of the day women are attracted to men. In fact, any man. If the society offers a choise, then it's our natural trait to go for the best reward we're able to get, but if a man and a woman were left on a deserted island, regardless of their looks or sexual preferences they'd end up having sex sooner or later.

Why are you talking to her?

"Thoughts become actions. Visible is made from invisible."

I used to believe in the freedom of outcome philosophy. The whole concept of it was glued into the back of my mind and I followed it with all my heart without even questioning it. The whole game of mine got the point of me having no more intentions of sleeping with girls I was talking to, even though I would have loved to have sex. Me being a total beginner, believing in the idea that the guy should not be dependent on the outcome, which is true, but as every other thing – should not be taken to the extreme. I was all out for self-amusement, therefore not giving a fuck about whether the girl likes me or not. Looking back now there were hundreds of girls who would have slept with me right then and there, if I had been a bit more knowledgeable and had some compatibility in my thoughts, knowing exactly why I'm going out in the first place and having a certain goal in mind to which I could strive towards. When you're too damn chill about your outcome, then in most cases it's easy to lose the desire for sex overall. Self-amusement should ideally be an important element of game, but it should never be the main goal. Outcome dependence is not a terrible mindset to have and even has great progress potential if we're talking about improving your game, and it's great for creating strong desire within girls to want to fuck you, but in terms of actually closing the deal and getting laid, it really comes up short.

"Always be thinking about how you're going to close the deal. This thought should be in the back of your head, not there to interrupt your current flow of fun, but also not be ignored."

Whenever you're talking to a woman, chatting her up on your phone, having a conversation at the bar or do pretty much anything that's putting you into interactions with girls, you must have a certain goal in mind, of why you're there to chat her up in the first place. My aim is to always convey value and make her have a great time, which includes having sex with me. I can't even emphasize the point of having a certain goal enough. Having an intention, knowing the direction of where you want to go with the girl and what you're there for in the first place is tremendously important.

Adopting the belief of being free from outcome will definitely help you to not worry about what might happen if you fuck up, it will diminish your approach anxiety and will make you express your own personality quite well, which is extremely suitable for a beginner. The traits that this belief lacks of are not making you focused on pulling, sometimes not even failing to see the right moment to pull due to being distracted by other factors, and failing to notice signs of she wanting to fuck you. There's not much wrong with the belief of freedom of outcome, but only if it's mixed with the intent of having sex and moving towards it as time progresses.

If your mere goal is to only have sex without caring for having fun nor enjoying your time there, then you'll most likely will, but not as much as a guy who's having loads of fun at the same time. Fun is an important component of pickup, which by having will boost your results instantly. Having the intention of wanting sex will help you a lot in terms of getting laid, but if we were to talk about your quality of time that you're spending, then it's not really worth much if you're not enjoying the time you spend getting these things that you wish for. Reaching sex through pickup is a rocky path, you'll feel tremendous amounts of frustration along the way, and that's pretty much guaranteed. Most of all, on the nights on which you're not able to pull, which will present themselves a lot even for advanced guys, you'll end up feeling poorly, which in turn will diminish your levels of enjoyment and fun. As you see, being too dependent on the outcome is certainly not a good way to live. The behaviours that follow this type of mindset also reek of negativity and neediness, which will diminish your chances of getting laid on a bad night even more, therefore preventing you from turning it around. Not focusing on fun and having a severe focus on sleeping with a girl will project neediness, which is unbelievably unattractive. All this being said -what is the right way to approach this matter? How does the mindset of a successful pickup artist look like?

The ultimate mindset to be successful in pickup and also have a fucking blast with all your crazy and fun experiences is to have a **clear intent** of why you're going out, whatever the reason for it might be, and at the same time **enjoy** every little incident leading up to that experience. Do not be frustrated if things don't go the way you planned, but also do not be too indifferent. Go for the goals you set out to achieve, but don't care too much for them for the negative outcome to ruin your mood. It's a paradox and the answer is not completely clear. Ultimately we need both and one cannot exist without the other if you're trying to create a life of your dreams. A great pickup artist cannot operate without fun since his skills being incomplete. At the same time, without having in intent for the night and just partying it up is also not optimal, since you'll even if you're able to attract some females, which you most certainly will be, you will not pull since you lack of intent and will. It is possible to turn on your pickup skills at the end of the night and pull the girl that's having the most fun with you, but the act of getting into that habit of after being an extravagant party animal and fully enjoying your time to put some fun to aside to pull for the majority of guys only works in theory. It's all dependant on your mental state and how well are you able to control and focus yourself even after being stimulated for hours without a cause. This is also where different kinds of styles come into play, which is essential for each and every one of us to find. The greatest value in this book is to show you what's possible and give you different examples of styles so that you could find the one that's the most appealing to your own personal preference.

Regardless of different styles and methods the most optimal way in terms of keeping your happiness in check while also maximizing results is to prioritize fun while also having a certain end result to strive towards. Remember that without having a goal you're like a ship without a destination. If you desire to get girls but don't make it your destination, then you simply won't get there. You might have loads of fun during loafing, but in the end if your desire is to go from New York to Seville, you simply won't get there and get lost in a vortex. Think of the healthy road of pickup that will get you to the ultimate enlightenment as a log that needs to be crossed. Anyone can fall off at any time and fall into the category of either self-amusement which represents drunks and aimless fools while the other side is about diehard pickup which is certainly not fun and is not much different from a regular 9 to 5 job doing something that you hate for someone you don't respect. There are many other disastrous traps that surround this log apart from these two sides, but you will never have to worry about them if you're able to master the skill of mixing chasing your goals that You chose for yourself, with total enjoyment of your time in this world.

The rule I live by is to go out with the intent of having fun. This belief has done wonders with my happiness levels since to me, fun is also having sex. By prioritizing fun I'm having a great time from the beginning untill the end and also reach sex since it falls into the category of fun. I believe this to be the most optimal way to go about pickup. To me having fun is also about making money, working out, eating healthy and having a positive influence on the world. I do not need to force myself to succeed, it's already fun for me to succeed and work towards my dreams. So instead of having a confusing paradox in your hands and debating whether you should dance to have fun or approach a girl to get sex, I offer you this idea. In my eyes it will clear up all the confusion on how to go about setting goals and balancing it with fun. Simply make your work fun so you would not have to worry about it. As you see, this can be applied in every aspect of life and not just pickup.

Step 1: Choose your destination

Step 2: Make the journey fun

If I do these three things and still get rejected

- Approach the girl I like
- Use the "man to woman" type of communication opposed to friend to friend
- I'm adding value to her day by being relaxed, fun and confident while also goal oriented and trying to make something happen by offering her to spend amazing time with me

Then it's not my fault.

It's possible to make some short term changes and see if the girl is just playing hard to get and if so, then adjust your personality, your approach and everything else accordingly, but this kind of approach towards pickup takes an extraordinary amount of energy, will feel fake and even if it doesn't, then you won't feel good doing it. Either way, it's not optimal because it's not real and will be bad for the both of you. Possible, but not adviced unless you're a sex maniac, play the numbers game by being obsessed with your lay counter and prioritize sleeping with girls more than anything else.

As far as this three rule concept goes, I can always try again and approach her some other time because you should never give up untill you see some clear signs of her being unease with you around her, but for that specific moment I've done everything from my part.

By acting based on these three principles and executing them correctly, the girl will see your personality, your state of mind and you being interested in her. If she still rejects you after seeing these three things, then she's aware of you, but cannot accept for some other reason that's not about yourself, but something about her. Don't take it personally. As much as we'd like to believe all girls can be picked up, it's never true, not even in the case of being Leo DiCaprio. It's just not possible.

Usually with nightgame I see many girls who don't want to talk to me in the beginning, which results into some really short conversations or she just pushing me away right off the bat, but after few hours many of these girls will be all over me. You have to take their emotions to an account. Maybe they were still recovering from a rough day they had just then, maybe they were waiting for their date to show up. Either way do not take rejections personally. By conveying these three principles that I just shared in the beginning you've already done most of the job and if she still doesn't like you, look for ways to make small tweaks in your game or just realize that she was really busy doing something else or just in a bad mood. A lot of game is just trial and error. But if you don't approach, then there will be no rejections, but also no results. It's to be loved by some and hated by a few than to be neutral in the eyes of everyone. So just suck the fear up and approach. The rewards are unbearably amazing.

Big Goals vs Small Goals

"We become what we think about."

Since you've gotten this war, then you already know the importance of having big goals, dreaming big and striving towards reaching for the stars. Every person who has ever been great, who has been praised by thousands of people for his or her achievements, have had different perspectives on how one achieves success, but agree on this one specific idea: We are what we think about constantly every single day. Dreaming big is pretty much essential to reach big success whether it's in pickup, with financial goals, fitness or any other area of life that one decides to focus on. Since big dreams, tremendously grand goals and having the will to strive for achievements that many would call impossible according to all the great people who have ever lived are so important, then dreaming small, celebrating birthdays, going to dinner parties, talking to friend and family, enjoying food and everything else that's considered to be minor, seems to be relatively useless when one decides to embark on the journey of becoming one of the greats of his or her generation.

In pickup, a big dream would be to become really good at seducing women, be able to sleep with different high quality girls every single day and also grow as a person through self-development, since this is what pickup eventually leads towards, if one actually follows up on teachings and crosses the mark of being intermediate.

A small dream, equivalent to a simple desire that lasts for only few hours tops, would be to enjoy the evening, take pride and enjoyment in approaching every women including the ones that don't have the capability of a positive response, be happy over being able to hold a conversation with a complete stranger for longer periods of time than before or to simplify – make a little bit of progress every single day and be happy about it. Having small dreams, even just acknowledging these sorts of meaningless occurences, seems utterly pointless and even silly to think about if one has this grand idea, a vast vision of the life that he is about to embark on very soon. Even though having a grand vision and striving for greatness is going to make you successful, it will not make you happy in any shape or form and will most likely embark the individual that's on this path on being addicted to external stimulus and different substances that offer relief without having to spend any energy on getting to that state of higher self on your own.

In order to find the most optimal road to walk on, one must realize how important balancing these two sides really is. In order to live a happy and fulfilling life by becoming successful, it's essential to think big and small at the same time every single day. Think bigger than the day you did before, but at the same time smaller than you did yesterday. If you only think big you'll never set small micro actionable goals. You'll always be lost in big dreams that will take you years if not even more to complete. In other hand, if you think small, then you'll be only thinking about the day that you're currently living in, you'll keep your head too far down and are not able make choises accordingly to create a much better future. There is no "one way" answer. One must apply both and have live them in harmony with each other.

In terms of picking up women, the best mindset to have is to have a goal to enjoy your night by moving in the right direction. One must develop a deep pleasure in improving his game and meeting cool new people by destroying your fears and living life on your terms without letting anxieties control you, and doing this all with a big smile on his face. Now that's a wonderful life. Learning pickup will provide you with the life of your dreams, it will fulfil all your desires if you only choose to experience it for real by letting go of your ego, your perceptions and adopt the ways of enlightenment. All it takes is just that one good night on which you have all the right ideas in place and working in perfect harmony with each other. It will get you hooked on positive stimulus and make you strive towards having success in an instant. Pickup can easily be one of the most positive influence drugs out there.

Balance your big goals by making your grind into pleasure.

Small town

"Don't like the place you're at? Leave."

First of all to make it perfectly clear, I did not grow up in a small town since Tallinn is actually the biggest city in Estonia, however, if you compare it to major superpower cities like London, Paris or Los Angeles, then there is really no competition. Picking up women in a major city will open up many new opportunities, the most important being the fact that the bigger the city, the more girls you're going to see, the more opportunities there are for you to fuck up, streets being full of hot women for tastes of all kind. One of the best parts about living in a really big city is that even if you happen to fuck up your relationships with some women, which you will and that's a hard fact, and by which I mean making really big mistakes that you're embarrassed about, then there is not much to worry about since you're most likely not going to see those women ever again. Big cities also have tons of other guys just like you going up to women, doing their approaches and you will most certainly not be the only one. Here's the deal though. 99% of those guys full out suck. They're terrible. They're disastrous. They're inexperienced. If you're able to distinguish yourself even just a little bit, you'll already be in the top 5 percentage of high value guys. Big city life can be easily compared to the small fish in a big pond model, where you will not be the best guy around since the changes of at least one guy being better than you out of let's say 7 million people is actually quite high. Whereas in a smaller city such as Tallinn with its 400 000 citizens there are not many who practise game and with few years you could literally become the next Hugh Hefner of your own home town. The smaller a city is, the less you have to worry about competition, but at the same time there are less girls, less chances to fuck up and also the mental shift of women is definitely not the same.

Taking action towards approaching women and being the so-called pickup guy in a small town is not really ideal for anyone who's after some great results in the dating game. The smaller the city is, the faster you'll build up a reputation, which is most cases is not optimal and will sink your potential upcoming results to the ground. For an example, a really good friend of mine is from a really small town, around 20 000 citizens.

Ever since he discovered that picking up women is actually really damn realistic, it only took him a few weeks untill he managed to creep out almost every single young woman in the entire village and destroy the chances of them ever hooking up with him. It's not so much about the women not being into him, which was most certainly not the case, but it was about this guy having such a low quality reputation in their small society, therefore girls even if they had been into him, would still not hook up simply because the whole city would look at the girl through the same lenses as well. After a while, after hammering it out even harder throughout endless rejections and being the laughingstock of the whole town, the whole situation got so bad that he literally had to move to a bigger playground. It's very possible to game with everyone knowing who you are and have that fuckboy reputation, girls knowing who you are and what to expect from you, but in order to do some an extremely strong frame is highly required, which is almost impossible to have as a beginner without any reference experiences behind under your belt. Needless to say, for every single beginner a small town for the purposes of pickup is always harder to manage.

Even though moving to a bigger town will bring more opportunities to approach women developing a devastating reputation, the fact you're moving into a bigger playground does not mean you're going to be successful either. Chances are that if you are no successful in a small town, you will not be successful in a big town either. Ultimately this comes down to how small of a place you've got there and the approach you've decided to take regarding pickup, since these kind of differences are one of the key factors and decide whether one should move or not.

I believe you can become successful with dating in any place you could possibly be reading this at this very moment. Despite the high potential of developing a reputation in a small town, especially as a beginner, people ultimately don't really care that much. We are all covered up in our little dramas, problems and anxieties, so paying attention to some guy who's running around the city acting like a pickup artist is the least of their worries. If anything then they're going to be jealous for not having the same drive as you do. No publicity is bad publicity and in the end it all comes down to how you approach this matter. Besides, even if there is someone who has taken high interest in your endeavours, his or her opinion does not even matter simply because of old wisdom from the great Roman emperor Marcus Aurelius – the person who's too engaged in someone else's personal business has no life of their own. Why would you ever be offended or even just listen to a person who is all about criticising the doers, yet does very little to excel themselves.

If you do game in a small town, you'll most likely be the only one. Other guys either don't even know about pickup since this kind of endeavour is not for the lower kind, of those who are less ambitious and are not making the most out of their time. Some of them do know about pickup, but don't want to be shown in a bad light, they don't want to be found out, they don't want to lose their suprise factor. If you're one of these so-called village people, then you could look at your situation as a problem, but in a way it's really an advantage. By the way, women in small towns face the same dilemma – shortage of available men. You're ultimately all in the same boat.

At the end of the day every single place where you can find girls to talk to will imrpove your game. However, if you're serious about pickup, get out of that village, small town or whatever it is, do everything in your power to choose one of the biggest cities you could possibly find in your area or even further, and then pretentiously make the leap of faith. The course of your upcoming life comes down to priorities and goals.

Here's my game

The most advanced pickup artists, if you ask them about the most important thing that we should be focusing on apart from leaving the house, they'll usually say congruence. An alignment with your thoughts, words and actions, all working together for the same purpose. They should be all unified. If you go about meeting girls, most guys do want to get laid, there is no question about it, but at the same time they also want to be accepted by the girl, to get validation from the girl, not have some other guy next to her be mad at you for approaching her, to be accepted by the people around them and by the society as a whole. There are like five different goals right here, therefore the congruence is nowhere to be found. A part of you is promotion oriented, that wants to have fun, but another part of you is prevention oriented which tries to protect you, therefore creating confliction within your thoughts, which transfers into your actions and words, making you seem insecure and not having the stuff sorted out in your head.

Back when I started to adopt the ways to live by from the pickup society, I went through phases that in most cases also many of you will have to face. By having different beliefs and goals, my style changed rapidly from an extravert with self-esteem issues to a socialising introvert with extreme confidence, but little to no will to prove anything to anybody, not even myself, therefore not even doing the required approaches to get laid. At the end of the day it's all about the place where your thoughts and actions are coming from.

When I go out, I go out with the intention of having a really great time. Let me say this again. I want to have a really great fucking time. Every inch in my body is aligned to the very same purpose of having fun. I might say things that piss people off, yet make someone besides me laugh their heart out. When I go out, I'm not worried about my self-image. The whole purpose of me being out there, partying it up, chatting with many different girls and breaking my social barriers, fears, anxieties and whatnot is to have the time of my life. The way how I can have the time of my life is by getting rid of this annoyingly ticklish feeling deep within myself that shows itself every time I feel resistance towards something. Almost every single guy on this planet feels this, since it's our body's survival system, it's a signal just like fear, that's showing us what should be done in terms of growth. Since growth can be really painful and unpleasant in many ways, we tend to think this feeling is there to protect us, which it is, but without adding some logical thinking into this mix of emotions, without having a leader that knows more than our emotions do, without all of this we get caught up in lower consciousness, the type of mindset that's not taking us anywhere in terms of success. One of the main points that we all should be aware of is our emotions like fear and anxiety, unwillingness and laziness being just emotions, which are easily controlled by our brain. Fear and anxiety are just signals that show us the area of which we need to improve in. So when I go out, I do everything that's appealing to me, starting from chatting up random girls to dancing in the middle of a street just because I feel like it, expressing myself and my personality, not giving a fuck about whether I'm being condemned by the society or not. If your goal is to have the time of your life, then social and behavioural freedom are an absolute necessity to have. I do things because I want to, not because it's the right thing to do. Funny enough, if you condition your brain to be on a high level of frequency, then the stuff that you want to do is right anyway.

Now...

It's time to reveal my style, the way I go about picking up girls, the things that I regularly use and that are part of my personality.

Ever since I started to choose my own style, it's been really important for me to mix two things – intensity and the ability to chill. I did succeed. I'm able to be really smooth, laid back, not caring about the outcome and just have lots of fun with the girl by making jokes, dancing, just talking about different tough topics and make them really fun for her so she could forget all her problems. At the same time I'm also able to maintain my intensity, being really intense, reeking of "I know what I want and I'm going to get it" vibe, projecting it through my eye contact, from my "don't give a fuck" body language, able to go in for the kiss any time when I want. When the kiss doesn't work out for whatever reason, I play it off by telling her it's a joke and continue to blabber about other things to take her attention away from my momentarily wrong move. My game is all about being the least attached man in the venue, yet the most engaging. The ability to not care what will happen, therefore not caring for the outcome and having no attachment to the upcoming occurences, yet giving my all to be the most engaging man out there, focusing on making the girl have a great time through interacting with me which will eventually leads to sex. I do give a fuck about the outcome, but I'm also entirely alright with any result as long as I give it my all.

Needless to say I still make mistakes. In fact I make a good portion of mistakes every time I go out with the intention to practise pickup. I used to be worried about action perfect and not fucking up, which made me insecure and really shy, really concerned about the outcome of any interaction. Nowadays I'm just putting myself out there, even at times when in terms of getting laid on that night I really shouldn't, when I realize that the girl I'm currently talking to, would not be into a guy like me. I know who I am and what I represent to the girl. I only spend money on women I really care about, which will take a deep level of connection that does not come easily and overnight. I might lose a few lays, but I will preserve the very same thing I've been working so hard to create – my authenticity, my charisma and my personality. I don't just change for people, I calibrate my actions. I'm never someone who I don't want to be. Famous actors and icons of the last century, Bill Murray and Jack Nicholson have been my role models in developing this exact mindset, by being one of the best actors of all time, able to transform into any character and at the same time still keeping his uniqueness with all trademarks.

My game is smooth, chill and intense – the perfect balance for a dark knight who's pretentiously ambitious. Guys have asked me why did I chose these traits and whether these are the best ones to adopt. The answer is simply: "I don't even care, since it does not matter." It's who I am thanks to all the fucked up experiences and also to all the fantastic times I've had, the movies I've seen, the books I've read, the people I've met and the values I've accumulated throughout my entire life. I've always wanted to be the master of influence from the very same moment I turned fifteen. Game is extremely mythical, full of different paradoxes and unspeakable spirituality. This is who I am. This is what I'll be doing untill I die. This is a big part of my legacy and it's free to be picked up by anybody who's interested in learning the ways of a sly man.

"If it's fun for you, do it."

I don't go out to get laid, I go out to just see what develops. Pickup is my form of art, it's the way I feel the most comfortable and also the most anxious to express myself. Pickup is something that is very scary to me and also the most fun thing for me to do at the same time, which I believe is the very same reason why I'm so bedazzled about it. I don't need to think about sex all the time since I assume every single girl wants to sleep with me and no matter what I do or focus on, they are always there to have fun with me. Is it true? Probably not. But does it help me? Tremendously. I'm completely aware of my blind spots, since I chose to have them for the sake of increasing my results.

"If it's not fun, then what's the point?"

A tremendously big mistake almost every new guy makes is not finishing his battle and giving up early without actually getting any reward out of the effort they put in. The only reason I became really good at pickup extremely fast was because I simply ran out of things to fail in. I tried everything I could think of, field tested every situation and method I could possibly find and ruined more personal relationships that any of my friends have ever had even when put together. I failed my way to success through walking the same road as Thomas Edison achieved his light bulb long time ago.

"I have not failed. I've just found 10,000 ways that won't work.

-T. Edison

It is my belief that failure is the only way to reach success since lessons that actually have the power to stick to you only come from our own experience and our ability to learn from them. We are not able to prepare for every occurrence, so failure is pretty inevitable. This is exactly where pickup becomes extremely handy and also teaches you to handle other areas of your life. It teaches you to handle situations you're not ready for by improving your skills of improvising to achieve a great result instead of having every step planned out and acting like a mechanized robot, which is the opposite of charisma. It's impossible to have every single step in your upcoming life planned out, since there will always be an element of randomness, but if you posess the skill of finding a solution to everything through chaos as pickup teaches, then you have the privilege to own the most expensive skill the world.

How to be a natural pickup artist

In pickup, there is so much crazy shit going on at all times, especially in clubs and bars. No matter in which country you're located in, the nightlife is most likely insane and seemingly surreal. To be in this kind of environment and still be constantly thinking of the pickup theories, why you should approach and even if you do, how will it play out – everything like this when learning the natural game will be completely redundant. In the nightlife environment where you can see the mayhem at every corner, random people making out, girls and guys dancing like maniacs, loud music pumping through your veins and the whole venue being just in total chaos, you will not be able to react fact enough.

A natural pickup artist has developed the ability to enjoy chaos.

We are all social creatures, all human beings are social creatures because this is how we are wired throughout our evolutionary progress. Still to this day we're born in tribes and we live in tribes. A human being needs to socialize in order to succeed in life, whether it's just staying alive or becoming the next Bill Gates, it's one of the most important parts of life overall. No great accomplishment is done alone. If it is, then it's not a great accomplishment. Everything is connected and the more people you're able to connect into your social circle, the more chances you've got of winning. In pickup, no matter how inadequately inexperienced you might be with women, no matter with how many females and people in general you've talked to in your life, at some level you are still able to sense if the interaction between you and the girl is going well or not. Hence we're all social creatures, there is a mechanism inside us that is able to detect danger. In the ancient times, since losing your tribe through not getting along with others was almost a certain death, humans developed a mechanism that will allow us to realize how we're doing with other people. We're ultimately all able to see if the other person is likeable towards us or not, if one learns to notice. We all have this sort of hardwire already inside us, meaning we're all able to realize this on some level or another. It is essential for one to learn the ways of tapping into it more often and use it to our advantage.

Natural game is all about throwing most pickup theories out of the brain, inject yourself with the ideas that help you express your personality without fear and start listening to your gut feeling much more often. Pickup theories are great for beginners since it gives them something adamant and strong to hold on to because of them being blind to social interactions, they've been rejected hard in the past, not having any knowledge on this subject or whatever the case might be, but once you've evolved to a high level, the more you think about getting laid, the less you'll get laid. The more theory you have, the less natural you seem. We all remember those high school womanizers who were getting laid from left and right almost every day while we were jacking off to our perfect imaginary girlfriend. Well, those guys did not practise pickup, they most likely did not even know about its existance. Those guys were out to have fun and sexual intercourse with underage girls was a big part of it in their teenage years. They believed they could, therefore they could.

The last thing you want is to have a mechanized behaviour and look like a freaking robot trying to impregnate a girl from earth for her to give birth to a some kind of an alien freak child. This is not what's going on of course, but this is exactly the vibe you give out if you're too much in your head and don't tap into your feelings to fully experience them by expressing them whenever you feel like it. As funny as this sounds, girls just want a normal guy, which translates into being the kind of a man who is confident and fun. This is what women see as being normal, without some weird pickup lines, without crazy over the top love gestures or anything else like that. Women just want a normal guy who is able to stand on his own and do it well. There are different types of guys out there, but despite our differences in style anyone can be labled as normal if his mind is in the right place. We're all different and by having the freedom to express ourselves freely and also having the right intent, we become the natural.

How to have effective natural game?

Natural game that's also very effective is all about becoming the cool guy who's good with girls, who feels like everything in life is just an experience that cannot be labled as good or bad, and most of all - who does not look at the nights of picking up women as some kind of a task to complete, but focuses on having fun himself. If a guy like this ends up with a girl, then it's just how things went and nothing more. The guy did not go out with an intent to only get laid, he might have had this in the back of his head as a side goal, but the overall focus was all on having fun.

A guy with natural game will go out, have fun and then will fuck a woman that he's fond of. There is no judgement, there is no anger, it's all about enjoying your time and being the cool, chill and engaging guy who girls could enjoy being around.

Natural game concept itself always explains that there are no techniques to learn since having specific techniques is not natural, it's mechanic and overly technical. In order to come off as a natural guy who is sex worthy and doesn't look like a pickup artist, you need to adapt these two traits. Be able to create fun and stay chill in the process.

To be fun, just do whatever you feel like doing and stimulate girls around you by giving them positive emotions and not take life as seriously as we're thought to see it. I live by the rule of if it already happened, then I might as well make fun of it. Some say it's disrespectful, rude and an asshole'ish thing to do, but I'd rather be all that than unhappy. Everything is just how we see it to be. It's the healthiest mindset to have about everything in life and is a solid foundation of happiness that will not be easily broken.

In order to be chill, the wise thing to do would be to check out the work of spiritual gurus such as Osho and Eckhart Tolle, since all these guys do is teach becoming chill and really present to the moment, absorbing everything around you without spending any energy on being judgemental and just going with the flow while feeling the vibe and truly enjoying every single moment we come across. It's the art of not giving a shit and enjoying every single occurrence, idea and every person that comes into the life of yours and seeing everything as a positive experience. The recipe of a healthy and enjoyable life.

A flawless natural is someone who enjoys life and loves to share their experience with the girls. A flawless natural is by any means not flawless and does make many mistakes, especially in terms of game, but since he is okay with his mistakes, knows they'll happen and accepts it, then that right there is what makes him flawless. There are no flaws, because there is no judgement and you won't come off as critical nor judgemental, you'll just be there for the girl to experience, you'll have that crazy attention drawing energy that just rubs off you and the girls want to sleep with your without you even doing anything.

Jack Nicholson, one of the greatest womanizers of all time, has mastered this idea perfectly. If you look at his style, you do not see any signs of using game, he is most definitely not a pickup artist nor does he not appear to be one. Yet, he is able to attract tons of women. Why is it so? Is it his money, or his looks, or his slow toned deep voice? The mere reason why he is getting these sorts of great results is because he looks real and totally in the heat of a moment, everything else that were just described are a bonus and nothing more. Jack looks authentic, he is someone who has his shit together and who just pulls you into his own world by just saying a few words, sometimes all it takes is just being around him. It's his masculine energy, that confidence and freedom. Jack's reality is so strong that one has no other choise than to just be drawn into it. Now that's a fucking flawless natural right there. No game, no techniques nor different methods, just authenticity and realness.

Relationship or Game?

"Masculine energy is about freedom, female energy us about trapping the masculine energy. By being trapped, masculine energy loses its power and attraction. Both parties contradict each other."

When I met my first girlfriend, the one with who I spent an entire year together, who moved in with me and who really had the ability to light up my day at any given moment whenever I felt down. We had a wonderful year together and really enjoyed each other's company. We constantly said to ourselves that we're in love. And we were. Truly. Yet, it does not matter how great your partner might be, if you're not fully commited to yourself and your dreams. The truest love that could ever be is the one that one have for himself. We are here to experience life, and if this ability is taken away from us, then one is unable to do successfully so no matter who is standing by him. It's the respect for yourself to not sacrifice own personal enjoyment for something that's not as valuable as yourself, and nothing ever is. Once, when an aspiring individual realizes this, he'll become something more than just a pawn. He'll be a king, of his own path.

My first strong relationship was really great with the exception of a grand dysfunction that eventually poisoned our bond. It was the result of me nothing being completely upfront with the girl I loved from the very moment I started dating her. As a pickup artist, the guy who's devoting hours of time every single day into learning the ways of being able to sleep with as many different high quality women as possible, acquiring information through books and video programs is not merely enough. The guy who wants to call himself a professional, also needs to live the life he's projecting on others and step out of this status of being a theory nerd.

Being in a committed relationship, it came to my attention that in order to have a successful partnership both parties should not go around and have sex with other people. It's not the traditional way. Therefore I quit going out, I quit flirting all together and became fully devoted on my girlfriend. I sacrificed my path that I had set out for myself to walk on to be with the woman I loved. Since picking up women was the thing I loved to do the most in my entire life, it gave me a sense of purpose, it teached me to enjoy life and be free just as masculine energy is supposed to be, not being able to practise the things that I preached and setting limitations on my dreams and controlling my desires began poisoning me from the inside. It was eating my heart out. I was alive, but I was not living. This life was unbearable for me, therefore I picked the rope up from where I left it and started going out once again, slowly in the beginning, flirting with women, getting sexual and kissing them, although not going all the way to sex. In my eyes that would have been cheating. There was a distinction with my congruence. My thoughts, words and actions were not all out for the same purpose as they usually should be. When your thoughts, words and actions don't go together, then you'll have a serious identity crisis at your hands.

One should always be very clear about his or her purpose. One needs to find out what his or her purpose in life could be. It does not have to be some grand and spiritual reason for you to live, the universe does not have to tell you anything as spiritual gurus often love to preach. Your life purpose is merely a choice that you'll make. Ask yourself what you want to do in life, what your perfect life would look like and start adjusting your current lifestyle accordingly to reach that point someday. It's not even hard, the majority is just too lazy to get busy on themselves. Most of us never realize the true power of devoting their life to themselves. For an example, my purpose that I've set out for myself is to enjoy my life to the fullest, which to me is becoming the best version of myself and empowering others around me for them to also have a better life just as me. I'm very clear about my purpose. The road I've decided to embark on in order to move towards accomplishing it, at least for right now, is through teaching guys who are in a weak position to be able to become a high value guy and learn the ways of interacting with the opposite sex. In order to do so, I must be a professional. In order to be a professional, I must live the life I'm here to teach. In order to live the life, I must follow my passion and not be in a committed relationship. In my case, monogamy is death, mentally and soon to be physically. The man who does not have a purpose or even worse, has one but completely ignores it, has really low value and he himself can feel it at all times. For someone like me, a committed relationship would be sacrificing my own personal enjoyment of life. This is a fact and it's not worth it.

Girls love a guy with a vision and purpose. Even though they'll try to trap you since female energy is all about trapping the masculine energy, it's not what they truly want. Men love to conquer and women love to conquer as well, but their form of conquering is being conquered, therefore once they're conquered, they're looking for new challenges.

Masculine energy is about being free, female energy is about trapping its freedom. When both parties get what they want, they'll lose attraction. It's kind of a paradox. In order to be happy, one must be on the right track. The result won't bring happiness, but the act of being on the right path will.

Your partner can either be an anchor or a booster. If your woman's vision is too small, if you can't bring her into your own life, onto your own path as a supportive character, if you're unable to share your world with her without becoming something she wants you to be, then find another woman. Be clear with your intent, be clear about your purpose. If your partner cannot accept that, then he or she is not right for you. It's an endless rat race that in order to be happy, must be accepted.

There is always a fine reason why anyone would emerge himself into learning pickup. It's either to find a girlfriend, to be able to sleep with a girl, to feel enough, to be respected by others... The list is long, and every single reason on can be tracked to one simple desire. We crave for happiness. I for an example had a strong desire to find a girlfriend, which I did. This feeling soon enough was replaced by having a new urge to improve my game and become the guy most women would love and respect, which in the end all came back to being able to respect and love myself. We tend to work on making others love us so we would be able to love ourselves, untill we realize it does not work that way. If you don't love yourself, others won't love you either and if others do love you, you will still not be able to love yourself since you don't love yourself.

"The girl loves that you're on your path. By coming off from it she'll slowly lose attraction."

One can't just reach the higher level of consciousness by fixing inner problems without trying to fix them first from outside. Even if one understands the concept of nothing else having the power to fix your life but you, he'll still must go through the process of finding that out for himself, therefore self-development, external, will be a necessity. We learn the most from our own actions.

Be completely honest with yourself. If it happens to be in your best interests to experiment, flirt with different girls every day, not be commited to anyone and just explore your options to get a feel for what you really like, then don't get into a commited relationship no matter how great the girl might be. There is only one outcome, which is a waste of precious time, which is spent locking yourself into a can and not coming out before one wakes up and realizes this very same thing. The concept of relationships is one of my most overlooked parts of whole dating advice, since guys find this hard to believe, but everyone who have gone through the path of getting a girlfriend not out of abundance, but out of scarcity, will turn soft, become bitter and break up at some point in one way or the other. It's good to have hard and painful experiences from which you can learn from, but I'm here to offer you a shortcut by telling you exactly how it's going to be, so when you're going through it yourself, you can look back at my advice and realize I was right, therefore making it easier to cope with breakup and move on to bigger and better things. The first woman you meet is rarely the right one. I'll take the liberty of saying it's never the right one. There are tons of people who won't agree with me on this subject, but this is my hard, deeply learned and also experienced lesson that I've stumbled upon by making this mistake more than just once.

As far as relationships go, you're pretty much embarking on a free ground. By implementing this mindset and wisdom that's being brainwashed into you by this book you don't even need any advice on how to keep a girl, how to entertain her so she would not cheat on you and how to act if she does. If a woman leaves you, it's no problem at all since you'll have these skillsets of meeting a new potential mate every single time you step out of the house, or even through online. Besides, being a man of purpose and with pickup skills, you'll realize how dating works, get a good idea on how the female mind works and know what to do without looking for any marriage counsellors or psychologists. Being a man of purpose, women rarely want to leave you anyway, unless they have a solid reason.

The Reason Why You Should Break Up With Your Partner RIGHT NOW

"It's a necessity to visit both ends of the spectrum to know what you're talking about."

Like so many of us, I used to be a major fast food junkie. I really loved to eat all kinds of shit, since it made me feel good. Whether my parents asked why I'm putting so much junk into my body, I always had the same answer: "It tastes good!" We eat food that tastes good simply because it makes us feel good. Fast food gave me the ability to cope with the horrors of everyday life, which at that point were huge. Fast food made me feel sane, it made me be happier, and it helped me deal with the stress, which is all good! The bad thing is that my health levels were going down, I could not handle anything that made me sweat, my mindset was really shitty due to the energy that I put in my body being shit, therefore my grades were dropping, I did not have any ambitions and was setting myself up for failure.

Long story short – fast food made it a bit easier to cope with life, it gave me some sort of satisfaction and took away some daily pain that was forced on me from reality by giving short term pleasure for long term failure. Although, I probably would have never embarked on this journey of self-discovery and self-empowerment if I hadn't been at the bottom. Therefore I cannot really look at it as a negative, but more of a necessity. How would anyone really know what's good and bad without having both sides tested out on themselves. Anybody who hasn't lived the life they're talking about is simply inadequate to teach. Don't tell me working out and being in shape is good, if you haven't been out of shape yourself and seen the other end of the spectrum. Same goes vice versa.

Exactly the same thing with me trying to pick up jogging, long distance running. Instead of withstanding and giving my all to become better at sports, to make myself stronger and more endurable, I used to quit right when it started to get hard, therefore making very little progress, not losing any weight and pretentiously staying in the same spot for almost two years due to not training hard enough. Sure, it was easier, but if I had pushed harder and gave better food for my body and mind to think more clearly to see this sooner, I'd had been much better off in terms of feeling like a king, feeling like being able to take on the world, having high self-esteem, being confidence and attracting good things to come in my way in general. As the late Greg Plitt used to say:

"A small ounce of pain produces a lifetime of pride."

You can either feel shitty for your entire life, or feel very shitty for an extremely short period of your life and going through it begin to live like a king. Which one does sounds better to you?

Some substances such as heroin are so obvious, since we all know heroin is really bad for our health in every single way. We all know drugs can get us tremendously high, giving something for a brief moment, but they're going to take from us in the long run. But, what about those negative substances that are really subtle? I'm talking about the things that take more from you than they give, but since they are doing it so slowly that we simply don't notice it. I'm talking about the things with which the timeline of influence is more stretched out, so it's harder to see the effects. The easiest example for me to give is to use hair growth. We don't see it, but it's happening all the time, untill, at one point we realise how long our hair really is. I like this call this concept poison dripping, slowly killing us, and we don't even notice it once the whole bath water has been replaced by poison that has been dripping for the past five years. With heroin, you'll see how fucked up your life will be within months, but with things such as bad relationships and useless habits, they do not necessarily hurt you right away, but they are slowly digging a grave maybe not for you, but for your dreams, your upcoming accomplishments and your future happiness.

Unhealthy food, unhealthy personal relationships, unhealthy emotions, unhealthy social influences, unhealthy habits – there is no obvious way of telling that these are hurting you, therefore you can't effectively tell right away. These are literally little drips of poison in our everyday life that eventually add up and kill us in one way of another. If it was something major such as heroin, alcohol or an extremely abusive parent, there is an easy way of getting rid of them, so to say "chopping the head off a dragon", but if they're small and hardly noticeable, then it's really difficult to see the harm they're causing untill on that one day you realize how fucked up your life has been, midlife crisis and all that.

The essence of getting tricked by these poison drips is that some kind of a person or any type of external influence comes into your life and in your mind you think he or she or it will provide you with some type of satisfaction, relief, help or good emotions. By choosing to intertwine yourself with this person or substance or influence or whatever it is, you're actually losing your ability to remove yourself from, for an example, this person, because you become dependent on that same individual. Let's take any sort of candy. For most of us, it tastes really damn good. Let's also say you bought it while it was on a discounted price. What your brain does is it starts to make rationalizations on why you should eat it.

It's cheap, therefore you're saving money. It's sweet and tasty, therefore you're going to enjoy eating it. You've been working out hard in the past few days, therefore you deserve it. Now what starts to happen with you is that you literally become dumber, since your willpower levels are going down, you're telling your brain that it's okay to eat candy, therefore increasing the chances of you also buying it the next time, therefore slowly becoming fat and obese without even realising. When you get fat, then it lowers your self-esteem. So imagine yourself being really over the top fat, having no willpower and low self-esteem, so to be able to get off from eating this junk food you'd have to feel really shitty for a long time to develop this new habit of eating healthy. You'd be just doing so bad at life that candy is the one thing that would provide relief, which makes it really easy for you to quit the diet at any point. What happened in this case is that you made the decision to partner up with candy, you're getting short-term pleasure and candy is slowly taking your life over by making you invest more energy towards it and starting to control your life. Your work will suffer, your relationships will suffer and everything will start going downhill. Basically, you're developing an addiction to negative stimulus that will destroy you in the long run in return for short-term pleasure that you don't even fully enjoy anymore since deep down you have this feeling of knowing that you have messed up. You're trading your life for negative addiction towards something shitty and guilt will follow. Maybe back in the day you used to read many books, and now, you've lost your willpower, you're focusing more on short-term pleasure and totally have lost the interest in books. Now that does not sound good at all.

How could this be happening? How could I have never known about this?

You did not know about it because of one basic delusion. You thought of yourself as this independent island, who does not get affected by the outside world. This is not the reality.

Think of yourself as a cell who has different influences coming through the membrane into you, but at the same time you're also influencing the outside world by giving some sort of input, which is really insignificant, but still something. The outside world has an effect on you, and you have an effect on the outside world.

To be completely aware of this and actually do something to fix these small factors in your life for the most optimal outcome, ask yourself this serious question: What foods should you partner up with? Should you pick something that tastes really good for a moment and is cheaper, but ends up as your body fat that will look and feel absolutely terrible and that's really hard to lose, or should you partner up with healthy foods?

Should you partner up with friends, who bring you up, or friends who bring you down?

Should you partner with emotions patterns, that eventually become addictions that are positive or with the ones that are negative?

Which ideas should you partner up with?

What kind of a guy or a girl are you going to partner up with?

Poison dripping within a relationship is an evolutionary thing, it's built in ourselves as men and women to get what we want. Men do it to women and women do it to men. Is it important for you to understand how this works? Fuck yes! Figuring out the ways of how men and women think, what makes them attracted to each other and how this whole concept of relationship works is essential regardless of your path in life. One could be the guy curing cancer or in the middle of creating a spaceship that will eventually fly us all to Mars, and completely blow the chances of it ever happening, because failure to understand these sorts of principles of what creates attraction and what women are really all about caused him to get attached to a girl who did not feel the same way, and be eventually pushed off his glorious path or so-called destiny, if you will. But, if you know and eventually understand the entire process of our psychology, you can avoid falling downhill.

The way men do the poison dripping on women is women's femininity is supported by their environment. Men are quite insecure when it comes to women, meaning their goal is to trap the woman and make her "his slave". A man doesn't like to see the girl go out and her girl-and guyfriends, dance with them and have fun, since man is scared of losing her to someone else. This happens especially when we believe we're in love, which makes us off-puttingly needy. A man gets insecure when his woman has a social life, has many cool girlfriends to hang out with, does cool things such as clubbing and camping and so forth. To summarize it all up, a man will be insecure when his partner is engaging in activities that does not revolve around him. A man works really hard to make her slowly ditch her social life and become the so-called house wife, who he could just have sex with whenever he wants to and to keep her around for housework. Men need the feeling of accomplishment, of being able to conquer a woman and then add her to the collection on their wall, figuratively of course. Men try to alienate women from all that so they could get all the attention. But then, when a man gets what he wants, he will lose all the attraction that made him approach that woman in the first place, which is followed by whining and complaining, because she's not that cool independent woman anymore.

A man tries slowly, without even realising, to make women to be available for him only. When his able to achieve this, they'll lose attraction and get bored, to which follows whining and complaining about the girl not being interesting or outgoing, and just being plain out boring for his taste. It's just like creating a painting by yourself, and then crying about it not being the way you wanted it to be. We are extremely counterintuitive beings, both men and women. We think we desire something, but in reality by getting closer to it, our attraction towards that special someone starts to fade. The more we win, the less we appreciate winning.

If you happen to find the right relationship, the one that's specifically tailored for your own needs and desires, then you'll be able to live the life that would otherwise with an incompetent partner not be possible, such as an open relationship, having regular threesomes with her friends, or it could be a monogamous relationship. The options are almost limitless and yours to choose from. Relationships with the right people can support you in ways of which you will never understand before actually being in a healthy one yourself. I personally know many people who have accomplished massive amounts by being in a relationship, that's not what I'm against at all. Relationships can be really powerful, but like most things in life, there are tons of people who fail at them.

Real answers

Do you think your women wants you to make millions of dollars? Do you think your women wants you to be really fit and attractive? Do you think your women wants you to be confident, powerful and charismatic?

The answer is in most cases a hard "No".

This seems very counterintuitive. You'd think that girls like money and good-looking guys, so they want you to look good by going to the gym and make money. In my experience, this is really against the agenda of most women in relationships. Sure, they all want a guy with those traits before actually being in a relationship with one, but after they've achieved it, most women will try to bring the guy down to their level. If both of you, the girl who you're in relationship with and you, start on the same level, and suddenly you become this badass guy who is winning in life and starts growing like mad whereas the girl is most likely staying to be the same and has hard time catching up. As you start to win at life, your entire state of being will go up and you'll start to be much more attractive, positive, outgoing and leader-like. It just becomes and upwards spiral. If you're winning at life and you know it, your self-esteem and confidence will be high and as a guy, you will naturally start approaching random women simply because you feel great and that's what men's psychology tells them to do when they're in such state. Men are built to never be satisfied with one women, unless they've been brainwashed by that one women to think that she's the one, or they're too weak to actually go for things that they want in life. Do you know how many guys masturbate despite having a functional wife? Literally 99,99% of them! This is not because they do not like their women, it's mainly because they are not satisfied with one for the rest of their life. The only man who does not cheat on his wife is the one that has accepted being sad and not living life to the fullest. Sad, but true.

As a man, by approaching many different women, my mind begins to open up, I become more creative and much happier because I'm pretentiously fulfilling my real evolutionary desires as a man. I just keep getting better and better and the quality of women I'm hanging around with, will increase.

Now going back to the married man, when his woman sees him becoming this winner and growing much faster than her, she, without even realising, starts to poison the man by trying to project beta qualities on him by using sentences such as:

"I love your big belly! It's so cute!"

"You don't need to work out, you're not fat at all."

"Oh I love that you have a hobby and play video games! You should enjoy yourself more often!"

"Don't go out today, stay in with me and let's watch a movie."

"Please skip going to the club just for today and stay in with me. I want to spend time with you."

In conclusion, whenever a man's state goes higher than woman's, she will find it hard relating to him since the girl is not there on that level yet herself, therefore she becomes insecure and is afraid of losing him to someone of higher quality that her, therefore she unknowingly tries to take him down to her level and making rationalizations such as the man not spending enough time with her, man being too caught up on work, man becoming too obsessed with fitness and gym and so on. She makes you feel like you're ignoring her, you don't love her and you're not caring for her enough. She makes you think you're a bad husband or a bad boyfriend. Even when you finally decide to take her out to an event with some really cool people that you had the privilege to know thanks to your efforts in self-development, and who are above her level, she'll be just pouting in a corner. She won't get along with you, nor your lifestyle.

In the other hand, if you're starting to fall on a lower level than her, for instance maybe you got fired, became overly fat, are not satisfied with your life or fail to be happy and so on, the woman will become more supportive. Our partners, even friends and family are incredibly supportive when you're doing badly, but when you're doing well, they'll get scared because they feel like they're losing you to a better crowd, to a better life. Nobody wants to be left behind.

By being poison dripped little by little every day, the new reality becomes your reality without you even realising why you're feeling so down, and you forget what it's like to feel amazing again. We wake up one day and realize how we've been wasting the majority of our lives. This is why so many of us don't understand why they're unhappy. We've forgot how to feel great again just as in childhood. As a child, we all feel great, playing on the playground with fellow kids, having the time of our life, whereas our parents poison drip us by changing out values and making us bitter, not because they're bad people, but because they're human, and as humans we're stupid and could not even be educated on all matters of life even if we wanted to because there is so much information and so little time. Needless to say, there is an extremely small chance of your parents realising how to effectively raise a child to be a "super human", always happy and at the same time really successful in life. Instead, the people who're successful, usually have some kind of a complex, anger, guilt or need to prove something to someone, and therefore work their ass off and become really successful. Yes, it may look great outside, but inside, many of them are just kids that have been badly hurt. When one operates on a lower level on consciousness, it's not possible to have a great life no matter how it might look externally.

The reason why we're doing this, poisoning each other unconsciously depending on who's growing and who's not, is because that slow poison drip is designed to erode your mental state. If a guy's state gets eroded by his girlfriend or wife, he is unable to go and sleep with other women. It's basically just a form of protection for the other half against not being left alone.

The only way how a relationship can ever be healthy is by two sides GROWING TOGETHER, without exceptions. If one of you gets left behind, the other one must realise it by being aware of this entire concept and help his or her partner to reach your level. If she cannot follow, then she will destroy you whether she wants it or not due to being a human. If she is able to climb with you, or even higher and then help you up too, then you two should stay together for sure. This case however is literally one in a million. Most marriages don't work out. Most relationships don't work out, or if they do, then the couple has been unhappy for a long time. If you look at our world, then how many people actually climb and do really amazing things with their lives? How many Steve Jobs' are there? How many Einstein's are there? Not many. Most of us are poison dripping each other, therefore keeping each other from growing just to save ourselves from the pain of breaking up and stepping outside of our comfort zone.

So many of us are in a bad relationship without even realising it. Our partners are killing us piece by piece every single day and then, one day, we wake up and realise how much we've actually missed in exchange for being with the guy or girl we love. People like to glorify staying married for a long time and taking one for the team so to say, but in reality it's one of the most stupid things you could ever do in your entire life. There is nothing glorifying in finding an excuse to not work on yourself and stay together with the same person because it's a path that you already know, therefore it being easier. The only way to be free and live a life of awesomeness, one must rethink his or her choises, realise whether they're getting more than giving, and really be rational about it from an individual standpoint. After all, if a guy is giving up your dreams just to raise a child with some bitch who chose to have sex with him out of desperation or any other negative reason, and him being too weak to dump her and find someone who's more suitable for his goals, it's not really a good life now is it? Your partner should be helping you reach your life goals instead of being one of them. If you make your girlfriend or your boyfriend to be as important as your own life, you've already failed. Ultimately, if you do happen to choose a woman over yourself, then your partner will lose attraction towards you regardless, since you've given up on yourself as an individual.

For most of us, after we've broken up with someone, we get this instant urge to get back together with her. This feeling takes place merely because that's the easy thing to for us emotionally, since our mental support system does not want to go through the pain of breakup. In the end, the pain is what makes us grow and a person and will take us to the higher levels of life, if we choose to let it. A little bit of pain produces a lifetime of pride. Think of your own relationship, either with sexual partners, friends or just foods and habits and emotions, see what's working, see what's helping you and make the right choise, which is not always the easy one. Ultimately we all know what's right and wrong for us, it's just damn hard to admit it thanks to our ego trying to protect his identity and forcing us to not let go of the idea that it has created for ourselves. Realizing that the stories we have of ourselves, the ideas of which we think we can and can't do are actually really inaccurate and that we've been living in a lie this whole time is really scary. Ignorance is bliss.

"It's easy to break up with someone, when you realize this relationship is toxic not just for yourself, but also for the other person. Then it's not just about you anymore, but about the well-being of both parties."

As far as real and healthy relationships go, if you're a person looking for something long term, then do not put up any type of front. Don't worry about whether the girl is attracted to you or not, don't even indulge into the small ounces of pickup. Use the knowledge, but do not worry about it. If the girl does not like you for you with all the plusses and minuses, then there is no point in wanting her. A relationship is supposed to be your personal safe space, where you're able to rewind and relax after a long day of beastmode. You should feel comfortable in your underwear, having a mess all over the room while your perfect girl is walking in. That's the sign of a healthy relationship. Also, it's important to make sure that she has a purpose in life as well other than you. David Deida has said that a man's purpose must be being successful in life, whereas a girl's purpose must be the supporting the man. There is a certain element of truth in it, but for a successful and happy life for both sides, a woman should also have something going on for her life aside from supporting her man. She has to have a purpose of her own, despite what any other lifestyle or dating guru might say. As one goes through different levels of higher consciousness, he'll come to this realisation eventually.

The Magic Pill: Part Two

"The negative attitudes start to decompose once action is taken. Sometimes, to get on the other side, you just have to push through it by using hard force."

To a guy who's into pickup no matter the stage he's in, whether it's beginner or advanced, there is nothing more harmful than the pickup artist batting average. This whole concept is about calculating how many approaches does it take to get laid, how many women have you slept with, how many more women do I have to talk with to reach the lay count of a hundred, how long does it take to sleep with hundred girls or even just one girl for that being and so forth. All of these sound like fair questions. Most men and women would love to know the answers, especially the guys that are just starting out in their pickup journey or are on their way of crossing that line for the first time. To know exactly how many women do you have to socialise with in order to reach sex gives you a specific game plan that you could follow. It's like having a precise goal, and by having one your journey will be much simpler. Guys who ask this question with a serious intent of actually finding out the exact number, are either beginners or are not into pickup at all, since approaching is work and it's smart to minimise your energy output and not do any more than you have to, and at the same time get the maximum reward possible. We would love to study the method that would let you have to approach the least number and have the most sex possible. After all, who wouldn't want to work less and get more? It's our wet dream. Sounds great, right. This is exactly what people want. The quick fix. The magic pill. Because having to approach tons and tons of women all the time is not even skill, it's just a numbers game that everyone are able to do.

I'll be completely honest and tell you how most nights go, even if you're a really wonderful PUA by using the example of myself. Usually I go out, talk to a ton of people, socialise and have loads of fun. I talk to lots of different girls and have more fun than I ever could have sitting at home in whoever's company. Most nights I'll probably make out with many different girls, get numbers, both solid and flaky that I will try anyway just for the sake of trying. Sometimes I get laid only a couple of times in a month. Sometimes I have a dry spell for months where I don't get laid at all. This result just plays out this way and there are several reasons for this. Maybe I'm busy with work, maybe I'm not feeling good, maybe I'm having crossroads in life and can't figure out what I want, maybe I'm just going out to dance and don't care much for pulling girls so I don't focus on it. Maybe I'm spending time with a girl who really wants to fuck me, but I have to get up early and have to ditch her. Maybe I'm busy enough the next day and won't call her, so the attraction just dies out due to not throwing any logs into the fire. Or, I might be on a run, where everything in my life is going great, business is doing well, I'm eating healthy and just feeling like I'm on the top of things. On those periods I might get laid at least five times per week, since I'm in the right mood and have the time to be able to bang it out. Some nights, when I'm feeling like an absolute king right away without having the need of warming up to socialising, I'll go out and have sex with the first girl I meet in the matter of minutes. Then there are some nights where I hammer it out for seven hours without any solid results. I might be tired, in a bad mood, frustrated like no other, but I will not give up. Sometimes it still doesn't work out even if you don't give up. That's life. There is an element of randomness in pickup, there are tons of factors that are out of your control. In the beginning I claimed that I'm able to have sex every single night, which is true, but it's true only if I'm fully submerged in it, if every inch of my body is focused on picking up a woman of my liking and if I throw everything else such as work, health and sometimes even fun to the background. I'm talking about the periods where I'm fully launched into pickup. Those are the times when I'm able to pull every single night. When my heart is not totally in it, then the chances of going home alone have tremendously increased, and not because of my skill level, but because of my desire and the lack of willingness to succeed.

The periods of relapse are a big part of the journey. They're not negative, they're transformational and in the end will skyrocket you to new and higher levels than you operated in before. It's not a straight line, it's rocky. Since they're going to happen either way, then we should might as well enjoy them.

The reason why the pickup batting average has destroyed the sex lives of so many guys is because this sort of belief forces you into a negative frame of thinking, which includes having ideas such as you don't like socialising and you want everyone to like you. Those people who look at the numbers rather than focusing on the vibe and feelings and being present to the moment, fail to realize that socialising is extremely fun and a key part of pickup. Pickup can be defined differently depending on who we ask, but there is only one healthy way of seeing it without actually fucking up your mental state.

The healthy definition of pickup is learning how to have fun and be free with social interactions while getting sex as a byproduct of that.

If I was only out for sex, I would just keep messaging my fuck buddies and not even leave the house at all. Luckily this is not what I'm about, since this is not what life is about, at least not to me. I'm a firm believer that life is what you want it to be, but we have to admit some options are just better than others. This is one of them. Sex is not the prize, it's a bonus. Freedom and fun are the real prize.

I pick up women because it's fun. The pure fact of it being fun is going to get you laid. If you don't find socialising fun, then you do not find life to be fun. Socialising is a big part of our culture, it's how we've survived for so long. Socialising is written all up in our genetic code, it's who we all ultimately are. If anyone happens to be denying this, then he or she is being bitter and is also struggling with the idea of enjoying life to the fullest as we're designed to. You can either believe some dark marketer who sells you a product that supposedly teaches you how to manipulate women into sleeping with you only to realize that you will become even unhappier than before, or you can learn it the right way, through acceptance. The road is long, the road is hard and it will test you more than you could imagine. But everything that you're going through, is worth going through.

Most guys reading this right now don't feel comfortable learning this. Most guys want to stay in their little cave, play World Of Warcraft and stay in their comfort zone. That's perfectly fine if you really want that for yourself, but the thing you have to realize is there ain't no other shortcuts other than the small ticks and tips that I talk about in this book. In order to finally be free to socialise, to have fun with other people, to get sex and to become a more powerful human being, these steps cannot be skipped by some manipulation method. It's about who you become throughout the process.

A guy who enjoys socialising will have fun with everybody, especially with himself for expressing his realness and accepts himself the way he is, yet strives to be better by each day. A guy like that is authentic and extremely charismatic. The only reason a guy like this would get rejected is either the girl being really busy with something else so she does not have any time to devote, or her having some serious mental blockages that are keeping her from taking any chances on guys that would actually treat her good. There are many women out there who despise you no matter who you are, which is caused by their own mental disorders, whether they're diagnosed or undiagnosed, big or small, visible to the eye or not. Chemistry between men and women is real, and you're not going to have it with every single woman. You can play on their desires and on the fact that you're a man and she's a woman, and you two are bound to have sex at some point when left alone on a deserted island since that's how our psychology works, and then create that situation where you two could be on this metaphorical island, meaning you can isolate her and play on the biological attributes, but if you're choosing a girlfriend, a wife or just about anyone with who you could spend more than just one night together, then you got to look for the ones that you have chemistry with. If you haven't had many girls in your life, you'll mistake your desires for chemistry, this is why it's essential for you to go out and learn pickup to be able to spot the real woman that's right for you from the extra-large pool of useless candidates.

If you're going to be yourself, then are everyone going to like you? Not in a million years. It takes some serious amount of courage to be the true you. When you start being yourself, then you'll have to accept that some people are going to dislike you and some are going to love you. It's always better to have those who love and hate you instead of surrounding yourself with this grey area where everyone around you are neutral. That's by far one of the worst things we, as humans, could ever do to ourselves. Rather experience the two ends of the spectrum than none at all.

For those of you who are truly eager to find out the best method for achieving everything in life…

Here's your magic pill. Learn to put hard, smart work and fun together by rewiring your neurological patterns and you'll find yourself achieving everything you could ever wish for.

For All of You Who Chase Perfection

If you're a person who's after perfection in your endeavours and who often experiences a lot of stress for not completing the tasks given to you perfectly, then this section is definitely for you.

I am a perfectionist. Everything I do must be completed perfectly. Since my skill set is far from perfection, it's literally impossible to achieve the goals I'm setting up for myself. Here's the thing though – the perfect skill set does not exist, at least not in the way we're expecting it to be. To be perfect in something or even everything means that we do not make any mistakes what so ever. Living without making any mistakes is a pipe dream, because as you know we all make countless mistakes every single day. It's literally gotten to the point where we don't even notice making them.

<u>Let's say you're in college.</u> In this case, perfection would mean that you'll get maximum points in every single test. Possible, but unlikely. No matter how hard you'll study, you will probably mess up at least one thing in a year that will prevent you to get that perfect report card. Maybe you'll decide to go out to meet with your buddies on a new year's eve and end up drinking a few cocktails. Maybe the alcohol you're consuming destroys an important brain cell that will make you lose the point out of a hundred in a test that's happening few days later.

"Perfection is not attainable, but if we chase perfection we can catch excellence." - Vince Lombardi

Okay, let's say this does not happen and your brain cells are all alive and well. But instead of drinking you'll stay up late on the night before the test to study. In result of this you'll get less sleep than your body needs and end up with a fuzzy brain in the morning. This is not an ideal state for you to write your test in and will probably make you lose some points. Let's say this does not happen either and you're in a great state for writing an exam and your groundwork has been the best it can be as far as studying goes. If you keep this up, you'll end up with no hobbies and without a satisfying social life. Yes, you'll achieve your dream for college, but you'll lack in other areas of your life. By lacking in other areas of your life you will not feel good and that's a given. A scientist whose personal life is a complete mess and has many troubles with her relationships will not produce the best work, let alone the perfection.

Now if you were to focus on your personal life, your work will suffer. It's going to be horrible, but it will most certainly not be perfect because you just haven't been spending that much time on it. Priorities. You can always do more and when you do more, you'll get better, but keep in mind that by excelling in one area, another will suffer. Perfection is not realistic. There is no end result, there's just progress. Since perfection means ones skill, endeavour or whatever it might be is entirely completed without shortcomings, and since nothing can ever be fully completed, perfection is unrealistic.

There is a special kind of state that's the closest to perfection. Since it's best we are able to achieve, it can very well be called perfection. Here it is...

The subtle art of curing perfectionism is being okay with your imperfection. Be perfectly fine being imperfect. Achieve perfection by being imperfect. We do not need to do everything right nor should be expected to. It's much more beautiful to fail and then succeed the next time. Failing makes us desire the thing even more, therefore making it even more valuable and worth spending our time on. This is the way how I can still be a perfectionist, just in a different and healthier way. Shift your focus from being always right to always being. It will implement a drastic change in your life and will make living more enjoyable. I live by the rule that I don't need anything, but I should want everything. This will allow me to enjoy everything I have, including my failures aka learning experiences, but in the other hand always strive for more. To me this is the combination of being a perfectionist and also a realist. It's the best place to be at.

"Perfection itself is imperfection."

Vladimir Horowitz

The side effects of success

"Day by day I'm getting more attraction from high-class women and less from low-class. Exact same with friends. This got me thinking on a post that I saw few days ago. The idea of it was that some people just shine too bright and low-class is not capable of accepting such positivity. An interesting thought."

This was the idea that I posted to Facebook a while back. It's the damnedest thing. I've been noticing this kind of shift for a long time now. The more I improve myself, the more specific types of people start to avoid me. I've lost tons of friends, potential relationships and just acquaintances purely for no other reason than this. I've taken the liberty to even ask them why they're avoiding me. The answer goes something like this:

"You've changed."

"I don't know. I just don't feel comfortable with you anymore."

"We don't have much to talk about."

"You're a doushebag."

Sometimes people even just plain out ignore me. I do have many controversial posts under my belt, so it's quite self-explanatory, although the reasoning behind this is much more simple.

One of my most praised mentors, Owen Cook, did a seminar on this very same subject in the beginning of this year. The seminar was purely dedicated on his past, where did he come from, what he was like and how he got to the place he is at now, making millions off teaching guys how to become better with women. Long story short – it's a road from one end of the spectrum to another. Basically, he came from a low guy status and rose up into the 0,1%. It's a "from zero to hero" type of story. The way how this is relevant to what I'm talking about right now is his mindset when he was on his lowest point.

"When someone came up to me with positivity, I could not bear it for any longer than 20 minutes max. It was unbearable for me to stay around

someone like that and I just had a deep urge to leave. But when someone was blaming, badmouthing, criticising either our government, politicians, saying that life is unfair, then I could talk for hours. I could complain for hours."

All these are not exactly his words since I had to pimp these up a bit due to his occasional rambling which goes totally out of context, but you'll get the idea. A person coming from low mentality perspective will not be able to handle much positivity because that's not how he's wired. An individual whose thinking pattern is wired to respond and relate to negativity, then it's no wonder he is unable to get along with people who are all about positive vibes. If that individual was able to handle the positive vibes, if he was able to relate to them, then he would not be in such disastrous life situations. The simple idea of we are what we think about all day long. Negative thoughts produce negative results and vice versa.

"We attract what we are" rule applies here perfectly, which is a big concept of Tony Robbins, the most famous motivational speaker of our time, books such as the Law of Attraction and so forth. For an example, if you're mentally on the 7th level, then you will not connect with people who are on the 3rd level. These two minds are just not wired in the same way and both of you will happen to contradict each other. It's like watching a diehard scientist and a Muslim argue about the origins of our human race. One says it's the cause of evolution, the other way says it is god's will and creation. These two people will not be able to stay in the same room with each other without stepping on a few toes. Almost every single time when such different ends of the spectrum collide, both of these individuals after the conversation is over, are left in a pretty frustrating state.

One day we all have to accept the fact that some people are going to reject us only because we shine too bright for them. And that's okay. Keep on shining. If you're sad about losing your friends and your partner leaving you for the reason of you being out of their class, then all you can do is to find new ones that are on the same level as you. If the tree is growing but the roots aren't working on creating a more solid foundation to hold that tree, then the whole thing is not gonna stay together for very long, the roots will begin to fail and the tree will fall over. The best way to look at it is them having respect for you, and knowing when to get out of your way, bailing out because they realized that they do not have the chops to handle the new you to the point of where the relationship would be healthy and not farfetched.

All relationship whether their friendly or something more are simply a value exchange. If one side stops offering value, then it's out of proportion and soon to be doomed. This is exactly what happened in my case. My old friends and acquaintances stopped offering value to me because they are stuck in their own world that's not growing nor going to anywhere new. A person like me, who's into self-development and dedicates his life on becoming the best version of himself is always expanding, learning new tips and tricks, in other words moving on to new and better things, has no business in hanging out with people who are stuck in their own paradigm, which are not taking them to any great places and only serve the purpose of easing the pain that the world causes. A coping mechanism is not supposed to hang out with a thriving mechanism. These things are no good fit together and will make both sides feel unease.

Keep in mind that I did not ditch anyone from my social circle. Everyone who left from my circle, chose to do so on their own without having any pressure from me. Everyone made their own choise, and this was theirs. Why is that so? Looking at me, seeing me going somewhere with my life, watching me destroy my own comfort zones to grow stronger are all making them feel insecure and left behind. They did not ditch me because I levelled up, they ditched me because they didn't have the strenght to keep up. They did not stop talking to me because I levelled up, they stopped because every time we got together and exchanged a few words, I reminded them of everything they're not, yet could be if actions was taken. I represent a reality check that makes them feel responsible for their own lives.

The idea of you pushing people away on your own will is a sign of operating on a lower consciousness. A person who does that is not acting out of love, but from personal ideas of receiving benefits. It's important to realize when the relationship or friendship is not healthy and should be cut apart, but at the other hand if one does it, then he is not in the state of acceptance and finds the influence coming from other being rather negative. This kind of individual tends to label everyone. As always, the best place to be at is in the middle, not forcing anyone to go in their separate way, but also being aware of who to hang out with and who is really not optimal or worth to be wasting your time on. The person with the highest brain capacity will accept everyone, enjoy everyone's company to some degree and be a person who is not judgemental. The perfect example is Bill Murray, a great American actor. Bill does not spend time with models, buy luxury cars or yachts nor does he have his own high class social circle. Bill travels the world, spends time with folks of all kinds and finds enjoyment from every single experience. He does not judge, he does not condemn, he simply experiences and that's all. Find joy in every single experience, respect people regardless of their success level and realize that this life of ours is here to offer us a mere experience of it. We're here to simply just be.

It's unneccessary to pity the friendships that are lost due to the reason of you shining too bright. These friendships and relationships were forged with wrong people who are no good fit for a wolf, therefore they were lost for a solid reason. A sheep cannot connect with a wolf and will always condemn him, whereas the wolf has his own reasons for being this way. Find new people who are worthy of you, crying over the old ones and thinking of ways on how to connect with them again will always be a step backwards, if you're looking at it from the standpoint of achieving major success. Anyone can learn from anybody, but in order to reach higher grounds in life, the people who we learn from should be filtered to a certain degree of your own choosing.

I'm still not convinced

"The biggest poison in us is regret. It's pure poison."

My business is is something that I really love doing. I teach guys how to seduce women and have an amazing dating life for the rest of their life. More importantly, I teach the healthy version of picking up women. I make people make themselves better through applying the stuff that I teach. I help people improve their own lives and reach levels that they never thought even exist outside of movies. My business is to make people happy.

Deep down we want ourselves to push through the adversity and become the person we always knew we could be. But our emotions, our circumstances and mostly our attitude will get in the way. Later on in life this feeling of "one day" is replaced by regret. In the end we only regret the chances we did not dare to take.

For the sake of your own personal health, if you're looking for major success with women, but feel lost and don't know what to do, or maybe you're already good, but strive to be better...pick up the teachings in this book and let them do the work for you. The path has been laid out in front of you. You just have to follow it.

Soon enough, if you decide to embark on this journey of seduction through self-discovery, are not giving up and keep hitting the iron untill the results that you wished for present themselves, you'll be in the top 0,1% of highly effective people in the world, and not just for developing the skillset of picking up women, but at life in general. Learning the ways of pickup will grant you a skillset that will make you successful also in life. These two concepts go together like bread and butter.

As it states in Eminem's hit song "Lose Yourself", we only have one life, one shot, one oppurtunity to experience life as an epic journey. The journey starts right when one decides to get up, start filling his head with positive vibes and the right kind of knowledge, and for the second and most important part – decides to take action and actually practice what he preaches. Even if by some chance this whole book turns out to be a hoax, if everything in this book turns out to be wrong, the guy who believes in it and takes action will still achieve major success by just adopting the thinking pattern of a wolf, a winner wolf. The power of the ideas in this book are so grand that even if everything turns out to be utter bullshit, then it still holds tremendous value for those who actually adopt these ideas. Life is all about trial and error, this is the most effective way of learning anything and finding out new laws and principles. The ideas in this book are the byproduct of reading biographies of rich, powerful and famous people, learning the reasons that have worked for successful people throughout ages, attending countless seminars of dating and self-development, seeing the patterns in all fields of life and find out that the laws of success in any field are ultimately all the same, and then going out to test them out and realize just how much value do these hold. The things that Socrates teaches, are totally valid to this point. The universal laws that are learned by exposing yourself to the right information and following up on testing them for your own to be convinced in their authenticity. The whole life is ultimately a grand experiment that's individual for each and every one of us. You have absolutely nothing to lose, but you have your whole life left to win.

Some really advanced stuff to destroy your negative emotions

"My goal is to snap you out of social conditioning, realize the truth about what's really going on in the world, and capitalize on it."

During us growing up, most of our ideas and beliefs that define who you are have been socially conditioned. They have been learned. Nobody has been born with a package of knowledge, it's all learned as we go on with our lives. Your drive, the things that you desire are either defined on a subconscious level and can also be directly based on how you grow up. Everything about our want factor has a deeper meaning and can be explained. As human beings we are made to thrive, because doing so requires us to survive. Without having our abilities conditioned to keep us from harm and survive, we would not even be where we are today. Surviving manifests itself in different ways.

When you go back a few thousand years being part of the group was crucial to survive. The result that we have from it is our biology, our DNA has this concept hardwired in us. In ancient times, if you suddenly went back in time, didn't try to fit in and in result of acting so be rejected by a group, you'd be left without support which determined whether a man lived or died. Under those extreme circumstances, unsuitable tough weather and dangerous predators being near, it was essential for anyone to be in a group. This is why the opinions that other people have of us, trying to fit in and by doing so either trying to impress people around us or do the opposite to not be considered as a threat depending on the situation, is something that every single average person holds in their life on a level of importance. It's a way to survive, but not to thrive.

Same principle goes for a tribe. If you're in a tribe and get enough power and authority from the other members, what happens is being the one who doesn't follow orders, but creates them, will make you an alpha male, leader, boss. You will start to lead and taking the people with you in a direction you believe is right. Their entire fate is dependent on the alpha's judgement call. This will affect the tribe and is called social conditioning. You see these kind of people with animal pack mentality everywhere around us in the society. Almost every single person we see if conditioned to be like that. Animals and we, humans, ultimately have the same dynamics, same mechanisms of being able to survive.

The reason why I'm explaining this is because it's really crucial to know these dynamics. Most importantly, understanding the reasoning behind everything allows you to overcome them and alter them in a way it's beneficial for your life. Not everything in our mechanism is still valid and relevant in our time. Many traits that we have, were extremely useful in the old times, when we did not have cities nor civilizations, but are completely dull and irrelevant today. The reason why one could know these things is thanks to the information provided to us by neuroscience and evolutionary biology, which most likely the hold the biggest amount of value in them as far as our species is concerned. One of the biggest problems is when I talk and do my best to explain these sorts of things, for a big part the extent to which you can process this information, the extent to which you're able to really understand this concept is much defined by how much neuron activity you have in the more advanced part of the brain, which is dependent on your lifestyle and your level of subconscious.

I'll start by explaining the big dysfunction that we currently are experiencing every single day.

A lot of people go through life trying to fit in, trying to impress others, trying to live a life that other people want to live. On a subconscious level you really desire to be a part of a bigger group, you really desire to fit in. Being part of the family, friendships or a relationship and so on. These things are really defined by how we grew up.

What I'm trying to explain you here is that all your emotions, everything you experience in your daily life have a reason. Every single emotion you have can be explained, even the most dysfunctional ones. They all have a reason why they happen.

Fear is a big part of our evolution, being able to survive and make decisions which will allow us to endure. When you go back in time and have a certain fear, then it most cases it's necessary to survive. Being afraid of a tiger, another tribe and whatnot. Fear has allowed us to adapt with reality and grow as a species.

As we grew, we became more self-aware and self-conscious, we began to create ideas and concepts thanks to our ability to speak. We began to construct more complex concepts in our brain. It all makes sense.

In times during the Stone Age and around there, when we experienced an occurrence that we could not explain, it brought us a lot of fear. To cope with that fear we created certain concepts to be able to understand what happened, whether it's religion or other advanced spiritual ideas or something else entirely. Every time we found an idea that explained it to us, because when we're able to explain the fear, it allows us to get rid of it.

In a zoo when you see a lion, you might be scared at first, but when you realize that you have glass between you and the animal you suddenly become less afraid. Fear is suddenly gone. Someone pointing a gun at you will trigger fear, but when you realize it's just a toy, the fear will disappear relatively quickly.

We have the ability to overwrite our fears, if we can make ourselves understand what the cause is despite it being either true or false. Everything has a reason, but even by believing in the wrong reason we still offer our brain an explaining and kill that certain fear. For an example god might not exist, but even if we tell ourselves he does and he protects us, many of us still find peace in their mind.

But if you don't have a reason, if you don't know why your fear is there, you will try to find another concept that can cope with it that could process this emotion that comes about with fear, with social conditioning, with love etc. The problem is that this mechanism that I'm explaining to you right now is not something that's flawless. The system is outdated due to our fast paced evolution in the past few thousand years.

When we first came from very primitive beings and then suddenly discovered language and were able to communicate and such, we did not understand why we had all these fast technologies, all these fast developments, all fears that really define life in a really drastic way. On a fundamental level we're still quite primitive. We don't have much understanding. Over the last 100 years when science became more socially accepted and more of us adapted this way of thinking, being more logical. It was at that period of time when we had an extremely fast growth period and started to develop so much as a species. The problem is that when we grow up and are exposed to certain beliefs, certain knowledge – the only thing that we're aware of is what we're exposed to. What we are being showed by our parents, our society and our environment in general, this is pretty much all we know. So when I talk about evolutionary biology and this long road of what we actually are, many of us don't even understand these things because they simply don't think about this. We have our own problems, our thinking is very direct like how to come up with rent money for this month, how to make that girl I work with like me back and such, and we fail to see the bigger picture. There is no bigger awareness in what your place is in all this shit storm that we call life. This is because it's never been thought about, it's not part of your neural network and it's not part of your awareness because you have not been exposed to it.

It is my goal to explain here where our fears come from and why we feel the way we feel and how understanding these fears and knowing why they're there you can overcome them and do the things that will get you ahead in life. The same way knowing that the gun that is being pointed at you is a toy can take away certain toys, the same applies to a lot of these dysfunctional beliefs we've adapted to cope with emotions and feelings we could not explain otherwise.

It is very important to realize that a lot of these understandings is the ability to look at your processes, to look at yourself as a third person without choosing sides and letting your paradigm affect your judgement. If you're too much warped in your own world view, you will not be able to process what I'm explaining. In order to understand my next concept you really need to be able to let go from your day-to-day routine way of thinking and take distance from it, at least for a little while.
This is crucial if you want to understand what I'm about to explain.

If a person lives an unhealthy life such as eat processed fast food and doesn't work out and keep himself in good shape, he'll most likely doesn't have enough cognitive power to process this information. It will go past him. If we don't stimulate these parts of ourselves that have the ability to process this information, then our behaviour will be more "animal" like. It is perfectly fine if you happen to categorize yourself as this guy or girl, I'm not here to criticise anyone, but I'm saying you have the ability to understand these concepts and these ideas if you're able to be in a very active awareness state of mind, which is correlated through a healthy lifestyle. Working out and eating healthy has been two of the most important tools that allow people to be more clear-headed and to be able to think.

Before, when I was explaining certain concepts like having fears and anxieties, you we're able to easily relate. These things will easily vibe with most of the people, they're easy to identify yourself with.

What I'm about to explain now, will require you to take distance from your belief system and your daily life. Upcoming information is hard to process otherwise. I invite you to use the part of your brain that's more advanced. I'm going to explain to you how our brain works and if you're caught up in the primitive part of our brain and think more impulsive, then you don't have the more advanced parts of your brain active and not recognize these mistakes that we have in our wiring. Overall in a nutshell, it's all about looking at our processes as an outsider. We develop this ability at the age of 15ish, so if you're quite young, then this concept can be really difficult for you to understand, and same goes for the people who are too caught up in their own world and are unable to see things from an outsider's perspective.

Everybody have the ability to be a king in their own way, every single person in our world has the ability to do that. As hard it is for some of us to understand that, everybody can do it. It's all about understanding the dynamics of ourselves, so we could outgrow from the errors of our mechanism and learn to deal with them to find lifelong success.

If you look at our brain with all its functions, then we've come a long way. If you focus on the physical part of the brain then you will see that the more primitive parts of our brain are in the centre and they've got layers on them. It's like the primitive side is the stone inside of a cherry and as we've evolved, different layers have appeared that cover the foundation, the stone. These layers are our advanced parts of our brain. As the brain grew, more advanced parts are the prefrontal cortex and such that for an example allow you to process language. Most parts that are more advanced and speak or to reason have come later in evolution. Primitive sides, the stone inside the cherry if you will, where also feelings and fears are located is where our subconsciousness lies. Subconscious is just as part of us as our conscious, but because it doesn't have these advanced parts to be able to think and speak, it experiences and expresses itself in feelings and fears. Your prefrontal cortex, the advanced part of the brain has the ability to affect these feelings and fears. Just as the example with the toy gun, at first we feel fear, then our advanced part of the brain kicks in and destroys the fear. So you first experience the stone inside of a cherry and then feel these layers that have been built on it. The moment your prefrontal cortex realises the gun is just a toy, the fear will be gone completely.

This whole thing means we are able to control our fears, our feelings and everything else associated with them. But in order to control them, we must understand them just like you understand that the gun is a toy and not a real one. Your primitive part of the brain is not able to explain the cause of your emotions, that job is for your prefrontal cortex, the advanced side of our brain.

The problem here is that since emotions are first experienced and then afterwards being understood and contextualised.

Hundred years ago neuroscience was not even a field of science. Only recently we've been able to go through crazy paradigm shifts that can really redesign how we look at ourselves in a way that's much more fulfilling and much more aligned with reality. So at first you experience at your emotions and then you become aware or them. There is nothing that tells us this, there is no instinct, there are no programs that tell us this process and how it works. It's only recently through neuroscience we begin to understand why for an example up for feeling a particular way such as anger towards yourself does not make sense. Many of us often times feel angry for feeling a certain way, feeling anger towards not succeeding in something like a marathon run despite practising for years or not getting a promotion even though you were working harder than the other guy. This is because we don't understand what's actually happening in our brain. We experience emotions before we're able to process them and decide whether it's justified or not. This idea makes you be aware of this and not beat yourself up for something that's not worth it because we're built to feel such emotions, but we don't have to identify ourselves with them.

Your emotions just **are**. They're not good or bad. They exist and that's it. Nature did not label anything as good or bad, but we did. Being able to understand that fully will change your life completely.

"I advise all of you to work out and eat healthy. It's not just because of looking good and living longer. Good quality food is essential for your advanced part of the brain to work more efficiently and exercise will also make you more attached to it. It's not just being fit and living longer, it's about your brain power as well."

The biggest problem for all of us, regardless of our race, our gender any other visual que that separates us, the biggest problem is the same for everybody. Our biggest issue is beating ourselves up over our feelings, because we do not understand how they work. We tend to take our emotions for granted and not rationalize at all. This type of behaviour will make us do stupid things, not use our advanced part of the brain and pretty much run around like animals in a world full of others just like us.

All these big corporation leaders, all the inspirational high-class people who we look up to, understand this idea that emotions just are and the only thing that matters is how we react to them. You cannot be successful without understanding this idea, since our emotions will always fight the ideas that are uncomfortable to adapt. They might have different perspectives and use different words to describe it, but the point will always remain the same. It's hard to start working out, it's hard to go for a 3am run, it's hard to work 18 hours for 5 days straight. All of these activities are extremely uncomfortable, but in many cases very much needed since they build the character, they build willpower and change our brains paradigm to something that will prioritize success over petty little feelings. To be able to control our own emotions by taking a step back, looking at the situation from a whole another perspective, making up our mind deciding what the right thing for us to do is without paying attention to emotions like fear and anger which exist no matter what, coming back to the real world and do the right thing, is the right thing.

Humans are not flawed, we just put too much faith on our outdated emotional state without actually realizing why it's so and what to do about it. Not controlling your emotional state will take you through like doing literally nothing, since our emotions prioritize staying alive and feeling good, but success needs you to step outside of your comfort zone and do something new for a change, which for our emotions seems really dangerous. We need to rationalize and really think of the situation, since we all can come up with an answer despite our educational differences. We all have the ability to make a right decision. Use the full power of what has been given to us, especially at this day and age where information is mostly free and accessible.

The only thing we need to be able to deal with our issues is to understand, where they come from and understand our relationship with them, how and why they work the way they do. This requires looking at ourselves as a third person, which requires eating healthy and working out to feed your advanced parts of the brain. It starts with increasing your blood flow through these two ways and allows you to think more with reason.

It starts with living a healthy lifestyle, which will create a healthy mind, which will be the reasoning behind your success and happiness.

Another very important insight so you'd be able to tackle this even harder, is the extent to which you experience an emotion that gets connected to a concept. What I mean with this is the way your brain works, whenever you experience an emotion whether it's fear, anger or whatever, you try to connect in with an idea. Same principle works when you look at a thing or a person, you connect that also with an emotion. Emotions and concepts in our brain go hand in hand, they're connected to each other. The problem with this, as we are emotional beings, is that everything we experience is quite emotional. Everything that we experience starts in our primitive part of our brain, meaning it starts with feeling our emotions first and then being able to rationalize and interpret it. Every fear, every single desire and craving starts by feeling the emotion first after which it will get conceptualized by our advanced part of the brain. That's the process that happens only afterwards. If you understand that concepts are connected to your emotions, and emotions is what drives all your thinking on a subconscious level, you'll see how important it is to **detach** concepts from emotions. Most of us think using our emotion and therefore are not able to find the truth, improve their lives and become someone of high value. Your emotion might tell you to eat processed unhealthy foods, because they taste good, which will cause health problems and lowers your life quality.
That's not really a smart idea to listen to now is it? We all die at some point, it does not even matter whether it's sooner or later, so this is what we would be able to live with, but the fact that our quality of life goes

down is something that plays a big part in our happiness. I'm not just talking about health, fame, money and success here, I'm talking about not feeding your brain the right fuel so it would be able to understand the concepts that eventually create happiness.

When two guys are talking to each other about god, one having strong positive beliefs on god while the other one has fairly negative beliefs on god's existence, you two think you're talking about the same god, but in reality all you're doing is talking about your emotions. You're not finding the truth, you're just protecting your idea. You're protecting your ego.

First we experience, after which we contextualize.

Let's have another example. If I start talking to you about working out and eating healthy, and you have a negative experience with it, maybe a certain money grabbing and uninformative online workout program is not working for you or maybe you just despise people who take their lives more seriously than you due to your own mental blockages, then you won't even listen to me because you've already attached an emotion to the concept, therefore not finding out the truth. If you have a really positive outlook on working out and healthy foods, then you will take everything I say for granted without missing a few mistakes I might make in the process of explaining it. This last part is really common amongst beginners who have just gotten into health improvement after a severe personal history and suck in any information like a sponge without any bullshit filters. There is a tremendous power in doing, but the more you add smart thinking to doing, the faster you'll see your results and be able to avoid dead ends.

The only way how you can find the real answer is by detaching yourself from emotions. You can still experience them, take them for granted, be aware of having them, but do not identify yourself with them. They're not you, they just are. You are the cherry, not the stone. Stone is the core of which you embody and play with, like a surrogate. Separate your mind from your body, and use it to play around with the body. There two separate things.

To be able to grow as a person is your ability to detach yourself from beliefs on an emotional level. This allows you to through life and notice whenever a belief is flawed, whatever it might be, discard it and replace it with a stronger one. But if you go through life and you have a very strong emotion connected to that belief and you're confronted with that belief being flawed, and since on a subconscious level this belief is what drives you and makes you do the things you do, your ego will feel threatened and tries to protect itself by blocking out all the information that could help you to discover how much of a bullshit that idea really is. Some people still believe that earth is flat because of this very same concept I just explained. It's not like they can't let go of the idea that earth is flat, they can't let go of the emotion attached to the concept of earth being flat. They'd see that's it's incorrect, therefore their whole life has been a big lie. In these hypothetical situations the ego feels extremely threatened and signals your emptions to block out the ground-breaking information. A defence mechanism.

The reason why I'm explaining all of this in a book about dating and sleeping with beautiful women is to make you understand and realize that as hard it is to understand the world, as hard it is to make sense out of everything you experience in the world, as hard it is to find answers and why things are the way they are, everything has a reason. Most of people back in the old days had a reason and that was god. That was their explanation. That was their ability to explain their fear. It gave them a sense of peace and relief, because it was something they could trust. The beauty about science is that now we can have that same trust and that everything happens for a reason instead of god on a scientific level, on a level that's much more improved by the brightest minds of all time.

We have the ability to control and to rewire ourselves, the only thing we lack of is knowledge and understanding, which ultimately produce will. Everything in our life does make sense.

The ability to detach your feelings from your ideas will make you grow like crazy, this is the recipe for any success, to make millions and billions of euros, to become the next legend of our lifetime and so forth. Being impulsive and trusting our emotions at all times will make you impulsive and form dysfunctional ideas and make you believe in something that's not actually correct.

Everything that I talk about here is made to make you, the reader understand that everything you experience, can be controlled, if you just control your mind. No matter how you feel and no matter how you look at things, everything makes sense. Everything. Once one understands it, one is able to overcome it.

It's not our fault for not knowing this stuff right away, it's not your fault at all, but it is upon us to fix it. If failed to do so, it becomes our fault. By feeding the advanced part of the brain that starts with losing the ego, working out and eating healthy, one is able to understand and overcome it. By adopting this whole idea that I wrote about in this article into your brain – it will give you tremendous amount of power over life. A positive paradigm shift, the best thing that could ever happen to us. Not money, not fame, not love, but the right kind of paradigm shift – that's all we need for a happy life.

The Deep Truth

The thing about life is that it's not always easy and you cannot always win. At some point point it will hit you, and it will hit you really fucking hard. It might be anything, either a breakup, losing your job, death in the family, literally anything that holds value to you. There is no escaping pain and there is no escaping failure. These things will stay with you untill the end of time.

In this life of ours, tears are guaranteed. Every single one of us will cry at some point of their lives and just as when you think it cannot get any worse, it will. You will find yourself alone. You don't know what to do. You're paralyzed, unable to go on and keep asking yourself this one question:

Why?

This is the ultimate question and the answer depending on what it is will either make you or break you. We all fall down in life no matter how strong we are and we will fall down constantly. The only thing that separates the happy person from an unhappy person is able to give the right answer to the why and get up.

Ask yourself:

Why am I failing?

Why am I even getting into this situation?

Because you have a dream. You have goals that you want to reach. Every single person on this earth will get hurt and will get hurt A LOT. The happy person will understand this, accept it and gets hurt for the right reason – to improve and fulfil his or her dreams.

Ultimately we all need harsh experiences, we all need these breakups, missed opportunities and big failures. We need to go through heavy loss just to find something even better. The only way to get to the next phase is to get up and work, to get up and put yourself in the shitstorm once again, to open the wound again and let it kill you...

And arise from that as a stronger, better individual ready to take on the next oppurtunity. Life is full of luxuries, happiness and joy, but only for those, who get back up.

Wear your scars with pride, because you'll get many of them eventually. It's on us to make sure that those scars are worth something.

This is the deep truth that nobody else is going to hit you with.

www.ingramcontent.com/pod-product-compliance
Lightning Source LLC
Chambersburg PA
CBHW030418290526
45786CB00001B/37